COGNITIVE SYSTEMS

Human Cognitive Models in Systems Design

COGNITIVE SYSTEMS

Human Cognitive Models in Systems Design

Edited by

Chris Forsythe
Michael L. Bernard
Sandia National Laboratories

Timothy E. Goldsmith
University of New Mexico

LEA LAWRENCE ERLBAUM ASSOCIATES, PUBLISHERS
2006   Mahwah, New Jersey   London

Lawrence Erlbaum Associates, Inc., Publishers
10 Industrial Avenue
Mahwah, New Jersey 07430
www.erlbaum.com

Cover design by Kathryn Houghtaling Lacey

Library of Congress Cataloging-in-Publication Data

Cognitive systems : human cognitive models in systems design / edited by Chris Forsythe,
  Michael L. Bernard, Timothy E. Goldsmith.
     p. cm.
  Includes bibliographical references and index.
  ISBN 0-8058-5291-3 (alk. paper)
  1. Human-computer interaction. I. Forsythe, Chris. II. Bernard, Michael L.
III. Goldsmith, Timothy E.

QA76.9.H85C6445 2005
004'.01'9—dc22   2005040291
                                                                      CIP

Books published by Lawrence Erlbaum Associates are printed on acid-free paper,
and their bindings are chosen for strength and durability.

Printed in the United States of America
10 9 8 7 6 5 4 3 2 1

Contents

Contributors

Travis Bauer   Sandia National Laboratories

Zachary Benz   Sandia National Laboratories

Michael L. Bernard   Sandia National Laboratories

C. M. Chewar   Virginia Tech

Patrick Chipman   University of Memphis

David E. Copeland   University of Southern Mississippi

Michael A. Covington   The University of Georgia

Scott Dooley   Knowledge Analysis Technologies

Chris Forsythe   Sandia National Laboratories

Timothy E. Goldsmith   University of New Mexico

Arthur C. Graesser   University of Memphis

Brian C. Haynes   University of Memphis

Joseph Kimmel   Overland College & Sandia National Laboratories

Wilhelm E. Kincses   DaimlerChrysler

Amy Kruse   Strategic Analysis

Darrell Laham   Knowledge Analysis Technologies

Terran Lane   University of New Mexico

Joseph P. Magliano   Northern Illinois University

D. Scott McCrickard   Virginia Tech

Daniel C. McFarlane   Lockheed Martin

Rob Oberbrekling   Knowledge Analysis Technologies

Andrew Olney   University of Memphis

Gabriel A. Radvansky   University of Notre Dame

Dylan Schmorrow   Defense Advanced Projects Agency and Office of Naval Research

Patrick G. Xavier   Sandia National Laboratories

R. Michael Young   North Carolina State University

Preface

With each year that passes, it seems there is continual growth in the field of cognitive modeling. At Sandia National Laboratories, our first endeavors in this field occurred in 1999. Like many others, our motive was to create more realistic synthetic entities for simulation products. However, at some point along the way, we began to ask the question, What more could be done with computer models of human cognition?

Cognitive systems, as defined in the forthcoming chapters, was our answer to this question. It is difficult to trace the exact genesis of the idea, but the term *cognitive systems* began to be used to describe systems in which a machine is endowed with a humanlike cognitive model that provides the basis for interactions between the machine and its human users. Central to this idea is the notion that when two people interact, it is an interaction between two cognitive entities. Individuals adjust what they say and do in accordance with their awareness of other individuals' general knowledge. They use shared knowledge and past experiences to put current events within context. They recognize and respond to failures in comprehension and personal sensitivities. We began to ask, If a machine can be supplied a reasonably realistic cognitive model, might it similarly interact with users as a humanlike cognitive entity?

After several years of research and development inspired by these ideas, much of this in collaboration with Professor Tim Goldsmith of the University of New Mexico, we began to take the first steps toward building a community of researchers who were pursuing similar lines of inquiry. This took the form of a workshop sponsored by Sandia National Laboratories on July 1 to 3, 2003, in Santa Fe, New Mexico. At this workshop, we were extremely fortunate to have attracted an impressive array of participants who discussed cognitive systems from a range of perspectives that included: (a) physiological indicators of cognitive state, (b) computational cognitive modeling, (c) automated knowledge capture, (d) augmented cognition, and (e) product applications for cognitive systems.

The chapters in this book represent a subset of the individuals who participated in this first workshop. This book is not meant to serve as a proceedings for the workshop, but instead each contributor was asked to expand on the perspectives he or she brought to the workshop, provide a broad summary of his or her research and development, and, in general, help create a resource for those who are either pursuing a similar path, have recently taken an interest in the area, or merely want to answer their curiosity about the matter.

Since the initial event in July 2003, a second, much larger, workshop was held during the summer of 2004, and a third workshop was held in the summer of 2005, once again in Santa Fe, New Mexico. It is hoped that this book will serve as a primer to inspire others to explore the possibilities of creating systems in which machines interact as humanlike cognitive entities and the community that has emerged around the workshops will continue to grow.

PART ONE

INTRODUCTION

CHAPTER ONE

Cognitive Models to Cognitive Systems

Chris Forsythe
Patrick G. Xavier
Sandia National Laboratories

Although sometimes rooted in nature, the problems plaguing human existence, ranging from the societal to the mundane, almost universally involve a cognitive dimension. Assembly instructions may be barely decipherable. Software may behave in unexpected ways. An auto accident may follow from misinterpreting the intentions of another driver. The cure to a pervasive disease may remain just beyond reach due to the inability to grasp insights that appear obvious in hindsight.

In each of these examples, humans utilize their cognitive resources, including their unique knowledge and experience, to interpret stimuli within their environment and operate on the environment to accomplish various objectives. Throughout history, humans have created artifacts to bolster and expand the potential of their innate cognitive capacities. Spoken and written languages have allowed communication concerning objects that are not actually present or events that have not been personally experienced. Numbers have provided a means to reason about the world using commonly understood conventions. Computers have enabled the automation of basic cognitive processes and the storage of vast volumes of knowledge and experience.

Our inspiration in advancing ideas within the rubric of what we have termed *cognitive systems* owes to an awareness of the cognitive nature of the problems confounding human endeavors and a belief that fundamental progress in overcoming these problems requires a new artifact. We assert that cognitive systems, as described in the following sections, may be the artifact that irreversibly and positively changes how people interact with the world.

WHAT ARE COGNITIVE SYSTEMS

There have been numerous varied instances in which others have used the term *cognitive systems*, and there is no collective agreement with regard to a definition, scope, or best illustration. Duly conscious of this ambiguity, we have chosen to refer to the technologies described in the remainder of this chapter, and subsequent chapters of this book, as cognitive systems. Therefore, it is appropriate that our discussion begin with an explanation of how we have conceptualized a cognitive system, although our intent is not to argue for a common definition.

In defining a cognitive system, we have chosen to draw on the properties of the most common cognitive system and the one with which most of us have had the most experience: ourselves and the other humans with whom we interact. In the framework elaborated here, we assert that humans represent the prototypical cognitive system. We further assert that the objective in creating a machine-based cognitive system is to emulate the properties of human cognition that enable people to effectively engage the world and interact with other humans as fellow cognitive entities.

In our opinion, the most compelling case for the creation of cognitive systems is to enable machines to interact with humans in a knowing manner that is similar to the way in which humans interact with one another. To explain what we mean by this statement, consider the following example.

Imagine you have another human who serves as your aide. It is the objective of your aide to first follow you everywhere that you go, listen to every conversation to which you are a party, read everything that you have read, and remember everything that you have done, how you have done it, and the consequences of your actions. Second, it is the objective of your aide to do everything within his or her power to help you as you go through your day-to-day endeavors; however, this aide has the benefits of unlimited memory accompanied by perfect recall and the processing capabilities of the most powerful computing systems.

The characteristics that may be attributed to such an aide are the same characteristics that we would assert as generally descriptive of cognitive systems:

- They know what you know, including the underlying structure of your knowledge, and what you don't know.

- They know what you do and how you do it, including the knowledge implicit in your actions.
- They know about your past experiences and can properly place events within the context of past experiences.
- They can apply your unique knowledge and experiences to interpret events in a manner consistent with how you would interpret the same events.
- They recognize when you have learned and how learning has reshaped your knowledge of the world.
- They know the consequences of your past experiences and the resulting sensitivities, and they can anticipate how you will react to future situations.

One may rightly assert that humans are imperfect cognitive systems. Memory is fallible. People falsely attribute beliefs to others. People adopt superstitious behavior. However, one cannot disregard the remarkable effectiveness with which humans interact, particularly when placed in comparison with troublesome facets of human–machine interactions. Consider the case in which two individuals who have never met one another and speak different languages engage in mutually beneficial commerce. Second, consider the ease with which two long-time collaborators operate together mixing various levels of abstraction and drawing on shared past experiences. Finally, consider the nonintuitiveness of much commercial software, the seeming obtuseness of associated online help functions, and the misdirected behavior of automated features meant to assist the user. It is our intent with cognitive systems to emphasize those facets of human cognition that make for effective human interaction while compensating for certain shortcomings of the human cognitive apparatus through the processing power and faithful data storage and retrieval possible with computer systems.

At first blush, one may respond negatively to our description of a cognitive system on the basis of privacy concerns. It can be intimidating to imagine one's actions faithfully observed and remembered. One can postulate numerous scenarios in which such data are used for detrimental purposes. We must acknowledge that there are no easy answers for such concerns. Of course the developers of cognitive systems may take measures to ensure the user is always in control of their personal data collection and the access of others to that data. However, as has repeatedly been the case with technological innovation, broad adoption of cognitive systems will create new possibilities for both the opportunist and, of notable importance, those who will defend against these opportunists.

In answer to the question, "What is a cognitive system?", we have chosen the following delimitation. A cognitive system refers to a variety of software products that utilize plausible computational models of human cognitive processes as a basis for human–machine interactions. The intent is to reproduce cognitive mechanisms responsible for the effectiveness of human–human interaction so that the human–machine interaction becomes more like an interaction between a human and a humanlike cognitive entity. In short, a cognitive system consists of software that helps a machine interact with people in the way people interact with one another.

PLAUSIBLE COMPUTATIONAL MODELS
OF HUMAN COGNITION

In our definition of a cognitive system, we have placed a heavy emphasis on plausible computational models of human cognition. The goal is to attain the highest level of psychological plausibility that is practical for a given technology. This distinguishes cognitive systems from those that only emulate human surface features. For instance, a system may feature dialogue-based interaction with a humanlike avatar as the means to emulate a dialogue between the user and another human; however, the underlying structure for the software may be entirely rule-based, bearing little resemblance to human cognitive processes. From a different perspective, a system may utilize mainstream approaches from machine-based reasoning for problem-solving, information retrieval, user customization, or other intelligent functions. Yet these approaches are based loosely, or not at all, on human cognitive processes. Neither of these examples would clearly qualify as a cognitive system using the definition we have chosen.

Our preference is to avoid an unreasonably purist or dogmatic stance. Benefits may arise from using dialogue-based interaction and humanlike avatars as interfaces to cognitive systems that are otherwise based on plausible models of human cognition. Similarly, for a given cognitive system, all facets do not need to emulate human cognitive processes. For instance, our own approach uses the most expedient algorithmic techniques to acquire the knowledge that populates a plausible computational model of human knowledge representation and cognitive information processing, without attempting to model the mechanisms underlying human learning.

In our discussion, we have made repeated reference to plausibility as a critical attribute of the computational models utilized in cognitive systems. We acknowledge that plausibility can have many legitimate dimensions that may or may not be quantifiable. Furthermore, it is unrealistic to expect general agreement with regard to a standard for plausibility.

Our emphasis on plausibility is largely meant to distinguish cognitive systems from alternative approaches that either make no claim to emulate human cognitive processes, or cite human cognitive processes, but cannot show a clear correspondence between computational representations and scientific understanding of the mechanisms underlying human cognition. Given the latter statement, one may correctly conclude that plausibility represents a changing standard that evolves with associated scientific understanding. Thus, computational models that would have seemed plausible when knowledge of human cognition was almost exclusively the product of research in experimental psychology may now be suspect given the proliferation of knowledge concerning the mechanisms underlying human cognition that has become available from brain imaging and EEG studies.

Our own claims to plausibility derive from the methodology we have employed in designing and verifying our computational model. This methodology begins with a survey of the experimental literature concerning human cognitive processes and corresponding neurophysiological processes. From this survey, we identify functional characteristics. For instance, from the work of Klimesch and colleagues (e.g., Klimesch et al., 1997), we establish that:

Generally, there should be an increased desynchronization of activation in the upper alpha bandwidth (10–13 Hz) during periods in which semantic memory is engaged.

These characteristics then serve as functional design specifications. In designing the computational model, the intent is to engineer a design that in operation will satisfy a collection of functional specifications similar to the example given earlier. Once implemented, simulation scenarios may be developed that are consistent with the experimental procedures used in the studies on which specifications were based, and these simulation scenarios may be presented to the computational model to verify that the model responds consistent with specifications (i.e., the performance of the model in simulated scenarios corresponds to findings of the original studies). In full acknowledgment that the scientific literature does not provide a complete specification for human cognition, we contend that the path to plausibility lies in a process for model development that integrates scientific understanding with structured engineering practices.

It may be asked, "Is plausibility a necessary attribute for cognitive systems?" With the various manifestations of cognitive systems described in subsequent sections, there are many cases in which nothing precludes the use of models with weak plausibility or even models for which plausibility was never the intent. However, we would assert that plausibility is an essential attribute to attain a knowing and responsive human–machine interaction of the nature proposed here.

For a human–machine interaction that resembles the interaction between two cognitive entities, we first assert that the machine should possess an accurate model of the knowledge of a user(s). This assertion is
based on a desire for the machine to adjust its interactions with the user to
accommodate specific facets of the user's knowledge of and experience
with a task, system, or domain. Additionally, cognitive systems will be discussed that enable a user to compare his or her own knowledge with that
of other individuals (i.e., perhaps experts in a given domain). In either
case, we believe the most direct and parsimonious approach to accomplish an accurate model of the knowledge of a user is to base that model
on a plausible representation of the underlying structural properties of
human knowledge.

Second, we assert that the machine should possess an accurate model
of the cognitive processes of a user. With certain cognitive systems, the
machine will interact with the user on the basis of inferred cognitive operations. For example, the machine may adjust the salience of perceptual
cues to enhance the situation awareness of a user and facilitate recovery
from situation mode errors. Where inferences regarding a user's ongoing
cognitive processes are an essential facet of the cognitive system and erroneous inferences may have deleterious effects, we believe the correctness
of such inferences will be a direct product of the accuracy with which
models represent the corresponding cognitive operations of the user.

Finally, cognitive systems concepts are discussed that provide the user
with tools for simulating the behavior of individuals, groups, or populations. As an aide or synthetic mentor, the simulation may be based on a
specific individual and the user allowed to create scenarios and observe
the response of the simulated individual(s). Other concepts augment the
hypothetical reasoning of users by allowing them to create simulations involving groups or populations. Here the objective is to allow users to simulate hypothetical situations to gain an understanding of the range of possible outcomes and how various factors interact (e.g., an individual may
run several simulations to see how highway traffic could be affected by a
public event). In each of these cases, the accuracy and usefulness of tools
will depend on the accuracy with which they forecast human behavior. We
assert that plausible cognitive models are necessary to attain a realistic
portrayal of human behavior, including the complex interactions between
different individuals and groups.

ESSENTIALS FOR A PLAUSIBLE COGNITIVE MODEL

The preceding section offered a brief description of the development
process on which we base claims concerning the plausibility of our cognitive modeling framework. We do not assert that the framework developed

by our group is the only plausible computer model of human cognition. Our framework embodies a particular level of representation and a specific combination of cognitive processes. Nothing precludes other frameworks that operate at different levels of representation or emphasize alternative combinations of cognitive processes. Furthermore, the precise computational mechanisms for representing cognitive processes may vary across frameworks, with alternative frameworks producing equivalent outcomes. Although alternative models may provide for plausibility, we cannot overstate the importance that models be based on a systematic development process rooted in science concerning human cognition.

The following sections summarize properties of human cognition that we believe are fundamental and have included in our cognitive modeling framework. Figure 1.1 provides a graphical depiction of this framework. Our framework addresses a specific combination of cognitive processes, and there is varying overlap with other reasonably plausible models.

Concepts

The basic unit in our cognitive framework is the concept. Concepts correspond to the most elementary units of cognition, enabling an entity to recognize and respond to stimuli. It may be noted that here, *recognize* implies knowledge, which is consistent with the contention that cognition is knowledge-mediated action whether observable action or mental processes.

Within our framework, cognition begins with recognition of meaningful regularities within an entity's sensory experience of its external and/or internal world. These regularities may involve almost any stimuli detectable to the entity's sense organs, as well as combinations of stimuli that may span sensory modalities and temporal durations.

Many factors may contribute to a regularity being meaningful. These include association with reward, predictive value, causative relationship, distinguishing attribute, cue in guiding motor processes, and so on. The foregoing assumes an ability to acquire meaningful regularities and retain the knowledge needed for their subsequent recognition. Once learned, the internal representations of these regularities correspond to the concepts that serve as the basic unit for cognitive processes.

Semantic Memory

Within our cognitive framework, knowledge of concepts (i.e., regularities) is represented within semantic memory. However, an additional function of semantic memory is to store knowledge of the relatedness of concepts. *Relatedness* refers to the awareness that two concepts are somehow associ-

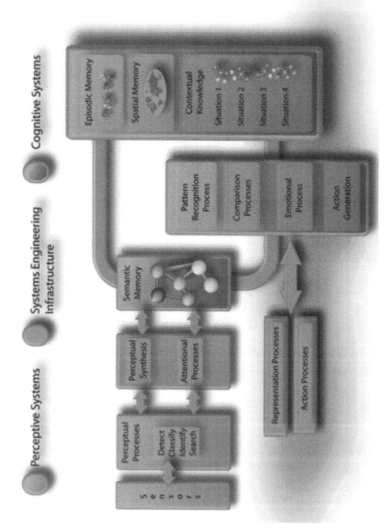

FIG. 1.1. This graphical depiction of the Sandia Cognitive Modeling Framework identifies the key components and interactions between these components.

ated—whether one is a property of the other, they are members of the same category, they operate together in some functional relationship, and so on.

Knowledge of the relatedness of concepts may be illustrated in many ways through experimental studies. Pairs of concepts may be presented and the person asked to rate their relatedness. A single concept may be presented followed by a pair of concepts and the person asked to indicate which of the pair is most related to the first concept. A person may be presented a single concept and asked to give a list of related concepts. These and other experimental methods indicate that people can readily access their knowledge of the relatedness of concepts; this knowledge is enduring, and different methods for collecting data concerning relatedness produce equivalent results concerning the relative relatedness of pairs of concepts (e.g., Schvaneveldt, 1990).

It has been estimated that a normal adult human has knowledge of at least 10,000 unique concepts and may have knowledge of 100,000 or more (Foltz et al., 1998). Given the numerous ways in which a concept may be associated with another concept and the numerous concepts with which any given concept may have an association, the structure for representing semantic memory must be extremely complex. Accordingly, we have adopted an approach in which the relationship between concepts is based on a representation of each concept as a vector in a high-dimensional space. The cosine similarity of vectors for a given pair of concepts provides the basis for the strength of the relationship between concepts. The relatedness of concepts derived in this manner then provides a basis for simulating the priming that occurs for a concept in response to the prior presentation of a related concept (e.g., Dagenbach, Horst, & Carr, 1990).

Context Recognition

Everyday experience is more than a complex array of differential concept activations. Instead we recognize patterns within this complex array. Within our cognitive modeling framework, we have referred to these patterns as *contexts*.

At a given moment in time, my overall experience of the world may consist of the somewhat separable experiences that I'm in my home, in my kitchen, eating breakfast. Home, kitchen, and eating breakfast may each represent a context. If we consider any one of these contexts, there are corresponding concepts (e.g., morning, orange juice, cereal, wearing pajamas, reading the newspaper, etc.).

Each of these concepts is predictive of the context "eating breakfast," but in isolation it is unlikely that any of these concepts alone would be sufficient for a meaningful inference. However, to the extent that the concepts present in a given scenario correspond to the pattern associated with the context "eating breakfast," it may be inferred that the context is "eating breakfast."

As illustrated, a given scenario may consist of multiple contexts that occur simultaneously (e.g., in my home, in my kitchen, and eating breakfast). Additionally, contexts may involve differing levels of abstraction (e.g., in my home and in my kitchen).

Much of our understanding of how people use their knowledge of contexts to interpret everyday experience is based on research concerning narrative and film comprehension (e.g. Magliano, Miller, & Zwaan, 2001; Zwaan & Radvansky, 1998). This research has shown that, while reading a story or watching a movie, people recognize transitions that correspond to progressions from one context to another. For instance, in reading a story, if the physical location of a primary character changes or if the story abruptly moves forward or backward in time, there is a distinct sense that the context has changed. As characters enter and leave the story, there is a similar sense of transition in contexts. Similarly, given actions aimed at attaining some goal, once the goal is attained or intentionally abandoned, it is perceived that there has been a change in context.

Findings from narrative and film comprehension have suggested five dimensions that are predictive of shifts from one context to another. These dimensions may be roughly described as follows:

- Time—transitions correspond to discontinuities or temporal boundaries separating meaningful blocks of time (e.g., end of the workday);
- Place—transitions correspond to discontinuities or boundaries separating distinct locations (e.g., walk out the front door transitioning from being inside my home to my front yard);
- Entities or objects—transitions correspond to the arrivals or departures and significant transformations of people, animals, or things,
- Causation—transitions correspond to the beginning and/or end of sequences of events that are inferred to constitute a causal sequence; and
- Intention—transitions correspond to the beginning or end of a series of events in which an entity operates to achieve a goal and either attains or abandons the goal.

In our modeling framework, we have adopted a structure for the representation of contexts that includes each of the dimensions described before and an additional dimension for which transitions correspond to shifts in emotional state. A known context may be based on one or a combination of these dimensions.

In our modeling framework, recognition that a transition has occurred with regard to one or more of the dimensions providing the structure for contextual knowledge is based on the activation of concepts within semantic memory. Activation of a concept corresponding to the temporal dimension (e.g., quitting time) may serve as the cue for a transition between one context (e.g., work) to another context (e.g., going home). This is accomplished through a context recognition process based on evidence accumulation. Here the relevance (i.e., evidence derived from the activation of concepts within semantic memory) of contexts to the current situation is continually updated. Transitions between contexts occur when evidence for a context exceeds or falls below the threshold for recognition. The experience of a given situation is then based on the combination of contexts that each exceeds some threshold for recognition.

There is an additional feature of the context recognition mechanisms that should be mentioned. There is knowledge accompanying contexts that concerns expectations. Knowledge of expectations consists of concepts that are likely to occur in conjunction with a context. For example, coffee would be an expectation for the context "eating breakfast." Consequently, given that other concepts provide sufficient evidence for recognition that the context is "eating breakfast," any dark liquid within sufficient proximity is likely to be perceived as coffee. Expectations correspond to a "top–down" influence and lead to a priming of concepts in semantic memory, which may occur despite an absence of corresponding sensory events, following recognition of a given context (e.g., Biederman, 1981; Perfetti & Roth, 1981).

Episodic Memory

As we progress through life, we create a record of our experiences. This record is referred to as *episodic* or *autobiographical memory*. Here we make a distinction in that *episodic memory* refers to the actual record of events stored to memory, whereas *autobiographical memory* refers to the recall that occurs as a product of constructive processes involved in accessing the episodic record.

Episodic memory is particularly important to modeling cognition in that it supports two functions. First, when an ongoing experience does not correspond with any known context, the model can refer to episodic memory to identify similar past experiences as an alternative to context recognition. Second, through its record of experiences, episodic memory provides a medium for learning mechanisms that acquire knowledge of new contexts through recognition of recurrent events.

Our own instantiation of episodic memory consists of a record of experience based on the activation of other components of the model. The record is not continuous, but instead certain events may trigger an entry to episodic memory. For instance, entries correspond to the recognition of a context or the transition from one context to another. Likewise, activation of concepts in semantic memory may also trigger an entry, as well as activation of other components that have not yet been described (i.e., comparator and emotional processes). An entry to episodic memory consists of a reference to items activated at the time corresponding to the entry and a record of the relative activation of each item. For instance, with semantic memory, this would consist of the concepts that were activated and their relative levels of activation.

The contents of episodic memory are not stored as distinct episodes with clearly defined beginnings and ends, but instead are represented as a continuous record of events. For any given point in time, the episodic record may consist of several simultaneously activated contexts. Episodes are a product of episodic memory retrieval. Based on retrieval cues, a slice of the episodic memory record is recalled that may have a distinct beginning or end, with the beginning and end typically corresponding to transitions associated with particularly salient contexts. Thus, in our framework, episodes are a product of episodic memory retrieval, and not the basis for structuring episodic memory.

Episodic recall utilizes an evidence accumulation-based mechanism similar to that previously described for context recognition. In particular, the episodic memory record is evaluated with regard to the relative correspondence to one or more memory retrieval cues. For example, if the retrieval cues consist of "baseball game" and "cold night," the episodic record would be evaluated with regard to the correspondence to these cues. Periods involving both cues, in general, would receive more evidence than other time intervals containing one or neither cue. For periods in which both cues occur, the evidence for a time interval would be a function of the level of activation associated with each cue during the time interval. For example, if it were an extremely cold night with significant discomfort, "cold night" may have been an extremely salient cue.

However, of tremendous significance, the episodic record has a level of accessibility associated with it that modifies the evidence derived for a given time interval with respect to such factors as the amount of time that has passed. Recall occurs for the time interval or intervals receiving the most evidence.

At recall, an episode derived from the episodic record may be replayed with activation of the constituent elements of the episode. For example, concepts in semantic memory may be activated (Menon et al., 2002). Similarly, although not incorporated in our current models, given a perceptual memory containing rich representations of perceptual entities, these perceptual representations would be activated (Vaidya et al., 2002). It is worth noting that the activation of constituent elements of episodic memory is somewhat consistent with events as they occurred at the time of the episode, but is also a product of current knowledge. As a result, the recalled experience may differ in some regards from the original experience (Levine et al., 2001).

Comparator

When presented a surprising or out-of-context stimulus, there is a distinct electrophysiological response. This has been demonstrated extensively with oddball paradigms, in which a subject is given a series of similar stimuli (e.g., tones of a particular frequency and amplitude) and interspersed within this series are a few highly dissimilar stimuli (Rugg & Coles, 1995). Similarly, a related neurophysiological response occurs in conjunction with a subject's recognition that they have committed an error (Holroyd, Dien, & Coles, 1998). It has been proposed that these responses reflect a learning mechanism that is highly sensitive to either context shifts or negative feedback with regard to assumed context (Luu & Tucker, 2002).

The comparator within our modeling framework serves a similar function. Specifically, the comparator monitors ongoing context recognition processes and maintains an awareness of current contexts, including expectations associated with each context. The comparator also monitors semantic memory and the concepts that are activated. The comparator is triggered when one or more concepts are activated in semantic memory that are inconsistent with the current context(s). Additionally, an adjustable threshold is provided that allows the model to be more or less sensitive to out-of-context events to enable situational influences (e.g., lowered sensitivity following positive events or successful goal attainment and heightened sensitivity following negative events or failed goal attainment) or individual differences (Mizuki et al., 1992).

When the comparator is triggered, there is heightened attention placed on the out-of-context event. This occurs through a boost in activation for the out-of-context concept in semantic memory, accompanied by a generalized dampening of the activation of all other concepts. As a result, in some cases, the model may abandon the context that had been previously recognized. In other cases, the evidence may be sufficient that a recognized context is not abandoned despite the out-of-context event although the experience may prompt learning that incorporates the previously out-of-context event, or acquisition of a new context.

In this discussion, emphasis has been placed on the comparator monitoring semantic memory activation. It should be noted that the comparator may similarly monitor other components (e.g., perceptual processes, goal attainment).

Emotional Processes

Our modeling framework has made provisions for separate components that each correspond to distinct emotional processes (LeDoux, 1998). For instance, a model may be configured that has distinct components for emotions corresponding to pleasure, dysphoria, frustration-anger, fear, anxiety, and disgust. Each emotion may have a behavioral correlate, but in the current framework the greatest impact of emotional processes occurs through its influence on information processing.

Concepts within semantic memory and contexts within contextual knowledge may be associated with an emotional process. For example, the concept *snake* may be associated with the emotional process corresponding to fear. When the concept *snake* is activated, this triggers the emotional process corresponding to fear. As a result, similar to the comparator described earlier, there is a heightened activation of the concept that triggered the emotional response accompanied by a generalized inhibition of other concepts (LeDoux, 1998). This serves to focus attention on the fear-inducing stimulus to the exclusion of other concepts and may prompt a reinterpretation of the ongoing context.

Perceptual-Motor Processes

At present, our modeling framework has employed interim mechanisms for the representation of perceptual and motor processes. For instance, with perceptual processes, we have implemented algorithms that correspond to each of the concepts in semantic memory. Data are supplied to these algorithms from appropriate sources, and the algorithms translate these data into corresponding values representing the occurrence or non-occurrence of concepts. As a result, concepts in semantic memory are activated at appropriate levels.

We do not assert that the perceptual mechanisms described here are plausible representations. Here we illustrate how a given cognitive system may combine components with varying degrees of plausibility. Our systems have emphasized the plausibility of context recognition and episodic memory processes. In contrast, systems focused on perceptual processes may employ a somewhat different combination of components with differing levels of plausibility.

Finally, within the current framework, we have only implemented rudimentary representations for action generation. With future versions, we believe that this component of the model will be of tremendous importance. Specifically, through a motor representation that incorporates procedural knowledge, the framework will be supplied the mechanisms essential for deliberative processes. At present, our modeling framework passively observes the world and applies its knowledge to interpret events. Subsequent versions will have the capacity to (a) carry out procedural operations, (b) assess the adequacy of their own knowledge and awareness of events, and (c) take measures to overcome inadequacies through acquiring additional knowledge and applying strategies that are self-perturbing as a means to promote alternative and/or unique interpretations of events.

Learning or Knowledge Capture

Learning is mentioned here as another illustration of the combination within a cognitive system of components and processes that vary in their plausibility. With the Sandia cognitive modeling framework, we have adopted a policy in which we place heavy emphasis on the plausibility of components such as semantic memory, episodic memory, and contextual knowledge. In contrast, we have set aside concerns for plausibility with regard to the mechanisms by which these components are populated with the knowledge of a specific individual (i.e., automated knowledge capture). Our approach has been to employ whatever learning algorithms seem most effective in acquiring the knowledge populating a cognitive model (see Bauer et al., chap. 7, this volume; Lane, chap. 11, this volume, for a description of mechanisms being developed for automated knowledge capture). However, considerable effort is exerted to ensure the plausibility of the representational structure and basic workings (i.e., memory storage and retrieval, application of knowledge to the interpretation of events, etc.) of these components.

ILLUSTRATIVE EXAMPLES OF COGNITIVE SYSTEMS

The final sections of this chapter describe various illustrations of cognitive systems. This represents only a sample from a broad range of possibilities. Subsequent chapters provide additional examples. Our intent here is to provide a general understanding of the breadth of opportunities to apply cognitive systems to enhance human effectiveness.

Operator Assistant for Error Detection and Recovery

Situation mode errors have been a factor in many catastrophic mishaps, and they represent a primary contributor to the accidents, errors, and misunderstandings that plague everyday human endeavors (Olson & Sarter, 2001). In general, there are three different manifestations of situation mode errors. In the first, a critical situation emerges and, for any of several reasons, the operator fails to recognize this occurrence. For example, an automobile driver may fail to notice various cues indicating that traffic will soon come to an abrupt halt due to highway construction. Second, an operator may recognize that a situation has developed that is deserving of their attention, but misinterpret the situation taking actions that are appropriate for the assumed situation, but inappropriate for the actual situation. For example, in response to an engine warning light, an automobile owner operating on the incorrect assumption that the oil level is low may overfill the oil reservoir. Finally, an operator may believe a situation exists and take associated actions when in fact there is no reason for the operator to deviate from his or her current course of action. For example, an automobile driver on a high-speed roadway may misinterpret an unusual configuration of traffic signals and unnecessarily brake to the surprise of surrounding drivers.

Factors contributing to situation mode errors include distraction, fatigue, boredom, attention capture, inadequate knowledge, and so on. Our own developments include a prototype operator assistant that serves to detect occurrences indicative of an operator situation mode error and facilitate error recovery (Forsythe et al., 2003). With this system, a cognitive model observes events maintaining an ongoing awareness of situations that exist. In the context of an AWACS simulation trainer, we have demonstrated 90% consistency between the real-time interpretation of events by our cognitive model and the interpretation of the operator on whom the cognitive model was based.

In our prototype system, we observe the operator's actions and use an eye tracker to acquire data concerning the operator's attention to visual cues. A discrepancy detector then assesses these data in light of the cognitive model's awareness of ongoing situations. The objective is to ascertain whether the operator has attended to cues critical for an appropriate awareness and response to ongoing situations, and whether the operator has taken expected actions, as opposed to actions that would not be expected given the cognitive model's interpretation of the ongoing situation. The discrepancy detector also considers the relative urgency of situations and the time that has passed since first detection of a situation without a corresponding operator response.

When conditions are detected indicative of a potential operator situation mode error, various corrective measures may be taken. In the prototype described here (see Fig. 1.2), we adjusted the saliency of visual cues (e.g., icons were prominently encircled). However, many other possibilities exist for the facilitation of error recovery (e.g., alerts, automated assistance, etc.)

It should be noted that the same system that accomplishes error detection and recovery might also be used as a training aid. In this case, an ex-

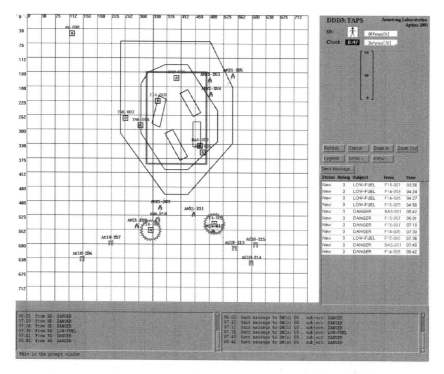

FIG. 1.2.   In this prototype, a cognitive model interprets events within the AWACS workstation simulation and a discrepancy detector identifies potential situation mode errors. As shown here, prominent circles highlight cues associated with an emerging situation for which the operator has not responded.

pert cognitive model would observe a trainee as he or she participates in simulation scenarios. Discrepancies would reflect occurrences in which the trainee responded in a manner inconsistent with the expert cognitive model's interpretation of events. These discrepancies would then provide the basis for training interventions.

Surveillance and Cognitive Collectives

Within limits, humans are generally very good at assessing a complex array of data and recognizing meaningful patterns or events within those data (Klein, 1997). However, as the number of data sources and associated breadth and variety of data exceed practical limits, humans are quickly faced with the common experience of information overload. The problem is exacerbated by the ever-expanding volumes of archival data. Consequently, people have coped by turning to a variety of automated alerting and data-mining solutions.

As an alternative to current algorithms used in surveillance and data mining, a cognitive model may serve the same function. In such systems, various data streams are assigned as input to the cognitive model and intermediate algorithms used to synthesize and convert data so they are consistent with the concepts or cues utilized by the cognitive model. Next, the cognitive model is supplied with various contexts that it recognizes. These may be contexts that span the range from extremely brief (i.e., milliseconds) to extremely long (i.e., years) temporal intervals. In addition to the recognition of contexts, cognitive models may also use the comparator as a mechanism to detect and alert users to anomalous events (e.g., deviant transaction).

The choice of a cognitive model may vary. For many applications, individuals would prefer their own cognitive model (e.g., observing news streams for stories of interest). However, in using a specific cognitive model, one is bound by the knowledge residing in that model. This is the same problem commonly faced with respect to the fact that any given individual is bound by the knowledge and experiences that they possess, with the accompanying biases and limitations (Blanchette & Dunbar, 2002; Clement & Richard, 1997). Therefore, as we have demonstrated in prototype systems, it is often desirable to use multiple cognitive models based on different individuals and perhaps individuals who represent very different perspectives (e.g., different disciplines, specialties, cultures, etc.).

In prototypes that we have developed (see Fig. 1.3), cognitive models based on experts from different domains of expertise observe data and respond to patterns specific to each cognitive model (Jordan et al., 2002). In addition, these cognitive models may also interact with one another to create what we have referred to as a *cognitive collective.*

Our prototype cognitive collectives have emphasized modes of interaction based on research concerning the interaction between individuals within group decision-making contexts (e.g., Bartolo, Dockrell, & Lunt, 2001; Gibson, 2001). First, there is thematic spreading activation. Separate cognitive models may respond to similar, yet distinct concepts (e.g., excessive spending relative to a mean and excessive spending relative to a threshold). These concepts may be assigned to a common theme. When one model observes a concept, there is priming of concepts in other models that fall within the same theme. If the concept being primed is not already activated, this priming serves to either partially activate the concept or lower the threshold for its activation.

Second, there is reminding. Two cognitive models may both respond to the same or two closely related concepts. However, the models may differentially assign significance to the concept(s) such that the effect of the

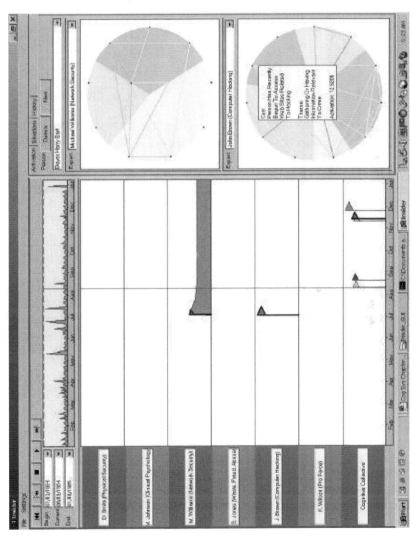

FIG. 1.3. This interface depicts the operation of multiple cognitive models for a period of one year. Flags indicate when a model has recognized a context of interest. Circle plots indicate specific concepts and patterns of concepts for which models responded, as well as priming of concepts by one another. A mouse-over opens a window with details concerning specific events. The bottom panel indicates the responses of a cognitive collective consisting of each of the six experts depicted in the above panels.

concept persists for a longer duration with one model relative to the other model (i.e., differential decay function). Through reminding, the cognitive model for which the concept has the greater persistence reminds (i.e., re-activates the concept) the other cognitive model of the concept once activation of the concept has diminished within the second cognitive model.

Through the combination of these mechanisms, the cognitive collective may allow significant events to be detected in cases where no single model is capable of recognizing a pattern on its own.

Memory Prosthetic

With regard to either factual or experiential knowledge, human memory possesses remarkable capacities. However, the functional value of specific memories is directly proportionate to their accessibility. It is a common frustration that we know the knowledge exists in our memory, but we cannot access it (e.g., Where did I leave my keys? What have I told this person and what have I not told this person? Where have I heard that before?). Many devices have been adopted to serve as memory prosthetics (e.g., organizers, to do lists, etc.). However, these devices require varying levels of investment by a user for them to be effective.

In an earlier section, we discussed the concept of an *aide*. This technology consists of a cognitive model that observes an individual and their transactions with various computing devices and acquires a reasonably accurate cognitive model of that individual's knowledge and experience. In one of its simplest manifestations, such an aide may serve as a memory prosthetic. Unlike current analogous memory prosthetics (e.g., Personal Data Assistants [PDAs]), an aide passively collects data requiring a minimum investment by the user.

As implemented in our PC-based prototypes, the aide collects a record of an individual's transactions that includes text generated and read by the user, as well as the user's keyboard and mouse activities. To query the aide, a user may either highlight a section of text or enter a text-based query. As shown in Fig. 1.4, in response to a query, the aide provides a list of semantically similar events (e.g., e-mails, documents, etc.). Additionally, the aide creates a bar chart in which events corresponding to the query are depicted on a time line. This feature allows the user to trace the genesis of an idea across time and note the ebbs and flows of activity related to a given topic.

Beyond facilitating recall, memory prosthetics may benefit users through mechanisms that provide a unique perspective on an individual's experiences. For instance, events may be placed on a landscape in which the x and y dimensions represent an index of semantic similarity and clusters of similar events produce a profile in the z dimension (see Fig. 1.5).

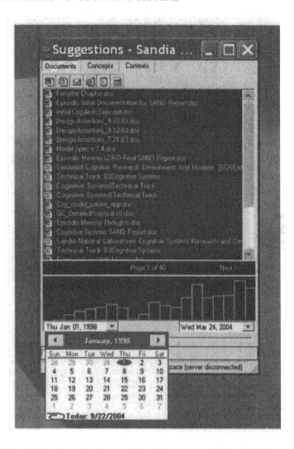

FIG. 1.4. The lead author's cognitive aide was queried using the text from the earlier section of this chapter describing semantic memory in the Sandia cognitive modeling framework. Files are listed in rank-order based on their semantic similarity to the text selected for the query. The bar chart shows the number of similar records from the past six years. By default, color coding indicates the relative similarity, however color coding is also used to indicate the relative recency of events.

Similarly, one or more documents may be selected as the basis for forming a context. Then once a context has been formed, current and archived records may be queried on the basis of their correspondence to the context. For example, a document describing a technical advance may be used to create a context and then other documents identified that describe the same or similar intellectual property. Finally, a specific time period may be selected and a record produced of activities that occurred during the selected time frame, as well as the key concepts and contexts that characterize activities during the selected time frame.

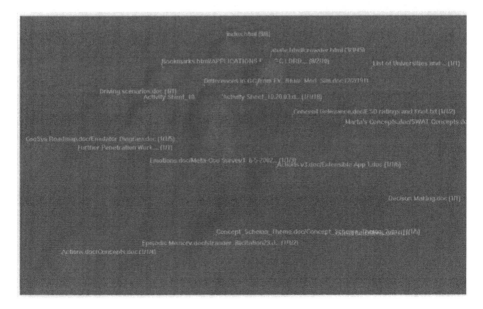

FIG. 1.5. A landscape visualization is used to depict the semantic similarity of documents created by a user.

Finally, whereas the utilities described so far have been focused on an individual user, the same capabilities may be extended to work with groups of individuals (e.g., peers, coworkers). Here an individual would make their aide available to others through some mechanism such as a peer-to-peer network. Other individuals could then submit queries to their colleague's aides to identify relevant events from their colleague's past experiences. For instance, a customer support representative troubleshooting a problem may query their colleagues' aides to see whether anyone else has seen anything similar.

Cognitive State Adaptation

Although far from perfect, humans exhibit a capacity to adjust their interactions with regard to the cognitive state of other individuals. In everyday dialogue, one may pause for a moment to allow other individuals to process a certain piece of information. In an automobile, a passenger may momentarily suspend their conversation as the driver undertakes a difficult maneuver. In response to apparent fatigue, one may slow the pace of an activity or propose taking a break. Where it is known that there is some sensitivity associated with a topic, one may choose their words more carefully than they might otherwise. These are all examples of adaptations that regularly occur within the context of human–human interactions, but are not part of typical human–machine interactions.

A family of technologies are proposed in which various measures are employed to gain an awareness of a user's ongoing cognitive state; based on this information, the machine appropriately adapts to the user's cognitive state (see Table 1.1). The following examples illustrate some of the many facets of cognitive state that may serve as the basis for system adaptations to a user, as well as the means by which systems may adapt (see Forsythe et al., chap 5, this volume, for related discussion of technologies for augmented cognition). In each case, the system employs a model of the user to determine the nature of its interaction with the user.

Through the DARPA Augmented Cognition program, we are currently working with DaimlerChrysler and other collaborators to implement cognitive state adaptation within an automotive application (see Kincses, chap. 10, this volume, for a detailed description of these activities). Vari-

TABLE 1.1
A Variety of Systems Are Proposed That Adapt
to the Cognitive State of the User

Data Sources	Cognitive State	System Adaptations
User actuation of controls	Tasks and goals, including relative urgency and progress toward goals	Adjust rate of information flow and associated scheduling
Eye-tracking and pupillary response	Awareness of stimuli or events	Adjust time profiles of automated systems
User head position	Situation interpretation or misinterpretation	Adaptive automation and/or allocation of tasks
User postural adjustments	Emotional state	Adjust saliency of information display elements
Physiological recordings	Impediments to normal cognitive functioning	System alerts
Physical location (e.g., GPS) and associated intelligence	Knowledge of domain or task(s)	Augmented context recognition and interpretation
System state variables	Skill levels or capabilities	User-tailored system support
External sensors	Actual and/or perceived physiological state	Adaptive training
Communications	Perceived roles and responsibilities	
User response to structured queries	Awareness of others	

Note. Such systems consist of three elements: data source(s), the cognitive state(s) detected or monitored, and the means by which the system adapts to the user's cognitive state. This table lists various possibilities with regard to each element. Specific systems may consist of different combinations of elements, as well as alternative means to address a given element.

ous data sources are interpreted by a cognitive model to provide an ongoing indication of the context(s) relevant to the driver (see Fig. 1.6). For instance, the driver may be changing lanes on a high-speed roadway to
overcome a slow-moving truck while attempting to adjust the climate
control system, cognizant that the fuel level is uncomfortably low. In the
prototype system being developed through these efforts, some data are
obtained from the automobile (e.g., steering wheel angle, lateral acceleration, and activation of controls). Other data are obtained from the operator (e.g., head turning, postural adjustments, and vocalizations). Furthermore, through EEG analysis, there is a basis for inferring relative levels of
workload corresponding to driving situations. Knowing these facets of the
driver's cognitive state, the system may appropriately adapt. For example,
interactions with the driver may emphasize the auditory modality when

FIG. 1.6.   This figure illustrates an early prototype developed in collaboration with DaimlerChrysler and the University of Pittsburgh through the
DARPA Augmented Cognition program. The objective is to enable a vehicle
to automatically adapt to the cognitive state of a driver. One component of
this system is the context manager which utilizes a cognitive model to provide an ongoing indication of the driving context. This figure illustrates a
cognitive model trained to use a variety of cues from the automobile and the
driver to distinguish the contexts of lane following, preparing to execute a
lane change and changing lanes.

the driver is engaged in visually demanding activities. The engagement of advanced safety systems may be adjusted so that alerts are issued earlier and automated features are activated sooner. Finally, the flow of information from the vehicle to the driver may be adapted so that low-urgency transactions are not initiated during demanding situations (e.g., incoming telephone calls may be blocked while attempting to merge with high-speed traffic).

In a second example, prototypes are currently being developed in which the system adapts to the knowledge of the user, as well as the user's learning experiences. Such systems require as an enabling factor the ability to automatically capture a reasonably accurate cognitive model of the knowledge of the user. We accomplish this using two, and potentially three, sources of data. First, text generated and read by the user is collected. Second, a record is created of the actions taken as the user interacts with the keyboard and mouse to activate various features within selected software environments. Finally, data may be collected that provide an indication of ongoing physiological processes (e.g., cardiac response, EEG, NIR imaging, etc.). Given these data, various approaches may then be employed to derive a model of the user's knowledge of a domain or task.

Once a model of a user is available, there are various ways in which a system may adapt. For instance, online technical support may be custom generated with respect to the user's actual knowledge of a software product. Based on facial recognition of positive and negative emotional responses, the conditions for initiating automated features may be adjusted so as to maximize user satisfaction and minimize frustration and annoyance. Finally, using EEG measures to detect patterns of localized activity consistent with learning (e.g., violations of expectations), training scenarios may be adapted to optimize presentation of specific course content.

Perceptual Representation

These technologies involve a variant of cognitive systems in which cognitive models are utilized as a basis for perceptual data representations. This may involve a visualization interface that allows the knowledge within a cognitive model to be explored or the operation of the cognitive model observed (see Fig. 1.3). In other cases, one or more components of a cognitive model may be utilized to transform data into meaningful representations.

One example involves a system designed to facilitate the recognition of anomalies within data and counteract the tendency to overestimate the co-occurrence of concepts, events, properties, and so on, for which there is some associative relationship (Jennings et al., 1982). A visual display

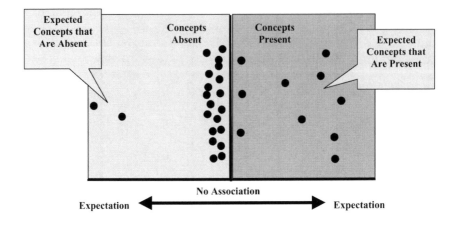

FIG. 1.7. Illustration of display concept that highlights expected concepts that are present, but perhaps more importantly, expected concepts that are absent.

may be created that highlights the absence of concepts highly associated with those concepts that are actually present. Given input concerning concepts present within some temporal or spatial block, a numeric value may be assigned to each concept such that concepts that are expected, based on their association with other concepts that are present, receive proportionately higher positive values. In contrast, concepts that are absent receive negative values with the magnitude a function of their association to concepts that are present.

For instance, because the concepts *desert* and *hot* have a relatively strong association, it is common to assume that all desert areas are hot, although temperatures may be mild in the high desert. Thus, using the case of desert and hot, if both conditions are present, both concepts would receive a positive value. In contrast, if desert is present, but hot is not present, a relatively large negative value would be assigned to hot because it would be expected given desert (see Fig. 1.7).

Human–Computer Interaction

As noted in an earlier section, we distinguish cognitive systems from those that merely utilize some form of humanlike visual representation (e.g., avatar-based interface) or means of communication (e.g., dialogue-based interaction). Instead a family of technologies is proposed in which a cognitive model provides a medium for human–computer interactions. However, we would expect that such technologies might often be enhanced by humanlike visual representations and means of communication.

Although the idea of using a cognitive model as a basis for human–computer interaction applies to a broad range of applications, here we focus on two of the more intriguing possibilities. The first involves technologies that utilize expert cognitive models in a role where they act as synthetic consultants, team members, or mentors. Such technologies were described previously for surveillance and the extension of error detection and recovery to training applications. However, such capabilities may similarly enable a user to query and pose unique problems to the expert cognitive model. In response, the model may provide an explanation of its cognitive processes based on the knowledge and experiences in its memory. For example, in the context of surveillance applications, an expert cognitive model might briefly account for the context(s) that was recognized, the pattern of concepts associated with the context and perhaps, past experience involving the recognized context, or other similar contexts. This could involve a dialogue-based discourse, but the interaction could also occur through some form of visualization or other mode of human–computer interaction.

Taken a step further, we have proposed concepts in which a user may assemble a group of expert cognitive models to form a synthetic council. In this case, the user may pose a scenario and observe the interaction between the synthetic experts as they apply their knowledge and experience to arrive at individual and collective interpretations of the situation. This represents an extension of the cognitive collective concept mentioned earlier. Furthermore, mechanisms may be employed to make the interaction between expert cognitive models explicit and comprehensible to the user in a manner that does not occur with comparable interactions with actual human experts.

Another variation on these ideas may be described as a synthetic mentor. Provided capabilities to acquire a reasonably accurate cognitive model of the knowledge of a user, this model may be compared to that of an expert serving in the role of a mentor. These comparisons would provide the mentor a basis for querying and challenging the user. For instance, where an association exists between two concepts in the mentor's model, but not in the protégée's model, the mentor may pose a series of questions to facilitate the protégée grasping the association. Likewise the mentor might re-create for the protégée relevant experiences of the mentor through either dialogue or simulations so the protégée becomes familiar with events giving rise to key facets of the mentor's knowledge.

Finally, there is the field of cognitive robotics in which various groups are borrowing ideas from human and animal cognition in creating robotic systems (e.g., Clark & Grush, 1999). In simulation, we have demonstrated the use of a cognitive model as a basis for interpreting environmental events by a robotic system—specifically, a swarm of robots programmed to enter a facility and follow a smoke gradient to locate its source (Schoenwald et al., 2002). However, as robotic systems are advanced for everyday applications, and in particular for use in homes and nonindustrial businesses, there is a potentially fruitful opportunity for a cognitive model to be utilized as the interface between the robot(s) and humans with whom the robot(s) must interact. This would create the opportunity for robotic systems to operate as cognitive entities, with the associated characteristics discussed previously, and human–robot interfaces to be developed that are more akin to a human–human interface than would otherwise be possible.

Knowledge as Commodity

The final illustration concerns a unique method of commerce that is enabled through cognitive systems technologies. As described in previous sections, once an individual's unique knowledge and experience can be captured and applied in a practical manner (e.g., surveillance, synthetic mentor, etc.), the individual's cognitive model may be packaged and traded as a commodity. For instance, a well-known expert may copyright his or her knowledge of a domain much like an artist copyrights his or her work. For example, when purchasing computer-aided design software, an engineer may select a dozen expert models from different domains that will come installed with the software. The engineer may then interact with these experts in a manner consistent with the ideas discussed in the preceding sections. Accordingly, experts may expect to receive a royalty each time their knowledge model is sold or upgraded (i.e., once an expert makes his or her knowledge available, he or she may choose to upgrade it every year or so). Finally, it becomes possible that vast libraries may be created containing models of different experts and expert knowledge sold to subscribers not unlike music CDs of artists are sold today.

CONCLUSION

The objective of this chapter has been to offer a general definition for *cognitive systems*, as well as the constituent components of cognitive systems, and present examples of systems that are consistent with this definition. Through a program of research and development at Sandia National Laboratories, we have made substantial investment in establishing the theoretical and technical foundations for cognitive systems and demonstrating the potential for cognitive systems through various prototype systems. In co-hosting the first Cognitive Systems Workshop in 2003, our intent was to provide a forum for individuals from other organizations pursuing similar paths to meet, discuss their respective ideas, and demonstrate their developments. Similarly, our goals for this book are to provide a vehicle to advance thinking and disseminate ideas concerning cognitive systems.

Arguably, many current technologies that have sought to enhance the effectiveness of humans working with machines have reached a point of diminishing returns where continued investment will only produce incremental gains. This applies to traditional areas of human–computer interaction, artificial intelligence, and data mining and visualization. We believe that the next major gains in human effectiveness will be the product of a reconceptualization of the problem and paradigmatic shift in the approaches taken to solve the problem. Cognitive systems are advanced as a candidate for this breakthrough in human–machine interaction.

If our prognosis is correct, the potential for cognitive systems is limited only by the imagination of developers and visionaries. It is with no reservations that we assert that, brought to maturity, cognitive systems could offer a breakthrough equivalent to the transition from command line to graphical user interfaces that occurred in the 1980s or the transition to Internet and network-based computing that began in the 1990s and has continued into the new millennium. We hope that the chapters throughout the remainder of this book serve to foster a similar optimism and enthusiasm for cognitive systems, and inspire researchers, students, developers, managers, and sponsors to contribute to this emerging field.

ACKNOWLEDGMENTS

This work was performed at Sandia National Laboratories. Sandia is a multiprogram laboratory operated by Sandia Corporation, a Lockheed-Martin Company, for the U.S. Department of Energy under Contract DE-AC04-94AL85000.

REFERENCES

Bartolo, P. A., Dockrell, J., & Lunt, J. (2001). Naturalistic decision making task process in multiprofessional assessment of disability. *Journal of Scholl Psychology, 39,* 499–519.

Biederman, I. (1981). On the semantics of a glance at a scene. In M. Kubovy & J. R. Pomerantz (Eds.), *Perceptual organization* (pp. 213–263). Hillsdale, NJ: Lawrence Erlbaum Associates.

Blanchette, I., & Dunbar, K. (2002). Representational change and analogy: How analogical inferences alter target representations. *Journal of Experimental Psychology-Learning, Memory and Cognition, 28*(4), 672–685.

Clark, A., & Grush, R. (1999). Toward a cognitive robotics. *Adaptive Behavior, 7*(1), 5–16.

Clement, E., & Richard, J. (1997). Knowledge of domain effects in problem representation: The case of Tower of Hanoi isomorphs. *Thinking and Reasoning, 3*(2), 133–157.

Dagenbach, D., Horst, S., & Carr, T. H. (1990). Adding new information to semantic memory: How much learning is enough to produce automatic priming. *Journal of Experimental Psychology-Learning Memory and Cognition, 16,* 581–591.

Foltz, P. W., Kintsch, W., & Landauer, T. K. (1998). The measurement of textual coherence with latent semantic analysis. *Discourse Processes, 25,* 285–307.

Forsythe, C., Bernard, M., Xavier, P., Abbott, R., Speed, A., & Brannon, N. (2003). *Using psychologically plausible cognitive models to enhance operator performance.* Proceedings of the 47th annual meeting of the Human Factors and Ergonomics Society, Denver, CO.

Gibson, C. B. (2001). From knowledge accumulation to accommodation. Cycles of collective recognition in work groups. *Journal of Organizational Behavior, 22,* 121–134.

Holroyd, C. B., Dien, J., & Coles, M. G. H. (1998). Error-related scalp potentials elicited by hand and foot movements: Evidence for an output-independent error-processing system in humans. *Neuroscience Letters, 242,* 65–68.

Jennings, D. L., Amabile, T. M., & Ross, L. (1982). Informal covariation assessment: Data-based versus theory-based judgments. In D. Kahneman, P. Slovic, & A. Tversky (Eds.), *Judgement under uncertainty: Heuristics and biases* (pp. 211–230). New York: Cambridge University Press.

Jordan, S., Forsythe, C., Speed, A., Wenner, C., & Goldsmith, T. E. (2002). *Extensibility of knowledge-based human-agent simulation.* SAND2002-3714, Sandia National Laboratories, Albuquerque, NM.

Klein, G. (1997). An overview of naturalistic decision making applications. In C. E. Zsambok & G. Klein (Eds.), *Naturalistic decision making* (pp. 49–59). Mahwah, NJ: Lawrence Erlbaum Associates.

Klimesch, W., Doppelmayr, M., Pachinger, T., & Russegger, H. (1997). Event-related desynchronization in the alpha band and the processing of semantic information. *Cognitive Brain Research, 6,* 83–94.

LeDoux, J. (1998). *The emotional brain: The mysterious underpinnings of emotional life.* New York: Touchstone.

Levine, L. J., Prohaska, V., Burgess, S. I., Rice, J. A., & Laulhere, T. M. (2001). Remembering past emotions: The role of current appraisals. *Cognition and Emotion, 15,* 393–417.

Luu, P., & Tucker, D. M. (2002). Self-regulation and the executive functions: Electrophysiological clues. In A. Zani & A. M. Preverbio (Eds.), *The cognitive electrophysiology of mind and brain* (pp. 199–223). San Diego: Academic Press.

Magliano, J. P., Miller, J., & Zwaan, R. A. (2001). Indexing space and time in film understanding. *Applied Cognitive Psychology, 15*(5), 533–545.

Menon, V., Boyett-Anderson, J. M., Schatzberg, A. F., & Reiss, A. L. (2002). Relating semantic and episodic memory systems. *Cognitive Brain Research, 13,* 261–265.

Mizuki, Y., Kajimura, N., Kai, S., Suetsugi, M., Ushijima, I., & Yamada, M. (1992). Differential responses to mental stress in high and low anxious normal humans assessed by frontal midline theta activity. *International Journal of Psychophysiology, 12,* 169–178.

Olson, W. A., & Sarter, N. B. (2001). Management by consent in human–machine systems: When and why it breaks down. *Human Factors, 43*(2), 255–266.

Perfetti, C. A., & Roth, S. F. (1981). Some of the interactive processes in reading and their role in reading skill. In A. M. Lesgold & C. A. Perfetti (Eds.), *Interactive processes in reading* (pp 269–297), Hillsdale NJ: Lawrence Erlbaum Associates.

Rugg, M. D., & Coles, M. G. H. (1995). *Electrophysiology of mind: Event-related potentials and cognition.* New York: Oxford University Press.

Schoenwald, D., Xavier, P., Thomas, E., Forsythe, C., & Parker, E. (2002, May 11–15). Simulation of a cognitive architecture for a distributed robotic sensing network. *Proceedings of International Society of Robotics and Automation,* Washington, DC.

Schvaneveldt, R. W. (1990). *Pathfinder associative networks: Studies in knowledge organization*, Norwood, NJ: Ablex.

Vaidya, C. J., Zhao, M., Desmond, J. E., & Gabrieli, J. D. E. (2002). Evidence for cortical encoding of specificity in episodic memory: Memory-induced re-activation of picture processing areas. *Neuropsychologia, 40*, 2136–2143.

Zwaan, R., & Radvansky, G. A. (1998). Situation models in language comprehension and memory. *Psychological Bulletin, 123*(2), 162–185.

PART TWO

THEORETICAL AND EMPIRICAL BASIS FOR COGNITIVE SYSTEMS

CHAPTER TWO

Situation Models in Comprehension, Memory, and Augmented Cognition

David E. Copeland
University of Southern Mississippi

Joseph P. Magliano
Northern Illinois University

Gabriel A. Radvansky
University of Notre Dame

This chapter is about how people understand situations and events, and how this understanding affects how they think about the world and their interaction with other people. The larger aim is to provide some insights into how augmented cognition can be better achieved by a more thorough understanding of how people conceive of and communicate about events. We do this by taking a perspective on event comprehension and memory known as situation model theory (Johnson-Laird, 1983; van Dijk & Kintsch, 1983; Zwaan & Radvansky, 1998). We first provide a brief overview of the critical components of situation model theory and the aim of efforts in augmented cognition. Then we discuss some research on how people are able to identify situations in which they interact with strangers. After this we describe how a person's understanding of a dynamic, ongoing event affects their ability to perform in that situation, in this case, an aerial combat simulation. Finally, we address issues of how the structure of the ongoing situation is aided or hindered by various types of augmented cognition assistance.

SITUATION MODEL THEORY

Situation models are mental simulations of real or possible worlds (Johnson-Laird, 1983) that isomorphically capture the elements and their interrelations of an event. First, a situation is embedded in a spatial-temporal framework. This is the location in space (or some virtual space, such as a chatroom) in which the situation unfolds and the span of time that the situation operates as a coherent whole. The spatial-temporal framework provides the context that defines a static situation (e.g., Bower & Morrow, 1990; Radvansky & Zacks, 1991; Radvansky, Zwaan, Federico, & Franklin, 1998).

Within the spatial-temporal framework of a situation model are a number of tokens that stand for the entities involved in that situation, such as people, animals, objects, abstract concepts, and so on. Associated with these tokens can be various properties that are relevant for the current situation, including external (e.g., physical) and internal (e.g., mental or emotional) properties. Finally, there are *structural relations* among the tokens, including spatial, social, and ownership relations. The probability that these components are included in the situation model is a function of the degree to which they involve an actual or likely interaction among those elements. The entities and their functional relations provide the content for the static situation (Radvansky & Copeland, 2000; Radvansky, Spieler, & Zacks, 1993). Entity properties are of less importance unless they provide information about the functional relations among the entities in the situation.

In addition to individual moments in time, a situation model can capture more dynamic aspects of an event. This can be done by joining a series of spatial-temporal frameworks by a collection of linking relations. These linking relations include temporal and causal relations and are presumably grounded in the tokens of the situation model that stand for the entities undergoing transition in the situation. During the first reading of a text, reading times increase when there are breaks in causal coherence (Magliano, Trabasso, & Graesser, 1999; Magliano, Zwaan, & Graesser, 1999; Zwaan, Magliano, & Graesser, 1995) and temporal contiguity (Magliano et al., 1999; Therriault & Rinck, in press; Zwaan, 1996; Zwaan et al., 1995). Causal and temporal connectivity are strong predictors of coherence judgments (Magliano et al., 1999). Furthermore, the degree of causal connectivity of story constituents is a primary predictor of recall and summarization (see van Den Broek, 1994).

Isomorphism

Most of the work on situation models has focused on text comprehension and memory. However, situation models should capture events of all sorts, including those that are experienced directly. This is consistent with recent discussions of embodied cognition and perceptual symbols (Barsalou, 1999; Glenberg, 1997; Wilson, 2002; Zwaan, 2004). We adopt the view that human cognition evolved operating in and adapting to complex environments. This requires an organism to mentally represent various aspects of the world, mentally manipulate that information, and store it for future use. This is an ability that humans have developed to a high degree.

The standard way to think about situation models is that they are built up from propositions that are used as a scaffolding to create them. Although this may occur in some cases, such as in reading, it seems implausible for nonhuman organisms. Instead it is more reasonable to assume that these beasts are using mental representations derived from the perceptual qualities immediately available. The abstraction of propositions is a more highly developed skill that may have emerged out of our use of language.

As such, the situation model is the more fundamental mental representation, whereas abstract propositions are more complex and fragile. This is reflected in their more rapid rate of forgetting (Kintsch, Welsch, Schmalhofer, & Zimny, 1990) and proneness to distortion. In line with this thinking, we view the characteristics of situation models observed in text comprehension research as reflective of a more general event comprehension and memory process.

Augmented Cognition

The work being reported here is being done in the context of the idea of developing an augmented cognition system. Essentially, this is a computer-based system that would augment a person's current cognitive processes of comprehension and memory by monitoring important information that is likely to be out of a person's current awareness, detecting discrepancies between a person's current mental state and the actual state of the world, and monitoring changes in the current situation to help the person avoid pitfalls that could arise.

For any augmented cognition system to operate effectively in the real world, it needs to efficiently capture critical aspects of the evolving and dynamic situation in which the person is embedded. This includes general aspects of situation structure, such as spatial-temporal location, entities that are actually or potentially being interacted with, the relations among those entities, and the flow of the situation over time. More important, such a system must take into account the mental state of the person, such as their goals and understanding of the state of affairs and course of events. In addition, the system should keep track of past behaviors for the purpose of learning from the past or at least reminding of past actions.

The work reported here is aimed at achieving these goals. The work on inferring a stranger's goals takes into account the broader aspects of the situation, characteristics of the person, as well as how the person is involved in the situation. The work on situation structure looks at how a person's interaction with an ongoing situation in the world is affected by aspects of the environment that are identified and defined by situation model theory. Finally, the work on augmenting cognition looks at how various types of assistance can influence performance in an ongoing situation. Specifically, it considers when the assistance is provided in terms of the structure of the situation, the nature of the assistance given, and the mental state of the person receiving the assistance.

Inferring Others' Goals

An augmented cognitive system capable of assisting a person must be able to recognize the goals of the person and situations faced. Although goals may vary widely, we assume that there is a relatively closed set of possible ones within a particular context. Furthermore, computer applications, Internet sites, document and e-mail content, locations at work, and times of day provide further constraints on goals. The degree to which these cues inform an augmented cognitive system of a person's goals can vary. For example, a computer application and the file content may be more indicative of a person's goal than the time of day when that document was created.

Situation model theory provides a framework for an augmented cognitive system to categorize and evaluate the informativeness of cues associated with people's goals. Just as readers must understand and represent evolving narrative situations to understand why characters do what they do, augmented cognitive systems must understand and represent the unfolding experienced events. As such, we assess the situations faced by a person that correspond to the spatial-temporal framework, entities, and linking relationships.

In the coarsest sense, assuming that a user has a laptop computer, personal digital assistant (PDA), or similar device, the spatial-temporal framework could provide cues to the user goals. For example, perhaps a user only works on certain goals in certain locations at particular times of day, such as downloading sports scores only when on the train to/from work. From a more sophisticated perspective, Internet sites may also serve as (virtual) spatial-temporal frameworks, which are further intimately tied to the goals of a user. Namely, we go to specific sites to gather information to meet our goals. Thus, it is important for an augmented cognitive system to understand the classes of goals associated with specific Web sites.

Computer Applications and Documents as Elements of Computer Situations

Applications are an interesting aspect of a computer use episode because they could be considered either a location or an entity. They may be locations in that users view programs as places in the local computer environment (e.g., "get out of the word processor and go into the spreadsheet"). However, applications could be considered a tool and, as such, an entity that a user interacts with. Applications could be informative of goals to the extent that applications can be used for specific purposes (e.g., Word processors are used to create documents, spreadsheets are used to store data for analyses). Ultimately it is an empirical issue to address how and when applications are perceived as tools or locations. As becomes clear later, different types of cues have different levels of informativeness with respect to identifying the unfolding situation.

We consider user documents (e.g., word processing files, spread sheets, e-mail messages) as entities. The contents of the documents produced by a user are extremely informative of a user's goals. For example, if one is writing a specific report, that document file should have a considerable amount of topic-relevant language (e.g., words and phrases). Furthermore, documents that are being created to achieve a larger goal should share semantic content to the extent that they contain the same content words and ideas. As such, it is important for an augmented cognitive system to be able to assess the contents of documents and determine the relations between them.

This analysis is not a trivial task. New advances in computational linguistics and semantic processing, such as latent semantic analysis (LSA), may make the analysis of document content feasible. LSA is both a method for extracting and representing word meanings from a large corpus of text as well as a theory of knowledge representation (Landauer & Dumais, 1997). LSA uses a statistical method of extracting, representing, and inferring the semantic similarity among words. It is beyond the scope of this chapter to provide a detailed discussion of LSA, but it is important to understand that it can be used to assess similarity between any two units of language (e.g., words, sentences). If an augmented cognitive system had a corpus of documents that reflected different goals that the user faces, LSA could be used to identify the goal addressed in a document by comparing it with its LSA corpus. Specifically, the likely goal could be determined by identifying other documents most related to the current one. One caveat is that this approach is contingent on there being a relatively closed set of goals that a computer user would address in the work environment, as well as the extent that the user draws on different words, concepts, and phrases when creating documents to address those goals.

Computer User Emotions. An important aspect of this process are the computer users—specifically, their emotional states. It is important for an augmented system to understand when a user needs assistance. However, such indicators vary in their ease of extraction. For example, it is relatively easy to record how hard a user punches the keys on a keyboard or mouse. Significantly greater force may be a sign of frustration. Other indicators of emotion are facial expressions (Ekman, 2003) and sitting position. However, recording and interpreting these signs requires sophisticated hardware and software.

Dynamic Relations Between Actions

The dynamics involved in monitoring the relations between actions of a user are complex. For example, suppose a user receives an e-mail, goes directly to a spreadsheet file, transfers numbers (e.g., copy and paste) from that file into a new e-mail message, and transmits it to the sender of the original message. It can be inferred that these events are causally related and are all related to a common goal initiated by the first e-mail. An augmented cognitive system should be able to infer these kinds of relations. This is particularly important when creating a record of the goal episodes of a user. However, developing the procedures for inducing these relations is not trivial.

INFERRING AN AGENT'S GOALS

Researchers at Northern Illinois University (Joe Magliano, Anne Britt, John Skowronsky, Dominik Guess, and Aaron Larson) and Sandia National Laboratories (Chris Forsythe) have conducted studies for the development of the situation recognition algorithms for an augmented cognitive system. The underlying assumption is that a system should recognize circumstances faced by a user in a psychologically plausible way and that situation model theory provides a framework for achieving this. Our strategy was to develop an experimental paradigm that would be similar to the problem faced by a situation recognition system. We were particularly interested in determining the procedures for evaluating the relative importance of the different situational components. Of specific interest was the idea that this situation recognition system would combine cues in a linear fashion, and we needed to assess the psychological viability of this assumption.

We chose an experimental situation that involved assessing the goals of strangers during unsolicited social interactions (i.e., the stranger initiates the interaction without an invitation to do so). We sampled a broad range of goals, such as the solicitation of goods or services (e.g., wanting money, help jump-starting a car, or to borrow an object), establishing social relationships (e.g., wants to become a friend or a romantic partner), and harming another (e.g., rob or kill). It is expected that the static elements of the situations associated with these stranger goals would be very different. For example, the time, location, characteristics of the stranger, actions of the stranger, and characteristics of oneself (e.g., dress or emotional response) would differ in situations in which strangers want to become a friend or romantic partner relative to situations in which the stranger wants to rob you. Presumably, people have schemas associated with various social goals that index the co-occurrence of these situational elements.

Experiment 1

The first experiment was done to elicit the features of the situations associated with stranger goals within the categories defined earlier. One-hundred sixty people were asked to imagine a scenario in which they are interacting with a stranger who has a particular goal (e.g., wants to become our friend, wants money, wants to rob us) and then answered a questionnaire that elicited information about the time and location of the interaction, the characteristics and actions of the stranger, and the characteristics of oneself (see the appendix for the general structure of the questionnaire). We then identified nonidiosyncratic cues associated with each goal (i.e., cues produced by more than one participant). This approach yielded a cue × goal matrix containing the frequency with which each cue was related to each goal. We used this matrix to calculate the strength and uniqueness of association between the cues and the goals (see equations), which provided a basis for further studies:

Equation 1: Strength of association (SA) = (Freq of cue_i for $goal_n$)/(total number of participants who considered $goal_n$)

Equation 2: Uniqueness of associations (UA) = (Freq of cue_i for $goal_n$)/ (Sum of the frequencies for cue_i for $goals_{1-9}$)

Presumably, some cues should be more informative than others. Furthermore, the relative informativeness of SA and UA may vary across cue categories. We conducted two additional studies to assess this.

Experiment 2

In Experiment 2, 133 people considered whether a stranger in various situations would have a particular goal (i.e., any given participant was asked to consider only one goal throughout the experiment). People were given one cue at a time and asked to judge how likely a stranger would have that goal given the presence of the cues. Participants made judgments for the cues elicited in Experiment 1. In this context, some cues should be more informative of a given goal than others. For each goal, a distinction was made between the cues elicited in Experiment 1 (i.e., informative of the goal) and those cues that were not. For each participant, the average predictability judgments were calculated for the diagnostic and nondiagnostic cues within each category (i.e., location, time, stranger characteristics, actions of the stranger, and characteristics of oneself).

A series of regression analyses were done to assess the informativeness of the SA and UA scores. The dependent measure was the average predictability judgment of the cue-goal pairs (i.e., there were 1,410 items of analysis because there were 141 cues in the matrix multiplied by 10 goals). The independent variables were the SA and UA scores for a given cue-goal paring. Regression analyses were done separately on each cue category, and the results are provided in Table 2.1. These results suggest that SA and UA have different degrees of importance across the cue categories. For the spatial-temporal framework cues (i.e., location and time of day), SA appears to be more important than UA. Specifically, locations and times associated with stranger goals were more predictive of them. As such, it is plausible because we interact with individuals with a wide variety of goals across a relatively limited set of locations and times. As such there are relatively few instances in which a location and time are uniquely associated with a goal. For example, various campus locations, such as the dorm, classroom, and cafeteria, tend to be highly associated with multiple goals (e.g., friendship, filling out a survey, religious conversion). The same is true for time. Certain times of the day tend to be highly associated, but not uniquely associated with specific goals (e.g., noontime is moderately to highly associated with friendship, romance, needing money, survey, and religious conversion).

For the entities, SA and UA function differently for characteristics of oneself and the stranger. These characteristics include emotional states (e.g., happy, sad, scared), facial expressions, dress (e.g., casual, formal), and objects that one is carrying (e.g., bookbag, clipboard, gun). The SA scores associated with oneself were predictive of a stranger's goals, whereas UA scores were not. In contrast, both SA and UA scores were predictive of a stranger's goal, but the regression coefficients indicate that UA

TABLE 2.1
Standardized Beta Coefficients and Variance Explained for Regression
Analyses Conducted on Each Cue Category for Experiment 1

Predictor Variable	Cue Category				
	Location	Time	Self	Stranger	Actions
Strength of association	0.34*	0.39*	0.21*	0.24*	0.27*
Uniqueness	0.15*	−0.06	0.11	0.43*	0.40*
Variance explained	20%	12%	7%	34%	39%

Note. *p < .05.

was more informative than SA. In these cases, many of the characteristics of an entity tended to be uniquely associated with a relatively small set of goals. For example, the cue of a stranger having a bible was only present for the religious conversion goals, and the cue of having a weapon was only present for the goal to rob or kill.

The most direct evidence for the role of linking relations involved the cues associated with a stranger's actions. Given that actions are understood by inferring causal links between those actions and a goal (e.g., Suh & Trabasso, 1993; Trabasso et al., 1989), it is reasonable to assume that these findings imply that people were inferring causal relations between the stated action and the goal they were considering. The regression analyses on the cues associated with the stranger action indicated that both SA and UA were predictive of a stranger's goal, but the coefficients suggest that UA was more informative. As with entity cues, many actions tend to be uniquely associated with specific goals. For example, asking whether someone has jumper cables was only present in the goal to get a jumpstart, and asking for a phone number was only present in the goal to establish a romantic relationship.

Experiment 3

Differences in the estimated variance explained in the regression analyses suggest that there are differences in the extent that the cues are informative of a stranger's goal. Both characteristics and actions of the stranger accounted for the most variance. Next was location, which accounted for more than time of day, which accounted for more than characteristics of oneself. Experiment 3 was done to further explore this informativeness hierarchy. The method used for Experiment 3 was similar to that used for Experiment 2, except that, here, 150 people were shown combinations of all cue categories. The informativeness of the cue categories varied from high to low. An informativeness score for a cue of a goal was calculated by summing its weighted SA and UA scores. The weights were determined by the regression coefficients for SA and UA that were derived from the regression analyses performed on the data from Experiment 2.

A series of regression analyses were done on the mean predictability judgments for each cue category combination for each goal. The predictor variables were the informativeness scores for each cue category. To estimate the variance explained by each global category specified by situation model theory (e.g., spatial-temporal framework, entities and properties, and linking relations), a series of two-step hierarchical analyses were done. In the first step, all variables were force entered into the equation except those that corresponded to the global category under consideration, and these variables were force entered in the second step. To esti-

TABLE 2.2
Standardized Beta Coefficients and Variance Explained for Regression
Analyses Conducted on Each Cue Category for Experiment 2

Predictor Variables	Beta Weight	Variance Explained
Spatial-temporal		1%*
Location	0.06	
Time	0.11*	
Entities		7%*
Stranger	0.29*	
Self	0.10*	
Linking relations		11%*
Stranger's actions	0.40*	
All variables		54%

Note.   *$p < .05$.

mate the variance accounted for by a global category, R^2 changes were calculated for the second step in the equations. Table 2.2 lists the estimated
variance explained for each global category and beta weights for each predictor variable. These results indicate that there are differences in the extent to which cue categories are informative of strangers' goals. Specifically, linking relations (as specified by a stranger's actions) accounted
for the most variance. The entities and properties accounted for the next
highest amount of variance. Both characteristics of the stranger and oneself were predictive of a strangers goal, but the beta weights suggest that
characteristics of the stranger are more informative that those of oneself.
Finally, the spatial-temporal framework accounted for the least amount of
variance. Time of day was a significant predictor, but location was not.

CONCLUSIONS

The results of these experiments contribute to the development of a context recognition component of augmented cognitive systems, with respect
to situation-goal elements of contexts. First, these results indicate that the
situation model theory can serve as a framework for identifying the cues
that should be monitored by an augmented system. Moreover, an augmented cognition system needs to be sensitive and able to compute the
relative informativeness of different cues that are monitored. Furthermore, the informativeness of a cue can be computed by determining
measures of SA and UA.

The data from Experiment 3 allow us to address the issue of whether a
system assumes that cues combine in a linear fashion. However, the question remains as to whether this is a psychologically valid assumption. The

regression equation for Experiment 3 assumes a linear relationship between cues and accounted for 55% of the variance. We plotted the average human judgments per item against the predicted scores derived by the regression equation. We assessed the extent to which quadratic and logarithmic functions describe this relationship. The quadratic equations accounted for 51% and the logarithmic function accounted for 43% of the variance. Thus, these results indicate that an assumption of a linear relationship between cues is reasonable.

SITUATION STRUCTURE AND PERFORMANCE

What we have discussed so far is the ability to identify the type of ongoing situation. Now we look at how a person's performance within that situation is affected by the dynamic structure of the ongoing events. We have a detailed analysis of an ongoing event—namely, a person's ability to successfully perform while playing a computer aerial combat game, and how this ability is influenced by a number of situational characteristics. This is important to the development of augmented cognition because any system that interacts with a person, and has the aim of accentuating their mental abilities, must understand the mental state of the individual and how that mental state is affected by the structure of the current environment and how dynamic aspects of that situation alter a person's understanding.

Experiment 4: Situation Structure and Performance

This section and the next are part of a larger study conducted by Seth Allen, David Copeland, Greer Kuras, Tiffany Milligan, G. A. Radvansky, Jenny Rinehart, Maureen Ritchie, and Brian Stouffer at the University of Notre Dame, as well as Chris Forsythe at Sandia National Laboratories. In this section, we focus primarily on the structure of the evolving situation and how this influences performance within that situation.

The Situation

For the purposes of this study, we had people play a video game. This was done to give people a dynamic situation in which to interact. The game chosen for this study was "Master of the Skies: The Red Ace." This is a World War I flight combat simulation in which the player is given various missions that involve destroying ground targets and shooting down enemy planes.

We coded performance for changes in the dynamic situation according to the principles outlined by situation model theory and assessed per-

formance as a function of achieving predefined goals. We assessed the occurrence and changes of situational elements during game play. In terms
of the spatial-temporal framework, because time was continuous, we did
not code for this component. Space was also continuous. However, unlike
time, there were various elements of the regions in which the space was
defined by clear landmarks, such as mountains, road intersections,
bridges, collections of buildings, airfields, rivers, and so forth. We divided
each combat zone into predefined regions based on these landmarks and
noted which region a player was in at any given moment in time.

As for the entity information, we coded the situations for four types of
entities: (a) allied planes, (b) enemy planes, (c) enemy targets, and (d) enemy anti-aircraft guns. Some of the relational information is implied by the
nature of the entities. For example, a friendly relation exists between the
pilot and the allied planes, and an adversarial relation exists between
the pilot and the enemy planes, targets, and anti-aircraft guns. We also explicitly coded spatial relations. Of primary interest was whether the entities were within a zone of interaction with the pilot or were distant and
there was no possibility of interaction.

This sort of situation is interesting because it allows us to also code situational characteristics of the person's actions within the situation—something that has not been possible with narrative text or film. For the pilot
we coded how (s)he interacted with the other entities. This included firing
machine guns, dropping bombs, or firing rockets. In this simulation, a pilot had the option of using the machine guns in every mission. However,
for any given mission, the plane was equipped with either bombs or rockets depending on the needs and goals of the mission.

Performance

The relationship between changes in situational dimensions and pilot
performance was assessed. Pilot success was determined by the number of
completed missions, enemy planes that were destroyed, enemy targets
that were destroyed, enemy anti-aircraft guns that were destroyed, and
hits taken by the pilot (i.e., from enemy fire). More generally, we looked at
performance in terms of (a) individual missions as a whole, and (b) ongoing performance by dividing actions into 5-second bins and assessing performance as a function of situational characteristics within those bins. As
such, mission success was only used in the mission analyses, and the other
dependent measures were used in both types of analyses.

Before looking at the influence of each situational component on performance, it should be noted that many of the data analyses were done using conditionalized subsets of data. For example, when looking at the ability of a pilot to destroy enemy targets, we only consider that subset of data

in which targets were actually present. Another component of this type of analysis was the idea of a *zone of interaction*. The regions in which pilots were flying were rather large. As such, not all entities in the space were relevant to the situation because some entities were far away. We assume that performance was more likely to be affected by entities that were relatively close to the person because these entities were in the foreground of the unfolding situation. This zone included an area around the player in which entities could affect the pilot (e.g., shoot him or her) or the pilot could affect them (e.g., shoot a target). For this task, in the upper right-hand corner of the screen was a display that essentially served as a radar screen with the pilot in the center and entities of interest (i.e., targets, enemy planes, allied planes, and anti-aircraft guns) indicated by various symbols. Entities that were far away were on the edge of this circle. Closer entities were within the circle. For our purposes, we defined the zone of interaction as being a circle whose circumference was halfway from the pilot's current position and the edge of the circle. Unless otherwise stated, or where it is implausible, all bin analyses are based on data selected for entities within the zone of interaction.

Spatial Framework. *Shifts in space* were defined as a player moving from one predefined region to another. Because this involved looking at transitions, we only looked at spatial shifts in the bin analyses. The results of these analyses are reported in Table 2.3. In terms of enemy entities, people were less successful at destroying enemy targets and anti-aircraft during a time that they had made a spatial shift than otherwise, although these differences did not reach significance, $t(14) = 1.69$, $p = .11$, and $t(14) = 1.39$, $p = .19$, respectively. There was no difference for destroying enemy planes, $t < 1$. This is consistent with the idea that spatial shifts can be disruptive to processing, much as what is observed in text processing, but this is more likely to be true when a person is interacting with entities rooted in the defined regions. In this case, the enemy targets and anti-aircraft guns were located in specific spatial regions, whereas the enemy planes were not. Thus, whether a person was moving across spatial re-

TABLE 2.3
Mean Performance for the Different Combat Dependent Measures
as a Function of Spatial Shifts in the Aerial Combat Study.
This Is Probability of Occurrence During a 5-Second Bin

Variable	Shift	No Shift
Enemy planes killed	.180	.176
Enemy targets destroyed	.196	.236
Enemy A.A. guns destroyed	.050	.079
Hits on pilot	.392	.370

gions when interacting with an enemy plane was of less importance. Finally, people were more likely to be hit by enemy gunfire when making a spatial shift than when not, although this difference also did not reach significance, $t(14) = 1.75$, $p = .10$.

Entity Variables. There were a number of entities in this situation with which the pilot could interact. These were: (a) allied fighters, (b) enemy fighters, (c) anti-aircraft guns, and (d) ground targets. We consider the influence of each of these entity types on performance.

For the allied fighters, because these were additional entities that were largely working to help satisfy the person's goals, it might be expected that their presence would facilitate performance. However, because people must be constantly monitoring the situation, it could also be that their presence could impede performance because this is an additional, dynamic element of the ongoing situation that the person must keep track of. The data are presented in Table 2.4. As can be seen in the attempt analysis, destroying enemy plane performance was significantly worse when allied planes were present than when they were not. Although this pattern was nominally present in the bin analysis, it did not reach significance. Conversely, although there was a nominal deficit in the attempt analysis for destroying enemy targets when allied planes were present, this pattern was significant in the bin analysis. Both of these types of analyses suggest that pilots were less likely to destroy enemy entities if there were allied planes present (in the zone for the bin analysis) than if there were not. This suggests that these additional entities can disrupt performance.

TABLE 2.4
Mean Performance for the Different Combat Dependent Measures
as a Function of Allied Plane Presence in the Aerial Combat Study.
This Is Rate of Occurrence for a Given Mission for the Attempt
Analysis and the Probability of Occurrence for the Bin Analysis

Variables	Present	Absent
Attempt analysis		
Mission success	.19	.20
Enemy planes killed	1.82	2.82*
Enemy targets destroyed	1.89	3.02
Enemy A.A. guns destroyed	.22	.02*
Hits on pilot	4.80	4.73
Bin analysis		
Enemy planes killed	.156	.169
Enemy targets destroyed	.237	.178*
Enemy A.A. guns destroyed	.130	.070*
Hits on pilot	.404	.354

Note. *$p < .05$.

It is unclear what to make of the anti-aircraft data given that in the attempt and bin analyses are somewhat conflicting. Part of this may be due to the relatively rare rate of anti-aircraft guns being destroyed for a mission, making the attempt analysis more suspect. The bin analysis is consistent with what is observed with the success of destroying ground targets.

Finally, it should be noted that the presence of allies did not influence the success of completing a mission or the ability to avoid being hit by enemy gunfire. This may have to do with the fact that enemy planes are the same type of entity as the allied planes, making it easier to coordinate that type of information, and that most of the hits pilots took were from enemy planes. Alternatively, it may also be that enemy planes were engaged with the allied planes as well as the pilot's.

What about entities working in opposition to the pilot? In this situation, these were enemy planes, targets, and anti-aircraft guns. To look at the influence of these entities on situation processing, we looked at the correlations between the number of entities of each type on the different performance measures (enemy planes killed, targets destroyed, anti-aircraft destroyed, and hits taken), again selecting only those data in which the entity of interest is in the zone of interaction during a 5-second bin. The results of these correlations are shown in Table 2.5.

A number of things can be clearly seen. First, for any given performance measure, there was a significant positive correlation with the number of entities involved for that task. For example, people were more likely to destroy an anti-aircraft gun when there were more of them in the zone of interaction ($r = .138$). This likely reflects that it is easier to hit a target when more are available.

Second, and more important, with regard to the entities that are not the focus of a given task, the more of these irrelevant entities there are, the less likely that a given task will be successfully completed. For example, the more enemy planes that were present in the zone of interaction, the

TABLE 2.5
Correlations of Performance for the Different Combat Dependent
Measures With the Number of Entities of Different Types
in the Aerial Combat Study

	Enemy Entities in the Zone of Interaction		
Variable	Planes	Targets	Anti-Aircraft
Enemy planes killed	.135*	−.087*	−.059*
Enemy targets destroyed	−.023	.135*	−.084*
Enemy A.A. guns destroyed	−.120*	−.029	.138*
Hits on pilot	.088*	.144*	.154*

Note. *$p < .05$.

less likely a pilot would successfully destroy an anti-aircraft gun that was also in that zone. Of the six correlations of this type, four of them were significant, and the other two were in the same direction. Finally, the number of entities of any type present in the zone of interaction also made it more likely that a person would be hit by enemy gunfire. Thus, the more entities that a person needed to track in the situation, the more difficult the task was.

Relational Information.   In this aerial combat simulation, there are a wide variety of interrelations among the entities, as well as between the pilot and the entities, that are going to influence a person's understanding of and performance in that situation. To provide an illustration of these influences, we look at relational information in the situation in two ways. The first is in terms of whether the person is actively interacting with entities in the situation, and the second is whether entities are in the zone of interaction.

With regard to the pilot's actions, there are two types of actions pilots can take in which they are clearly interacting with other entities in the situation. These are firing their machine guns and dropping a bomb or launching a rocket at a target. Because there will almost certainly be a positive correlation between taking these actions and destroying the enemy, we focus on the cost to the pilots—namely, the number of hits taken. For firing their machine guns, there was no correlation between whether the guns were being fired and hits being taken when there were enemy entities in the zone of interaction ($r = .004$, $p = .88$). This is likely because gunfire is usually directed at enemy planes. These planes can either be attacking the pilot or flying away. Thus, there is little relation between the pilots' actions and the consequence of those actions for this case. In contrast, for dropping bombs and firing rockets, there was a significant mean correlation between this activity and taking a hit ($r = .200, p < .001$). Thus, when a pilot was making a run on some target, he or she was more likely to be hit by gunfire, which usually came from some entity not currently the focus of the ongoing situation. As such, a person was more susceptible to damage when the situational structure in his or her mind opened him or her up to this possibility.

The other way to look at relational information is in terms of entities in the zone of interaction. Perhaps the comparison of most interest in this context is whether enemy planes are in the zone of interaction when the person is attacking enemy ground targets. In this case, the enemy planes are irrelevant entities that could disrupt the attack on the ground targets. What we did was look at those cases in which there were ground targets in the zone of interaction and there were enemy planes present somewhere in the situation. We looked at the success of destroying a target when the enemy planes were all out of the zone of interaction or when there were some present in the zone. What we found is that people were nominally more successful when there were no planes in the zone ($M = .218$ success), compared with when there were some ($M = .207$), but this difference was not significant, $t < 1$. Thus, although there was some support for the idea that the presence of other entities that can interact with a person in the situation can disrupt processing, the effect was minimal at best. What these findings may indicate is that when people are focused on one element of the situation (such as a target), people do not actively attend to and process other entities in the situation that are outside of the foreground of the situation model.

Combined Analyses. At this point, it is clear that there are a number of aspects of a situation that can influence how a person is actively processing and operating in the course of events. However, for more thorough understanding of the impact of situational structure on performance, it would be best to consider the combined influence of various factors, rather than individual pieces one at a time. This can be done in the current context by entering the data into a series of regression analyses that incorporate the variables described earlier.

We did four regression analyses, the results of which are reported in Table 2.6. By taking into account all of the factors we have discussed, although many of the previously reported results reemerged, there were some interesting differences. First, when spatial shifts were considered alone they did not have a significant impact on performance, but when more of the situation is considered there were two marginally significant influences. Specifically, spatial shifts were associated with a lower likelihood of destroying an enemy target and a lower likelihood of being hit by enemy gunfire. Essentially, it appears as if, during a spatial shift, people are less likely to engage with the enemy perhaps as a side effect of having to mentally manage the spatial shift.

TABLE 2.6
Regression Analyses Results, in Terms of Beta Weights,
for the Various Performance Measures in the Aerial Combat Study

Variable	Spatial Shifts	Allied Planes	Enemy Planes	Enemy Targets	A.A. Guns	Firing Guns	Bombs/ Rockets
Enemy plane killed	.007	−.021	.142*	−.074*	−.068*	—	—
Targets destroyed	−.042**	−.070*	−.005	.138*	−.063*	—	—
A.A. guns destroyed	−.030	.079	−.194**	−.183*	.198*	—	—
Hits on pilot	−.019**	−.061*	.141*	.127*	.124*	.004	.158*

*$p < .05$.
**$.05 < p < .10$.

In terms of the presence of entities in the situation, as was observed earlier, people were more likely to accomplish a given task (e.g., shoot down enemy planes) when there was more of that entity type present in the zone of interaction, as evidenced by the large positive beta weights (.142, .138, and .198, respectively). Again, the more things there were to destroy in the zone, the more likely this would happen. However, in terms of irrelevant entities, in every case where there is a significant or marginally significant effect, these additional entities had a disruptive influence on performance. This was also true for many of the nonsignificant effects as well.

Finally, in terms of the relational information captured by whether a person was actively interacting with entities in the situation, taking into account a broader view of the structure of the situation, it is seen that whether people are firing their machine guns did not influence their being hit by enemy gunfire, but they were much more vulnerable when they were focusing on a fixed target with their bombs or rockets.

Conclusions

This study illustrates that it is possible to take the principles and methods developed in research on situation models in language comprehension and memory and adapt them to ongoing situations in which the person is an active participant. Aspects of a situation that involve updating information about the ongoing event, or tracking multiple, similar aspects of the event, have the potential to disrupt processing. By providing this demonstration, we can identify cases in which the structure of the situation will both improve and, more important, diminish the performance of the person in achieving his or her goals. Taking this as the basis, we can now look at ways that we can augment a person's cognitive processes, using knowledge of the structure of the situation, by providing assistance to a person in an ongoing, developing, dynamic situation.

AUGMENTING COGNITION

In this section, we move from describing how the structure of a situation influences performance to a consideration of how providing assistance can help or harm people when they are interacting in these environments. This research looked at the impact of providing assistance to people while they were actively involved in a dynamic situation.

Overall, the results of three experiments are discussed. Experiment 4 looked at a situation in which, during an unfolding situation, people chose to provide assistance and the effectiveness of this assistance. This is a further analysis of the same study reported in the previous section. Experiment 5 was a more controlled study that looked at the impact of different types of assistance presented on a fixed schedule. Finally, Experiment 6 looked at the impact of different types of assistance as a function of the skill level of the person embedded in the situation. Thus, the person providing assistance is taking the role of an augmented cognition device, providing assistance based on the current state of the situation in which the person finds him or herself.

Experiment 4

In Experiment 4, we paired 30 people to form 15 player–coach teams. Each person was randomly assigned to each role. The two were seated in different rooms. The coach had a monitor to watch the game as it was played. In addition, both people wore headsets with microphones so they could hear the game and talk to each other. The game was played for three 45- to 60-minute sessions. Game play and conversations were recorded to DVD for later coding.

Comment Types

The coaches' comments were grouped into 10 categories. These categories segregated different types of information provided by the coach. A listing of these categories and examples of each are provided in Table 2.7. These 10 categories include the following: (a) *Episodic reminders* were comments that referred to a previous event or action in the game; (b) *misinterpretations* were comments in which the coach corrected a player's misinterpretation of the ongoing situation; (c) *knowledge gap* comments provided the player with general information about the situation that the player had forgotten; (d) *spatial attention* comments directed the

TABLE 2.7
Example and Proportions of Comments
of Each Type of Category for Experiment 4

Comment Category	Example Quote	Proportion
Episodic reminder	"Remember when you . . ."	.03
Misinterpretation	"Those are shells, not bullets."	.02
Knowledge gap	"Press 4 for the shotgun."	.08
Spatial attention	"It's to the left."	.11
Action suggestion	"Drop a bomb."	.20
Status attention	"Two targets remaining."	.29
Emotion control	"Calm down."	.01
Positive statement	"Good job Huggy-Bear!"	.11
Negative statement	"Stop crashing."	< .01
Other comments	"That shotgun is cool."	.15

player's attention to a location in the unfolding situation; (e) *action suggestions* were suggestions for movement or action within the situation; (f) *status attention* comments directed the player's attention to information about the status of the current situation (that were not spatial); (g) *emotion control* comments typically involved calming or comforting the player; (h) *positive statements* were supportive comments, typically after a successful action; (i) *negative statements* were comments that focus on negative actions or outcomes; and (j) *other comments* included anything that did not fit the first nine categories. Although most comments were easily classified into one category, some utterances contained information that could be placed in two categories. For example, "Fly to your left" provides both an action suggestion and spatial attention information.

The proportions of comments for each category type are listed in Table 2.7. As can be seen, the majority of comments were action suggestions, status attention, and spatial attention. These are important because they all focus on dynamic aspects of the ongoing situation. This suggests that the coaches were aware of the important components of the situations and could identify pieces that could be provided as assistance to the players.

Assistance and Success.   Let us now look at whether comments are related to performance success. Comments were given more often for successful ($M = .067$ comments/s) than unsuccessful missions ($M = .056$ comments/s), *Wilcoxon* $z = 2.04, p = .041, t(14) = 2.17, p < .05$. Looking at the various comment types, there was either no difference or comments occurred more often for successful than failed missions. However, the only statistically significant difference was for Status Attention comments, *Wilcoxon* $z = 2.445, p = .014, t(14) = 2.76, p = .02$. Thus, comments that augment a person's understanding of the ongoing situation provided the greatest benefit. An important further point is that comments were more beneficial for missions with goals of destroying ground targets ($M_{Success} = .072$ comments/s, $M_{Fail} = .058$ comments/s), *Wilcoxon* $z = 1.676, p = .094, t(14) = 1.75, p = .10$, than for destroying enemy planes ($M_{Success} = .063$ comments/s, $M_{Fail} = .082$ comments/s), *Wilcoxon* $z = 1.704, p = .088, t(14) = 1.82, p = .09$. This suggests that, although comments are helpful overall, the goal and type of situation affects whether comments help or harm performance. This is explored in more detail in Experiments 6 and 7.

Mission Types

The data were then analyzed in terms of the different types of missions people flew. These were classified as (a) single target, (b) multiple target, and (c) enemy plane missions. For single-target missions, the comments associated with success, other than positive reinforcement, *Wilcoxon z* = 3.045, *p* = .002, were increases of misinterpretations, *Wilcoxon z* = 1.577, *p* = .115, and action suggestions, *Wilcoxon z* = 1.306, *p* = .191. Thus, people benefited from corrections and ideas proposed by the coach. In addition to these relations, spatial attention comments were more likely to occur when the target was not destroyed, *Wilcoxon z* = 2.072, *p* = .038. It may be that directing the pilot's attention to regions of space other than the target is distracting or missions that a pilot is doing particularly poorly on are ones more likely to require a redirection of attention.

The pattern for multiple target missions differed from that for single target missions. Specifically, the comments associated with success, other than positive reinforcement, *Wilcoxon z* = 3.170, *p* = .002, were spatial attention, *Wilcoxon z* = 2.080, *p* = .038, and status attention, *Wilcoxon z* = 2.292, *p* = .022. The need to coordinate a plan of attack to take out targets in different locations placed different demands on the situation, which in turn affected the information provided by the coaches.

For missions that included no targets, only enemy planes, the only types of comments associated with success were positive reinforcement, *Wilcoxon z* = 3.296, *p* = .001, and emotion comments, *Wilcoxon z* = 1.890, *p* = .059. There were, however, fewer episodic, *Wilcoxon z* = 1.418, *p* = .156, and action suggestion comments, *Wilcoxon z* = 1.420, *p* = .156. Apparently, when the situation is extremely intense (these missions were described in the game as "Onslaughts"), coaches prefer to remain quiet. However, if they do provide information, it tends to hinder performance.

Comment Locations. Our analysis of when the comments occurred was based on the parsing of the events into five-second bins. That is, we considered what was happening in the situation, including whether comments occurred, for every 5-second interval of game play. To simplify things, we broke our variables down into three categories: (a) time-based, (b) pilot-based, and (c) external situation. Here we looked at whether there were any differences in when comments occurred.

Overall, comments were made by coaches in 26.8% of the bins. The *time-based variables* were day of testing, mission number, attempt within a mission, serial position of the attempt (from the start of the study), and bin within an attempt. Comments were more prevalent earlier in time, being more frequent during earlier days of testing, missions, attempts of a given mission, and overall. However, more comments were provided as the pilot progressed into a given mission. Thus, coaches provided less assistance as the pilots became more expert in this task, while providing increasing assistance as a given situation developed.

The *pilot-based variables* were gunfire, bomb/rocket launching, and taking a hit. Pilots were less likely to receive comments when they were actively engaged in firing their machine guns, *Wilcoxon z* = 2.783, *p* = .005. Episodic, *Wilcoxon z* = 2.273, *p* = .023, knowledge gap, *Wilcoxon z* = 2.982, *p* = .003, emotion, *Wilcoxon z* = 1.684, *p* = .092, negative, *Wilcoxon z* = 1.524, *p* = .128, and other comments, *Wilcoxon z* = 2.731, *p* = .006 all decreased during gunfire. The only two categories to show an increase in comments during gunfire were misinterpretations and positive statements, but neither were significant. An increase in misinterpretations is because the most common error was when the player mistakenly shot at an ally. An increase in positive statements is because the coach would praise the player just after successfully shooting down an enemy plane or target. There was no difference when they were dropping a bomb/shooting a rocket (usually at some ground-based target) or being hit by enemy gunfire.

The situation variables were number of other allied planes, number of enemy planes, number of enemy targets, and presence of anti-aircraft guns. Comment production was influenced by the number of allied planes. Specifically, when there were allied planes within the zone of interaction, there were more misinterpretations, knowledge gap, and emotion comments, *Wilcoxon z* = 2.955, *p* = .003, *Wilcoxon z* = 2.783, *p* = .005, and *Wilcoxon z* = 2.492, *p* = .013, respectively. As mentioned earlier, this is most likely due to instances when players mistakenly fired at an allied plane.

For the other comment categories, there was a general tendency for there to be fewer comments when allied planes were in the zone of interaction. However, the decrease only approached significance for spatial comments, *Wilcoxon z* = 1.790, *p* = .07. This suggests that coaches felt the players did not need to be as concerned with entities in other locations when there were allied planes to assist the player.

For enemy planes, there were fewer overall comments when enemy planes were in the zone of interaction than when they either were not in the zone, *Wilcoxon z* = 2.556, *p* = .011, or were absent from the situation, *Wilcoxon z* = 1.915, *p* = .056. Fewer comments occurred when enemy planes were in the zone of interaction for action suggestion, status attention, and other comments, *Wilcoxon z* = 2.50, *p* = .012, *Wilcoxon z* = 1.875, *p* = .061, and *Wilcoxon z* = 1.789, *p* = .074, respectively. These results are noteworthy because they demonstrate that comments decrease with the presence of dynamic agents that can potentially harm the pilot. Thus, it appears as if the coach recognizes that the player needs to focus at those times and should not be distracted.

For both targets and anti-aircraft guns, which are static entities, there tended to be a pattern in the opposite direction. That is, there were more comments when these entities were inside the zone of interaction than when they were not, although these differences were not significant. There were more status attention comments when both targets and anti-aircraft guns were in the zone of interaction, *Wilcoxon z* = 1.874, *p* = .061, and *Wilcoxon z* = 1.761, *p* = .078, respectively. Also, there were more positive comments when targets were in the zone, *Wilcoxon z* = 3.181, *p* = .001.

Experiment 5

The purpose of Experiments 5 and 6 was to explicitly manipulate comment types and assess their effects on performance. In both of these experiments, assistance was provided by an experimenter rather than another participant. In Experiment 5, there were 36 participants. After a brief practice period with one of the missions (4–6 minutes), subjects moved on to the experiment proper. In this study, we explicitly manipulated the types of comments people received on a particular mission, with the order of comment type and mission number counterbalanced across subjects. There were four comment-type conditions used (a) episodic reminders, (b) spatial directions, (c) status indicators, and (d) suggestions. Assistance falling into each of these categories was provided every 5 to 10 seconds during the ongoing event. In addition, there was a control condition in which no assistance was provided to serve as a baseline of performance. Within each condition, there were three missions flown, one of each of the following types: (a) destroy one or more targets, and (b) destroy enemy planes only (i.e., no targets). Each block lasted from 6 to 7 minutes, and the missions were rotated until the time had expired for that block.

The results are presented in Table 2.8. As can be seen, most assistance conditions did not differ from the control, except for a few spatial direc-

TABLE 2.8
Mean Performance for the Different Comment Conditions for
Different Types of Measurement of Performance in Experiment 5 of the
Augmented Cognition Series. Standard Deviations Are Listed in Parentheses

Variables	Control	Episodic	Spatial	Status	Suggest
E-planes destroyed	3.3 (2.5)	4.0 (2.9)	3.4 (3.2)	2.6 (1.9)	3.5 (2.7)
% Targets destroyed	29.5 (28.0)	21.4 (22.7)	17.1 (17.1)*	27.3 (27.7)	24.5 (27.3)
Wins	0.9 (1.0)	0.7 (0.9)	0.6 (0.6)*	0.7 (0.8)	1.0 (1.0)
Crashes	4.3 (2.0)	4.0 (1.6)	4.4 (1.7)	4.2 (1.6)	3.8 (1.7)
Hits	30.2 (8.2)	33.1 (10.9)	32.3 (8.6)	29.3 (10.6)	27.4 (8.5)

Note. *p < .05.
**.05 < p < .10 for comparisons to the Control condition.

tions conditions, which were in the wrong direction. Thus, if comments were affecting performance, they were having a negative effect. This is in marked contrast to what was observed in Experiment 4.

To further explore this, we examined the effects of assistance as a function of pilots' skill level. The specific idea was that it might be that the assistance would be helpful to less-skilled players relative to skilled players, and that this relationship was obscured when all of the people were considered together. To classify people based on skill, z scores were computed for each of the performance measures in the control condition. These values were then used to calculate an average z score across the five performance measures (the inverse scores were used for crashes and hits). Based on this method, 20 people were classified as *unskilled* (i.e., below the mean) and 16 as *skilled* (i.e., above the mean).

For the control condition, relative to skilled players, unskilled players destroyed fewer enemy planes ($M_U = 2.2$, $M_{SK} = 4.5$), had a smaller percentage of targets ($M_U = 18.3$, $M_{SK} = 43.4$), had fewer wins ($M_U = 0.3$, $M_{SK} = 1.8$), and had more crashes ($M_U = 5.4$, $M_{SK} = 2.9$), but did not differ for number of hits taken ($M_U = 32.2$, $M_{SK} = 27.8$), $F(1, 34) = 2.47, p = .13$.

The data separated on skill are listed in Table 2.9. As can be seen, there were cases for the unskilled group in which performance was significantly better when there was assistance provided. Interestingly, in contrast, for the skilled group, performance was worse for most measures when assistance was provided, especially for number of wins and crashes. In addition, the influence of comment type differed depending on the goal. Stat-

TABLE 2.9

Mean Performance for the Different Comment Conditions for Different Types of Measurement of Performance in Experiment 5 for the Unskilled and Skilled Players. Standard Deviations Are Listed in Parentheses

Variable	Control	Episodic	Spatial	Status	Suggest
Unskilled					
E-planes destroyed	2.2 (1.9)	3.0 (2.3)	2.7 (2.3)	2.3 (1.7)	3.1 (2.8)
% Targets destroyed	18.3 (16.2)	18.5 (21.0)	15.5 (15.6)	17.3 (22.5)	16.8 (19.8)
Wins	0.3 (0.4)	0.5 (0.7)**	0.5 (0.5)	0.4 (0.6)	0.8 (0.9)*
Crashes	5.4 (1.5)	4.1 (1.9)*	4.6 (1.8)	4.3 (1.6)**	4.1 (1.8)*
Hits	32.2 (8.1)	34.6 (12.7)	33.5 (9.8)	28.7 (10.4)	28.3 (8.4)
Skilled					
E-planes destroyed	4.5 (2.9)	5.2 (3.2)	4.3 (3.9)	3.0 (2.2)**	4.0 (2.6)
% Targets destroyed	43.4 (33.6)	25.0 (24.9)*	19.0 (19.0)*	39.8 (29.1)	34.1 (32.7)
Wins	1.8 (0.8)	0.9 (1.1)*	0.8 (0.8)*	1.1 (0.9)*	1.3 (1.1)**
Crashes	2.9 (1.7)	3.9 (1.3)**	4.2 (1.6)*	4.0 (1.6)*	3.6 (1.5)
Hits	27.8 (8.3)	31.4 (8.2)	30.8 (7.2)	30.2 (11.1)	26.3 (8.7)

Note. *$p < .05$.

**$.05 < p < .10$ for comparisons to the Control condition.

us attention comments assisted performance the most for target missions. However, for destroying enemy planes, status attention comments improved performance the least (or impaired performance the most).

These analyses suggest that frequent assistances of all types can impair performance in skilled individuals. In contrast, it can be somewhat beneficial to unskilled people. Experiment 6 explored this idea further, along with a manipulation of the quality of comments relative to the nature of the ongoing situation.

Experiment 6

Experiment 6 was similar to Experiment 5 with the following changes. First, instead of providing assistance every 5 to 10 seconds, people were only given assistance at times when it seemed apt. This turned out to be about every 12 to 15 seconds. Furthermore, people were divided into two groups. The first group ($n = 36$) heard comments that were related to the primary mission goal and were components of the situation that were important to the mission goal(s), but were not in the foreground of the situation (what the pilot was currently interacting with). For example, assistance was not provided about the number of bombs or rockets remaining until the player had five or fewer left. The second group ($n = 36$) was given information related to secondary goals (e.g., indicating distant enemy aircraft during a multiple ground target mission) or was already in the focus of the situation (e.g., advising the player to shoot at enemy planes directly in front of the pilot). As in Experiment 5, groups were further divided according to playing skill based on performance in the control condition.

The results from Experiment 6 are shown in Table 2.10. As can be seen, the unskilled group that received the helpful comments showed improvement relative to the control condition for both types of mission goals. The skilled group either showed no effect or a slight decrement in performance. For the obvious, or secondary goal, comments, performance for the unskilled group was unaffected, but with a slight improvement in terms of crashing and getting hit by enemy fire. This is because these comments tended to include warnings or locations of enemy planes for missions with targets. In contrast, the skilled group showed a dramatic decrease in performance with assistance.

In addition, consistent with Experiment 5, the types of comments, particularly status attention comments, had different levels of influence depending on the goal. Specifically, status attention comments are much more beneficial for goals dealing with static entities (e.g., targets) than with dynamic entities (e.g., enemy planes).

TABLE 2.10
Scores on Performance Measures in Experiment 6 Compared
to the Control Condition for Good Versus Bad Comments
and Unskilled Versus Skilled Players

	Control	Episodic	Spatial	Status	Suggest
Helpful Comments					
Unskilled					
E-Planes destroyed	1.18	2.34*	2.09**	1.62	2.26*
% Targets destroyed	0.11	0.15	0.27*	0.27*	0.14
Wins	0.09	0.50*	0.68*	0.55*	0.55*
Crashes	5.64	4.73**	4.36*	4.86	4.77**
Hits	36.50	34.86	33.05	29.86*	29.23*
Skilled					
E-Planes destroyed	3.35	2.74	3.36	2.40	3.38
% Targets destroyed	0.25	0.23	0.21	0.31	0.32
Wins	1.00	0.71	0.64	0.64	0.79
Crashes	3.43	3.93	5.36*	4.21	4.07
Hits	28.21	31.50	38.00*	34.57	35.43**
Obvious Comments					
Unskilled					
E-Planes destroyed	1.20	1.81	1.48	2.00	1.63
% Targets destroyed	0.15	0.13	0.13	0.18	0.12
Wins	0.30	0.25	0.50	0.40	0.30
Crashes	5.55	5.20	4.40*	4.60	4.65
Hits	41.40	38.90	30.85*	31.80*	30.65*
Skilled					
E-Planes destroyed	3.20	3.38	2.92	2.98	3.19
% Targets destroyed	0.32	0.18	0.21	0.33	0.22
Wins	1.38	0.63*	0.44*	0.75	0.31*
Crashes	3.19	4.25**	4.94*	4.25**	4.75*
Hits	30.25	34.13	38.06*	34.81	35.13

Note. *$p < .05$.
**$.05 < p < .10$.

EXPERIMENT SUMMARY

Overall, these results suggest that this sort of assistance can be beneficial to a person. However, this assistance should be provided strategically. This study illustrated at least three important aspects of providing comments. First, the skill level of the person is important. In Experiment 4, coaches provided more comments earlier in the situation, when it was assumed people were at a lower skill level. This was supported by the results of Experiments 4 and 5, where unskilled people benefitted from assistance. A second aspect is that the quality of the assistance affects performance with regard to how the assistance relates to the structure of the dynamic situation and the person's place within that situation. In Experiments 5 and 6, people showed more improvement when assistance was aimed at important, but peripheral, information, rather than information that was more likely to be in the foreground of the situation. A related idea is that assistance needs to be provided at the appropriate time. In Experiment 4, coaches provided fewer comments in more intense situations involving dynamic entities. Also, people showed a larger benefit (i.e., unskilled people) and a smaller impairment (i.e., skilled players) when the assistance were not provided constantly, but only as needed.

Finally, and most important, there was evidence that different types of assistance were more beneficial in different situations. For example, in all three experiments, the frequency or impact of status attention comments varied depending on the situation. Thus, the type of situation and the resulting goals show an important interaction with the types of assistance.

CONCLUSIONS

In this chapter, we have shown the value of using situation model theory as an approach for developing ideas and procedures within an augmented cognition framework, and the effectiveness of augmented cognition in ongoing situations. More specifically, we have shown that situation model theory can be used to develop protocols for identifying the situations in which a person is embedded. This would be important to an augmented cognition system, in the sense that the system needs to understand the environment a person is operating in, the functional structure of that environment, and what sorts of information will be useful to that person in that situation. We have also shown that people are affected by the structure of a dynamic situation. This is important to augmented cognition because the system needs to understand how the situation is structured and what consequences changes in the situation have on a person's ability to function effectively in the world. Finally, we have shown that providing assistance to a person as a surrogate for an augmented cognition system can boost performance. Much of this assistance was oriented around events occurring in the situation and did not refer to more general knowledge. Furthermore, we observed that this assistance was not uniformly beneficial. Instead it was only helpful when the person had lower skill in a task, and the comments were oriented toward components of the situation that were less likely to be in the foreground of a person's thinking. When these conditions were not met, the augment cognition either had no effect or was detrimental to performance.

ACKNOWLEDGMENTS

This research was supported in part by a grant from the Army Research Institute, ARMY-DASW01-02-K-0003 and funding from Chris Forsythe of Sandia National Laboratories.

APPENDIX

Imagine someone you don't know approaches you to <GOAL>. Think of one possible situation. We would like you to image the encounter in great detail and answer the following questions about it. Please consider each question carefully and list all the possibilities. For some of these items, you may not have anything to fill in. In those cases, please write "not relevant" (NR).

PART 1: Please think about the location of this situation and answer the following questions.

1. Where are you when the stranger approaches? Describe the location.
2. What time is it?
3. What day is it?
4. What season of the year is it?
5. Are you alone? If not, who may be with you?
6. Is the stranger alone? If not, who may be with the stranger?
7. What other activities or events are going on around you?
8. Please list anything that might have happened immediately prior to the event.
9. Are there any other descriptions that you think are important?

PART 2: Describe yourself in this situation. We need to know a basic description of you before the event takes place.

1. Describe how you are dressed (e.g., jacket, pants, skirt, hat, shoes).
2. Describe your appearance (e.g., clean, disheveled, tidy).
3. Describe how you feel (e.g., nervous, excited, angry, happy, fearful, relieved, disgusted).
4. What specific facial expression, if any, do you have?
5. What gestures or movements, if any, are you making?
6. List any of your characteristics that you believe are relevant to the situation (e.g., gender, race, age, hair).
7. What, if anything, are you holding?
8. What may be the stranger's impression of you?
9. Mention anything else you think is relevant.

PART 3: Describe the stranger in this situation. We need to know a basic description of the stranger before the event takes place.

1. Describe how the stranger is dressed (e.g., jacket, pants, skirt, hat, shoes).
2. Describe the stranger's appearance (e.g., clean, disheveled, tidy, stocky).
3. Describe how the stranger may feel (e.g., nervous, excited, angry, happy, fearful, relieved, disgusted).
4. What specific facial expression, if any, does the stranger have?
5. What gestures or movements, if any, is the stranger making?
6. List any of the stranger's characteristics that you believe are relevant to the situation (e.g., gender, race, age, mustache).
7. What, if anything, is the stranger holding (e.g., weapon, purse, map, food)?
8. What is your impression of the stranger?
9. Is the stranger a member of an organization or profession related to the encounter? If so, what is that?
10. Mention anything else you think is relevant (e.g., speech, mannerisms).

PART 4: Listing the stranger's goals, plans, and actions.

1. List all of the reasons you can think of for why the stranger wants to <GOAL>.
2. List all of the ways you can think of that the stranger plans to <GOAL>.
3. List out the sequence of actions taken by the stranger and by you over the course of the interaction.

REFERENCES

Barsalou, L. W. (1999). Perceptual symbol systems. *Behavioral and Brain Sciences, 22*, 577–660.

Bower, G. H., & Morrow, D. G. (1990). Mental models in narrative comprehension. *Science, 247*, 44–48.

Ekman, P. (2003). *Emotions revealed: Recognizing faces and feelings to improve communication and emotional life.* New York: Times Books/Holt.

Glenberg, A. M. (1997). What is memory for? *Behavioral and Brain Sciences, 20*, 1–55.

Johnson-Laird, P. N. (1983). *Mental models: Towards a cognitive science of language, inference, and consciousness.* Cambridge MA: Harvard University Press.

Kintsch, W., Welsch, D., Schmalhofer, F., & Zimny, S. (1990). Sentence memory: A theoretical analysis. *Journal of Memory and Language, 29,* 133–159.

Landauer, T. K., & Dumais, S. T. (1997). A solution to Plato's problem: The latent semantic analysis theory of acquisition, induction, and representation of knowledge. *Psychological Review, 104,* 211–240.

Magliano, J. P., Trabasso, T., & Graesser, A. C. (1999). Strategic processing during comprehension. *Journal of Educational Psychology, 91,* 615–629.

Magliano, J. P, Zwaan, R. A., & Graesser, A. (1999). The role of situational continuity in narrative understanding. In H. van Oostendorp & S. Goldman (Eds.), *The construction of mental representations during reading* (pp. 219–245). Mahwah, NJ: Lawrence Erlbaum Associates.

Radvansky, G. A., & Copeland, D. E. (2000). Functionality and spatial relations in situation models. *Memory & Cognition, 28,* 987–992.

Radvansky, G. A., Spieler, D. H., & Zacks, R. T. (1993). Mental model organization. *Journal of Experimental Psychology: Learning, Memory, and Cognition, 19,* 95–114.

Radvansky, G. A., & Zacks, R. T. (1991). Mental models and the fan effect. *Journal of Experimental Psychology: Learning, Memory, and Cognition, 17,* 940–953.

Radvansky, G. A., Zwaan, R. A., Federico, T., & Franklin, N. (1998). Retrieval from temporally organized situation models. *Journal of Experimental Psychology: Learning, Memory, and Cognition, 24,* 1224–1237.

Suh, S., & Trabasso, T. (1993). Inferences during reading: Converging evidence from discourse analysis, talk-aloud protocols, and recognition priming. *Journal of Memory and Language, 32,* 279–300.

Therriault, D. J., & Rinck, M. (in press). Multidimensional situation models. In F. Schmalhofer & C. Perfetti (Eds.), *Higher level language processes in the brain: Inference and comprehension processes* (pp.). Mahwah, NJ: Lawrence Erlbaum Associates.

Trabasso, T., Van den Broek, P., & Suh, S. Y. (1989). Logical necessity and transitivity of causal relations in stories. *Discourse Processes, 12,* 1–25.

van Den Broek, P. (1994). Comprehension and memory of narrative texts: Inferences and coherence. In M. A. Gernsbacher (Ed.), *Handbook of psycholinguistics* (pp. 539–588). San Diego, CA: Academic Press.

van Dijk, T. A., & Kintsch, W. (1983). *Strategies in discourse comprehension.* New York: Academic Press.

Wilson, M. (2002). Six views of embodied cognition. *Psychonomic Bulletin & Review, 9,* 625–636.

Zwaan, R. A. (1996). Processing narrative time shifts. *Journal of Experimental Psychology: Learning, Memory and Cognition, 22,* 1196–1207.

Zwaan, R. A. (2004). The immersed experiencer: Toward an embodied theory of language comprehension. *The Psychology of Learning and Motivation, 44.*

Zwaan, R. A., Magliano, J. P., & Graesser, A. C. (1995). Dimensions of situation model construction in narrative comprehension. *Journal of Experimental Psychology: Learning, Memory and Cognition, 21,* 386–397.

Zwaan, R. A., & Radvansky, G. A. (1998). Situation models in language comprehension and memory. *Psychological Bulletin, 123,* 162–185.

CHAPTER THREE

Designing Attention-Centric Notification Systems: Five HCI Challenges

D. Scott McCrickard
C. M. Chewar
Virginia Tech

Technological realities of multiple, ubiquitous information delivery streams for user notification often beg improved interface and usability in human–computer interaction (HCI). Many new HCI approaches hint at promising notification solutions, but the HCI field faces five important challenges that can be assisted by applied research in the cognitive systems community. When resolved, designers and researchers will have convenient access to basic research and guidelines, requirements engineering methods for notification interfaces, better and more usable predictive modeling for pre-attentive and dual-task interfaces, standard empirical evaluation procedures for notification systems, and conceptual frameworks for organizing reusable design and software components. This chapter provides an overview of these challenges and discusses some initial work undertaken in each area.

As we consider the general promise of adaptive interfaces, notification systems seem to be ideal for many situations. Notification systems are interfaces specifically designed to support user access to additional digital information from sources secondary to current activities (McCrickard, Czerwinski, & Bartram, 2003). Examples of notification systems include e-mail alert devices, instant messengers, and in-vehicle information systems. When these systems are blended with technologies that can track and infer priorities of user attention and workload characteristics (such as through eye gaze, physical and biomedical sensors, and user models), attentive user interfaces (AUIs) result (Vertegaal, Velichkovsky, & van der Veer,

1997). More specifically, when notification systems adapt information presentation and delivery to avoid overloading the user and to recommend content that may be of interest, we refer to these as attention-centric systems (Horvitz, 1999). The next section provides more information about user goals that relate to notification and introduces several examples of notification design artifacts and systems.

Reflecting on Forsythe's general vision of cognitive systems for interaction—where inferences from a user model or expert model provide opportunities for interaction that would expose users to alternate perspectives—we see roles for notification systems at each of the three levels. At the first level of this vision, the system acts as an aide that knows the user's priorities and interests and acts as a mediator of information. We already see examples of these types of systems emerging, such as the Scope notification system—an AUI that delivers alerts and provides an overview about incoming e-mail, calendar tasks, and other information based on learned user priorities and expectations of urgency (van Dantzich, Robbins, Horvitz, & Czerwinski, 2002). If Forsythe's vision is to be realized in the years to come, we will see notification systems emerge that also act as councils and oracles. As a council, a notification system would be an interface for an expert agent that possesses unique domain knowledge and engages users transparently, using a variety of paradigms to conduct dialogue-based and multimodal interaction. Oracles assume even more control over a user's implicit goals, seamlessly blending interaction responsibility among humans, agents, robots, and sensors. Success of notification systems that act as aides, councils, and oracles requires vast collections of empirically validated design artifacts, user models, and entity libraries. The challenges outlined in this chapter create the infrastructure necessary to accumulate such collections.

Our vision is part of a movement toward a science of design. In fall of 2003, the National Science Foundation (NSF) Directorate for Computer and Information Science and Engineering (CISE) sponsored a workshop toward the establishment of a Science of Design program, focusing on software-intensive systems. More than 50 prominent researchers, many from an HCI perspective, attended the workshop, and each contributed a brief position paper. As HCI consumers of cognitive science research, we use this initiative to help frame the requirements for cognitive systems development. Our general proposal is based on the recognition of a critical need to instantiate and operationalize a design method and environment that espouses hypothesis formation, testing, and iteration, co-evolution of problem specification and design solution, and progressive accumulation of design knowledge. Such an approach promises to inject a more rigorous, scientific approach to a discipline where it is lacking.

BACKGROUND—USER NOTIFICATION
GOALS AND SYSTEMS

The emerging discipline of notification systems provides an important area for the development of cognitive systems. Notification systems can be found in many implementation forms and on a variety of platforms. Perhaps classic desktop systems are the most readily identifiable—instant messengers, status programs, and stock tickers. However, other familiar examples hint at the range of potential systems, such as Weiser's dangling string representation of network traffic (Weiser & Brown, 1996), in-vehicle information systems (Tufano, Knee, & Spelt, 1996), ambient media (Ishii et al., 1998), collaboration tools (Carroll, Neale, Isenhour, Rosson, & McCrickard, 2003), and multimonitor displays (Grudin, 2001). Because notification systems are often light-weight tools (e.g., small peripheral displays in the corner of a desktop interface) that inform users about everyday information (e.g., airline ticket prices, news headlines, presence of collaborators or loved ones), designers are generally able to address important concerns with a relatively simple implementation effort. However, a user's initial acceptance and continued use of a notification system largely depends on satisfaction of their multitasking usage goals—leading to difficult design tradeoffs. Although many design efforts have emerged in recent years, techniques and methods for teaching, engineering, and evaluating usability for these types of interfaces have not been fully developed and evaluated—making this a design area ideal for focusing interdisciplinary research attention.

Early Design Efforts

In recent years, developers and researchers have demonstrated many innovative interface design approaches toward facilitating use of multiple simultaneous information sources. To introduce this research area, we provide examples of innovative systems and then discuss related work toward understanding psychological effects of these systems.

Several efforts can be characterized as attempts to deliver information of interest with small desktop applications, specifically designed to provide glanceable awareness without disturbing other tasks or becoming annoying. The Scope (van Dantzich et al., 2002), Sideshow (Cadiz, Venolia, Jancke, & Gupta, 2002), and Irwin (McCrickard, 1999) applications adopt this strategy. As an alternative to dedicating constrained screen space to tickering displays and other notification tools, Harrison demonstrates transparent user interface objects, where overlaid notification information objects have some degree of transparency and can provide awareness of additional information and enhanced context with minimal obfuscation of other objects (Harrison, Ishii, Vicente, & Buxton, 1995). Other desktop notification applications do not seem to attempt to prevent distraction, instead proactively providing prompts intended to guide or enhance activities. Microsoft's Office Assistant (Clippit) and Rhodes and Maes' (2000) Remembrance Agent are examples.

Other innovative work has demonstrated feasibility and utility of presenting notifications within a user's environment, although there are many different approaches here as well. Large screen displays are used in both MacIntyre's Kimera augmented office environment (MacIntyre et al., 2001) and efforts like Informative art (Redström, Skog, & Hallnäs, 2000), but there are fundamental differences in the objective amount of user attention necessary to extract information and gain meaning—sometimes there is great cost in terms of attention needed to process the information being displayed, whereas in other examples the information is subtly embedded in the environment. Techniques for subtly altering elements of the user's environment to convey information for background processing was demonstrated in the ambient ROOM and elsewhere with projections of water ripples, natural soundscapes, spinning pinwheels, patterns of light patches, and the Information Percolator's air bubbles (Dahley, Wisneski, & Ishii, 1998; Heiner, Hudson, & Tanaka, 1999; Ishii et al., 1998). Other work described how physical widgets can display information states with curious physical objects, such as an artificial flower arrangement (Greenberg & Fitchett, 2001). Although many of these examples are designed to enhance user efforts on desktop platforms, in classrooms, and in office environments (Mamykina, Mynatt, & Terry, 2001), similar research interest (and HCI expertise) often extends to cover more ubiquitous displays—vehicle and wearable navigation/information systems, heads-up displays (HUDs), and augmented reality applications. Collaboration tracking and groupware systems also tend to have multitasking design components that deliver information in divided-attention situations.

Information Design Studies

Understanding how to design aspects of these emerging systems has provided direction for several HCI research efforts. Some efforts within the community have focused on effective attention allocation by reducing distraction. Guidelines for in-vehicle information systems (IVIS) limit types of display interactions, restrict magnitude of display change, and display time (Bailey, Konstan, & Carlis, 2000; Green, 1999; Tufano et al., 1996). Other approaches have sought to optimize selection of attention demands by considering associated cost of user interruption and appropriately tailoring notification presentation (Maglio & Campbell, 2000). Horvitz's inference procedures for automated notification systems are one example—driven by his belief that human attention is the most valuable commodity in HCI (Horvitz, 1999; Horvitz, Jacobs, & Hovel, 1999; Horvitz, Kadie, Paek, & Hovel, 2003). Similarly, McFarlane describes a taxonomy and empirical study of the major dimensions and design tradeoffs related to interruption coordination methods (McFarlane, 1998, 2002).

In contrast to the approach of preserving attention as best as possible, other researchers have focused on optimizing the presentation of notification items that provide users some type of measurable utility (Wickens & Hollands, 2000). Empirical evaluations often simulate dual-task situations, asking participants to perform a primary task while reacting to secondary displays and measuring utility (benefits from acquiring the information) and costs (e.g., in task correctness and completion time). Several studies have investigated how to improve reaction to notifications using preattentive processing, which considers how information can be assimilated and understood rapidly by using colors, shapes, and motion (Bartram, Ware, & Calvert, 2001; Healey, Booth, & Enns, 1996; Healey & Enns, 1999). Earlier work examined moving and changing text as a method to present information, observing the perceptibility and readability of rapid serial visual presentations (RSVPs) of letters, strings, and words (Duchnicky & Kolers, 1983). Rather than optimizing displays for quick reaction, another approach has been to increase utility with information design options that allow deeper understanding and memorability (Kang & Muter, 1989). For example, Cutrell, Czerwinski, and Horvitz (2001) investigated impacts of messaging on primary task-related memory and performance

There may be some hope that these various efforts present diverse approaches to filling user needs, perhaps eventually converging to provide complete coverage of design challenges. However, there are no known mechanisms in place to facilitate collection and analysis of this design advice, either in the form of guidelines, tradeoffs, or system examples. Furthermore, the field lacks widely accepted usability engineering and evaluation processes that could be integrated into HCI education and cohesive research efforts.

An Underlying Conceptual Model
for Notification Design

Considering the commonalities in the systems like those introduced earlier, we have recognized a few general goals. In McCrickard, Catrambone, Chewar, and Stasko (2003), we noted an important distinction between notification systems and traditional HCI research, the attention-utility

theme, asserting that it is useful to think of attention as a constrained resource that can be traded for utility. This utility is enabled by perceiving
additional, valued information while performing other tasks. The success
of a notification system hinges on accurately supporting attention allocation between tasks while enabling utility through access to additional information. The attention-utility theme concisely captures the source of
scarcity (the attention of the user) along with the user's purpose in using
the notification system (utility associated with access to an additional
source of information). In McCrickard and Chewar (2003), we summarized attention benefits (e.g., understanding patterns, trends, and changes,
providing responses, prompting task transition; etc.) and situational cost
factors that notification system users generally expect.

Users ultimately use a notification system to gain benefits, which come
from specific types of utility and can result from associated user goals. We
recognize that the three general user goals of comprehension, reaction,
and interruption can be thought of as critical parameters—key measures
of system success that can be benchmarked through empirical testing to
reveal design progress (McCrickard, Chewar, Somervell, & Ndiwalana,
2003). These goals are unique in that the user is willing to sacrifice a certain amount of primary task attention to achieve them. Other important
system features and user needs must be typically supported in user interfaces to include privacy, reliability, and trust. These features can negatively
influence the amount of required attention without providing a distinct
benefit that independently motivates system use. The level of cost, determined by the amount of attention removed from ongoing tasks, may be el-
evated as a result of the situational factors (fully detailed in McCrickard &
Chewar, 2003).

With compatible tools and methods, user notification requirements
and/or interface usability can be abstracted, expressed, and compared
with three parameter ratings (an interruption/reaction/comprehension
[IRC] rating)—that is, designers without dual-task analysis expertise can
assess attention cost factors to determine target IRC levels for a new notification system. Factors such as a user's lack of skill in perceiving unfamiliar
or complex notification information may contribute to these parameters,
and objective ratings may not carry a constant value across different situations. With this rating and a general understanding of the user tasks supported by the notification system, a designer can access the repository of
design knowledge for appropriate information and interaction design
techniques (e.g., use of color, audio features, animation, screen size, transition of states, etc.), which have analytically and empirically derived IRC
ratings. Furthermore, usability evaluation methods, provided to designers
as part of the integrated system, are adaptable to specific combinations of
targeted parameter levels. User testing results can be conveniently added

back into the design knowledge repository and compared to target parameter levels to determine design success and build reusable HCI knowledge. This approach is discussed in greater detail as we describe five HCI challenges relating to cognitive system development.

THE FIVE HCI CHALLENGES

Improve Access to Basic Research and Guidelines

Certainly the challenge of designing effective notification systems is formidable when considering the range of possible psychological effects for diverse groups of users. As we reviewed earlier, researchers of basic psychological questions are making progress in understanding information and interaction techniques that are effective for dual-task situations. Unfortunately, these results tend to be outside the reach of ordinary interface designers because they lack the disciplinary background to decipher published articles in cognitive and experimental psychology and human factors. High-level summaries that might deliver useful guidelines tend not to be available.

Challenge 1: The HCI development community must have convenient access to basic research and guidelines for attention-centric notification design.

One of the fundamental goals of human-centric design is to equip interface developers with techniques that allow them to design more usable systems. Part of this goal is accomplished when designers can recognize points in the design cycle and user interactive experience that can benefit from mitigating psychological effects on the user. However, this goal is only fully accomplished when designers have at their disposal a variety of options that are informed by results from empirical testing and grounded in widely accepted theory. As researchers from psychology, human factors, and HCI, when we are unable to deliver such option sets to designers, we fail to provide a critical service to a key information consumer.

As the general software development community looks at the work that must be done to improve our practice as a science of design, we see many nuances contributing to the challenge that notification systems designers face. For example, Bonnie John surfaces many related considerations stemming from breakdowns in design teamwork that necessitate focus within a Science of Design program (John, 2003). On the premise that the software development community must provide nearly all of the infrastructure required for the interdisciplinary transfer of knowledge, she argues that significant research must be sponsored—to include process and tool support for enhancing contributions from interdisciplinary team members—helping to deliver knowledge from the behavioral sciences for prediction of design idea feasibility prior to extensive building or prototyping efforts.

Other observations from prominent researchers note the changing quality of design work in general—transition from a largely individual or small-group activity to a distributed, interdisciplinary team effort often involving redevelopment of an existing system. Jakob Nielsen, a principal of the Nielsen Norman Group and author of several influential books on usability engineering, predicts that the future trend of software development will involve offshore team implementation efforts guided by domestic user research and design work. Based on this prediction, distance between design and development functions will increase further, posing new challenges to designing usable and useful systems (Nielsen, 2003). These new business practices imply that the challenge of delivering basic research results to system developers will become increasingly more difficult in years to come.

Deliver Requirements-Engineering Methods

The second challenge addresses the core design process for software interfaces. Many contemporary approaches assist designers in applying design guidelines, and some of the more promising methods encourage iterative refinement through integrated testing and analysis. However, most people approach design as a purely creative process, lacking in structure and documentation, with the only product being the designed artifact. If we are to make progress toward Forsythe's vision and move toward attention-centric notification systems, we must look for processes that encourage designers to form and test hypotheses, preserving the knowledge gained through a channeled creative process.

> *Challenge 2: Processes and frameworks should be available for requirements engineering and development of interaction specifications for software engineers.*

Several prominent researchers provide thoughts on new requirements for methods that would center on three important themes that will enable the full potential of cognitive systems to be realized. The first theme is an argument for design methods that support an improved understanding of problem spaces. As noted by Turing Award winner Fred Brooks, "Often the hardest part of design is deciding what to design" because designers often lack a precise description of the problem to be solved (Brooks,

2003). Long-time software developer and AT&T researcher, Michael Jackson, elaborates: "A science of design must be at root a discipline of devising, understanding, populating, and exploiting [an] informal structure" so that software development problems can be decomposed into subproblems within known problem frames (Jackson, 2003).

Brooks also introduced a second theme for software development processes that embodies the movement to increase the scientific basis of design—tools must be available to present detailed option sets for design choices, ideally that assist in co-evolution of the problem as well as the design solution (Brooks, 2003). Several other prominent researchers echo and elaborate this sentiment. Warnier-prize winner Mary Shaw, co-director of the Sloane Software Engineering Center and author of seven books, argues for systematic guidance of design decisions, specifically those that express costs and benefits of software design and help designers consider user preferences (Shaw, 2003). CHI Lifetime Achievement Award winner, John M. Carroll, notes that this knowledge must focus on user activities in a way that leverages research from social sciences (Carroll, 2003). Colin Potts argues that knowledge should be accumulated by recording the "science of the designed" through artifact-as-phenomena investigations, modeled as pattern abstraction (Potts, 2003). These ideas are summarized in the second challenge for the cognitive systems research community as we strive to lay the groundwork for attention-centric notification systems.

Enhance and Expand Predictive Modeling Capabilities

As interface developers and HCI researchers consider ways to lower costs of software development yet develop highly usable systems, cognitive modeling may be compelling. Rather than invest in costly user testing, HCI professionals are often intrigued at the idea of discovering breakdowns in human information processing through automated methods. With cognitive architectures like ACT-R (Anderson, 1998), SOAR (Lewis, 1999), and EPIC (Kieras, Wood, & Meyer, 1997), which have been in development and appeared in the literature since the early 1990s, we have reason to hope that these architectures should provide design requirements insight for typical designers. Unfortunately, the systems based on the architectures currently available do not come close to meeting the needs of most notification system designers and researchers.

Challenge 3: Better and more usable predictive modeling for pre-attentive and dual-task interfaces must be available to HCI researchers and system developers.

Cognitive modeling has been successfully used to investigate specific design-related questions and support theory. One example probed typical user behavior with online help manuals (Peck & John, 1992), and studies of dual-task performance in driving situations with in-vehicle systems are fairly common (e.g., Salvucci, 2001). However, for these models to be effective, they must specify mechanisms and constraints related to human information processing and graphical user interface interactivity, such as limitations of human memory, attention, facilities, perceptual-motor operation characteristics, response selection limitations, and sensory perception performance abilities.

Constructing models that encapsulate these vast collections of theories and results of empirical studies is extremely complex and often forces models to be created to address narrow problems such as those introduced earlier. Not only do the problem domains that a given model may address tend to be narrow, but models also tend to be extremely difficult to configure and use for problem solving. Designers who are unfamiliar with the model face challenges in deciding whether the problem they are investigating can even be validly studied using the model. These are some of the key findings that resulted from our own study, in which a novice designer attempted to use three cognitive architectures to probe questions relating to notification system design (Turnbull, Chewar, & McCrickard, 2003). Although each of the three architectures exhibited usability and performance-positive features, none was able to support a novice designer's requirement to quickly learn and sufficiently customize a predictive model for a simple information design question that would be typical in early-stage design.

Standardize Empirical Evaluation Procedures

Although use of notification systems has become widespread in recent years, there are surprisingly few efforts within HCI literature that effectively evaluate usability of their information and interaction design. For example, some notification systems support collaborative activities and are studied from a computer-supported collaborative work (CSCW) perspective, whereas disparate agendas lead to inconsistent definitions of successful design, inhibiting cross-initiative influence. Perhaps a leading cause for the general lack of user studies in reporting system development efforts and innovative design solutions is the lack of training that software developers typically receive in designing experiments. Although some developers make the extra effort to test systems and report findings, this is often done with procedures that are not replicable or comparable in related efforts. This practice prevents long-term research growth and disciplinary cohesion. However, by helping software developers create reusable test platforms and instruments that can capture key usability concerns, researchers from disciplines that value empirical data collection can contribute to our long-term success.

Challenge 4: Usability engineers need assistance in developing standard and reusable evaluation procedures for notification system interfaces.

As one of the two important research challenges asserted by Abowd and Mynatt (2000) for the emerging interfaces for computing, they motivate the imperative for assessing progress toward real human needs with quantitative and qualitative evaluation methods that capture authentic context of system use, saying that research irrespective of the need for evaluation will have little impact in the HCI community. In response, this general message has guided the agenda of two workshops at major HCI conferences and special issues of journals. Within the notification systems research community, there has been encouraging momentum with the development of generic usability evaluation tools, especially for specific classes of systems. Heuristic evaluation methods have been adapted for both ambient displays (Mankoff et al., 2003) and large-screen information exhibits (Somervell, Wahid, & McCrickard, 2003). The key benefits of generic evaluation tools include the ability to easily compare and benchmark system performance, recognize progress toward reference tasks, and collect experience necessary for cost–benefit reengineering assessments (Whittaker, Terveen, & Nardi, 2000). Although there may be some concern that generic evaluation tools are not capable of providing rich and expressive results about a particular set of features, we have obtained results to the contrary in probing this general hypothesis (Somervell, Chewar, McCrickard, & Ndiwalana, 2003).

Provide Conceptual Frameworks for Design Reuse

The ability to reuse components from one design to the next represents cost savings in the form of both development efficiency and improved reliability for usability. However, the benefits of reuse are often only available after a practice has reached a sufficient level of maturity, apparent through establishment and acceptance of formal methods. With reusable components that have understood psychological effects on users, notification systems designers are able to create adaptive interfaces, appropriately tailoring presentation to accommodate the needs for interruption, reaction, and comprehension (McCrickard & Chewar, 2003). This adaptivity requires a rich set of reusable components that are well organized according to critical user concerns. Unfortunately, we have seen little indication that reuse even occurs on a system-to-system basis—a state that would allow designers to improve on the work of their predecessors and perhaps an achievable near-term goal on which to focus.

Challenge 5: Conceptual frameworks must be crafted to assist in organizing reusable design knowledge and software components—a necessity for design efficiency and long-term progress.

As we consider arguments made by prominent researchers that support the goal of improving designer tendencies to reuse design knowledge, two fundamental concepts provide a possible starting point. First, Carroll (2000) described how reusable statements about the psychological effects of a design artifact in use (claims within a claims analysis) can act as a hill climbing heuristic. By *hill climbing*, he meant achieving a progressively better design solution based on knowledge attained from previous efforts—a collection of existing claims forms the slope that has already been traversed and provides a basis for continued advancement. To hill climb, a designer focuses on mitigating downside effects of key claims through new design iterations while enhancing or maintaining upside effects. The foundation is improved as auditable claims are strengthened with increasingly compelling evidence derived through theory, user testing, and field study observation (Carroll, 2000). In the next section, we extend this concept to include co-evolutionary development of both the design and user's model.

As a second fundamental concept, we consider William Newman's notion of critical parameters, which provides us with a mechanism to measure our progress in hill climbing. To conduct meaningful modeling and usability evaluations that allow systems to become progressively better, and in response to his 1994 study of CHI paper contributions (Newman, 1994), Newman argued we first must define or adopt critical parameters or figures of merit that transcend specific applications and focus on the broader purpose of the technology (Newman, 1997; Newman, Taylor, Dance, & Taylor, 2000). He implied that well-selected critical parameters can function as benchmarks—"providing a direct and manageable measure of the design's ability to serve its purpose"—and indicate the units of measure for analytic methods that predict the success of an early design. Whittaker et al. (2000) extended his arguments to a proposed reference task agenda for HCI to increase community scientific focus. The convergence of these ideas provides the theoretical basis for a potential solution that we will proceed to discuss: The iterative process of gauging critical parameters, embodied in design artifacts and expressed with claims, guides the hill climbing process and provides an index for archived, reusable design knowledge.

TOWARD A SOLUTION TO LINK-UP
OUR NEW DISCIPLINE

Although there are many potential approaches for injecting scientific inquiry into HCI and the interface design process (e.g., Hix & Hartson, 1993), we augment the task-artifact framework, embedded in an iterative scenario-based design process, facilitating design knowledge hypothesis formation, tradeoff mitigation, and component reuse. We are developing a design environment specifically to assist novice developers with analyzing and constructing design rationale for notification systems. The IRC framework described earlier in the chapter provides the theoretical and technical underpinnings for the tools we are building and integrating.

Task-Artifact Framework and Usability Engineering

In the late 1980s, Carroll introduced a proposal for a systematic method to reconcile contrasting perspectives of hermeneutics and theory-based design (Carroll & Kellogg, 1989). This method was founded on the conjecture that successful HCI designs embody an assortment of psychological claims, determining the system's usability. In carrying out an analytical investigation for understanding a design in psychological terms, the task-artifact framework helps designers recognize tradeoffs implicit in the design as users form a goal, act toward its achievement, and evaluate progress. Articulating these tradeoffs as useful generalizations for future design work provides a mechanism for generative problem solving and design, integrating theory development with design evaluation (Carroll, Singley, & Rosson, 1992).

In the description of this process, Carroll noted that this tradeoff evaluation provides a method for mediated evaluation—a compromise that allows explicit goal formation in early stages of design, intrinsic evaluation and modification of goals throughout the design cycle, and inclusion of goal analysis in payoff evaluation. In later work, Carroll argued that the task-artifact framework, coupled with the use of scenarios to articulate user concerns and interface usage, provides a basis for an action science in HCI through the deliberate management of tradeoffs made explicit and assessment of basic tasks (Carroll & Rosson, 1992). Based on the task-artifact framework, Carroll developed a gradient of progressively powerful analysis techniques, starting with basic scenario-based design and task coverage through Norman's stages of action and extending to the process of claims analysis and hill climbing, a taxonomy of concept relations for mapping problem and design knowledge, and object-oriented design methods (e.g., class hierarchy generation and object point of view analysis; Carroll, Mack, Robertson, & Rosson, 1994). We review the basic techniques, which form our co-evolutionary design method.

Norman's Stages of Action and Conceptual Models

One classic theory in interface design literature is Norman's (1986) theory of action. Because user tasks are composed of psychological goals and intentions and are accomplished with control mechanisms to physically manipulate system states, he recognized two different expressions of a task (physical and psychological) that must be resolved within an HCI system. Norman established the idea that governing the usage experience is the consistency of two conceptual models—the design model held by the designer and the user's model based on the user's understanding of the system. Each model can be analyzed as stages of action, which describe the cyclical evaluation and execution of tasks across the Gulf of Execution and the Gulf of Evaluation. To facilitate a user's evaluation and execution of tasks, designers must develop conceptual models as they would develop the scaffolding of a bridge. Several factors contribute to each of these conceptual models. The design model should be inspired by a requirements analysis, including consideration of a user's background, situational context, and task-oriented goals. This model expresses the designer's understanding of user needs and is a representation of the intended functionality for the system. The user's model is formed by the user's understanding of the system image, the physical system, and its documentation.

The key idea we continue with is that Norman's view of the role of an interface designer is to develop the system image so that the user's model and design model are compatible. Scenario-based design (SBD) is an approach to interface development, providing an inquiry method to help designers reason about elements of a usage situation and receive participatory feedback from stakeholders. Through the development and sharing of narrative descriptions of users solving problems with designed systems, designers are able to create the scaffolding across Norman's Gulfs—and develop systems with design user's model compatibility. Enabling designers to compare these conceptual models, as well as research and improve suitable design artifacts, is a central goal of our work.

Claims Analysis

During any design process, many compromises are often made, but claims concisely articulate the positive and negative effects (tradeoffs) of a feature on a user in accomplishing a task. Claims address a variety of situational and interface aspects that affect the compatibility of the design and user's models, such as user satisfaction and feeling of reward, color and object layout, and strength of affordances. To ensure interface usability, developers can focus on developing and validating key claims associated with essential tasks to be supported by the interface. The process of making claims about the problem context, the general activities addressed by the interface, and the information and interaction design techniques is called *claims analysis*—a design method for mediated evaluation that produces a testable and refutable record of design rationale. In this manner, claims list a set of hypotheses about a scenario or design artifact and "open up a process of critique and refinement" (Carroll, 1994).

Related work by Sutcliffe has developed theories and methods for design reuse in the requirements generation stage (Sutcliffe, 2000). Based on his work with Carroll, he argued that HCI research should focus on producing designer-digestible packets of HCI knowledge in the form of claims, grounded on solid theory and allowing general reuse (Sutcliffe & Carroll, 1999). To this end, Sutcliffe's Domain Theory provides a structure of abstraction, formal definitions, reuse program evaluation metrics, and generic tasks that can be used to catalogue design information—an implementation road map extendible to any design domain that is employed in plans for our design tool.

A Notification Systems Claims Library

We designed and implemented a claims library for notification systems artifacts and design knowledge, which uses Domain Theory (Sutcliffe, 2002) components and IRC rating framework (McCrickard, Chewar, Somervell, & Ndiwalana, 2003) as an index. The claims library serves as an underlying component for the system, where an example of a claim in simplest form could be:

> *Use of tickering text-based animation to display news headlines in a small desktop window preserves user focus on a primary task, while allowing long-term awareness BUT (-) is not suitable for rapid recognition of and reaction to urgent information*

Claims are grounded by empirical testing or observation, so a designer of a notification system may compare this claim with claims related to use of in-place animation techniques, such as fading and blasting. To simplify the process, we can abstract a claim and focus on critical parameters relating information presentation to effects on information processing (IRC)— user's interruption, reaction, and comprehension:

> *Tickering text-based animation* ∈ {*low interruption, low reaction, moderate comprehension*}

Full claims records that are stored in our design knowledge repository can be quite detailed, so appropriate generalization practices and search tools must adequately support an abstraction-specification process. Other publications from our group detail the approaches and findings in more depth (Chewar, Bachetti, McCrickard, & Booker, 2004; Payne et al., 2003; Wahid, Allgood, Chewar, & McCrickard, 2004).

Requirements Analysis—Understanding the Design Model

This series of steps within the requirements analysis module starts with the problem scenario and results in a template for connecting problem claims by stage of action. The tasks, information characteristics, user background, and other aspects of the situation from requirements gathering in this step, combined with previous design knowledge, formulate the design model. Within the module, various processes assist the designer, such as selection of basic tasks, hierarchical task analysis, matching of requirements to standard task models, and decomposing a task model to stages of action.

Enhancing Claim Development and Reuse Through Participatory Negotiation

When designers sit down with users in a participatory design session, there are many possible negotiation points. In our work, we focus on scenarios, claims, and hierarchical task analysis diagrams, combining participatory design with the LINK-UP system, thus enabling reuse of claims to be accomplished in a participatory negotiation session.

This module integrates a participatory design negotiation technique with the claim development and reuse process in the LINK-UP system. Starting with problem claims in the stage of action templates, which emerges from the requirements analysis module, this module facilitates designers in presenting their understanding of requirements to stakeholders and receiving specific feedback. Tools within this module allow a designer to build a participatory negotiation session and allow a stakeholder to take part in one.

Expressing and Analyzing a System Image With Claims

After a designer develops a system image (either through the full implementation of a working system or a minimally functional prototype), this tool allows description of the key interface features with design claims. Revisiting the stage of action template holding the problem claims, the designer links each problem claim to a scenario and several design claims (information or interaction). Design claims can be reused completely or in part from claims within the repository or entered as original entries. Whether new or reused, a key process within this module is the association of artifact representations (screen shots, pictures, etc.) with claims. This process of specifying the design claims and representing prototype artifacts expresses the system image.

Automatically Creating Empirical Tests for Claims Evaluation

As designers proceed through the design process, they generate a huge collection of claims. Sometimes individual claims include empirical supporting evidence, but often they do not, and rarely are all sets of associated claims in the interface adequately validated. This presents an issue in designing and developing empirical tests to investigate the quality of the interface.

Designers and evaluators want to select sets of claims most appropriate and desired for user testing. Claims are grouped within and sequenced among the different stages of action. This module helps with the selection of information and interaction usage scenarios, creation of a test script as an input file for an automated test platform, and generation of an output file from the platform that could then append a claim record with the derived parameter values. The testing procedures supported by the tool are compatible with literature on critical parameters, reference tasks, and standard lab-based procedures for interface testing.

Visualizing Claim Linkages in LINK-UP

This module visualizes the changes an interface has gone through while being developed. The visualization specifically depicts the claims and scenarios that were used for an interface over time, showing the evolution of claims and scenarios and the relationships that are formed and working closely with the other modules.

Integrated Design Knowledge Reuse

A main advantage of the LINK-UP system is that it provides continuous and integrated access to the design knowledge repository, facilitating knowledge reuse. The design knowledge repository will build directly on a working prototype system that is based on Sutcliffe's (2000) Domain Theory. Through access to the claims database, designers will be able to build from and test previous design results. They will also be able to contribute to a growing body of knowledge. To enable these features in a manner that preserves content quality and user trust, the system also includes accounts and profiles of designers and expert administrators. Expert access to the claims database allows full claims administration, association of claims with related theories, example systems, design artifacts, and other meta-analysis and knowledge management features, such as a claims entry, editing, rating, and commenting features for designers.

In summary, the LINK-UP system provides a Web-based interface to guide the usability engineering process for a notification system. Designers interact with five major design support tools (including support for requirements analysis and negotiation, analytical and empirical testing, and design knowledge access), saving and building on progressive session results throughout the process. A set of claims (serving as design hypotheses) and associated critical parameters (serving as engineering targets and results) guide design progress within a single design and through a meta-analysis of several systems. The design knowledge repository will grow and improve through use, becoming a living record of notification systems research.

LOOKING TO THE FUTURE

Within this chapter, we have described a research area worthy of sustained interest from the cognitive systems community—attention-centric notification systems. As a research area, the study of notification systems can act as an incubator for the development of Forsythe's vision about the levels of cognitive system maturity. To focus this development in a way that will assist the software developer in making useful and usable systems for a wide diversity of users, we have introduced five challenges to guide research and practical exploration between HCI and cognitive systems research: (a) convenient access to basic research and guidelines, (b) requirements engineering methods for notification interfaces, (c) better and more usable predictive modeling for pre-attentive and dual-task interfaces, (d) standard empirical evaluation procedures for notification systems, and (e) conceptual frameworks for organizing reusable design and software components.

We also describe our initial work toward building infrastructure to overcome these five challenges, focusing on notification system development. We described LINK-UP, a design environment grounded on years of theory and method development within HCI—providing a mechanism to integrate interdisciplinary expertise from the cognitive systems research community. Claims and the claims library act as a repository that allows convenient access to basic research and guidelines, while the modules parallel a lifecycle development iteration and provide a process for requirements engineering guided by this basic research. We are already integrating standard empirical evaluation tools, extensible so that as we and others develop usable cognitive architectures they can be integrated as well. The activities carried out through the LINK-UP system provide access to and interaction with reusable design components organized based on our theoretical framework. We think that approaches like this may provide the scientific basis necessary for exciting interdisciplinary advancement through many fields of design, with notification systems serving as an initial model.

REFERENCES

Abowd, G. D., & Mynatt, E. D. (2000). Charting past, present, and future research in ubiquitous computing. *ACM Transactions on Computer-Human Interaction, 7,* 29–58.

Anderson, J. (1998). *The atomic components of thought.* Mahwah, NJ: Lawrence Erlbaum Associates.

Bailey, B. P., Konstan, J. A., & Carlis, J. V. (2000). The effects of interruptions on task performance, annoyance, and anxiety in the user interface. In *Proceedings of the IFIP TC.13 International Conference on Human-Computer Interaction* (INTERACT 2001, pp. 593–601), Tokyo, Japan.

Bartram, L., Ware, C., & Calvert, T. (2001). Moving icons: Detection and distraction. In *Proceedings of the IFIP TC.13 International Conference on Human-Computer Interaction* (INTERACT 2001, pp. 57–165), Tokyo, Japan.

Brooks, F. (2003). *Is there a design of design?* Position paper for the NSF Invitational Workshsop on Science of Design: Software-Intensive Systems, Airlie Center, VA.

Cadiz, J. J., Venolia, G., Jancke, G., & Gupta, A. (2002). Designing and deploying an information awareness interface. In *Proceedings of the 2002 ACM Conference on Computer Supported Cooperative Work* (pp. 314–323). New Orleans, LA: ACM.

Carroll, J. M. (1994). Making use: A design representation. *Communications of the ACM, 37*(12), 28–35.

Carroll, J. M. (2000). *Making use: Scenario-based design of human-computer interactions.* Cambridge, MA: MIT Press.

Carroll, J. M. (2003). *Activity as the object of design.* Position paper for the NSF Invitational Workshsop on Science of Design: Software-Intensive Systems, Airlie Center, VA.

Carroll, J. M., & Kellogg, W. A. (1989). Artifact as theory-nexus: Hermeneutics meets theory-based design. In *Proceedings of the ACM Conference on Human Factors in Computing Systems* (CHI 1989, pp. 7–14), Austin, TX.

Carroll, J. M., Mack, R. L., Robertson, S., & Rosson, M. B. (1994). Binding object to scenarios of use. *International Journal of Human-Computer Studies, 22*(2), 243–276.

Carroll, J. M., Neale, D. C., Isenhour, P. I., Rosson, M. B., & McCrickard, D. S. (2003). Notification and awareness: Synchronizing task-oriented collaborative activity. *International Journal of Human-Computer Studies, 8*(5), 605–632.

Carroll, J. M., & Rosson, M. B. (1992). Getting around the task-artifact cycle: How to make claims and design by scenario. *ACM Transactions on Information Systems (TOIS), 10*(2), 181–202.

Carroll, J. M., Singley, M. K., & Rosson, M. B. (1992). Integrating theory development with design evaluation. *Behavior and Information Technology, 11,* 247–255.

Chewar, C. M., Bachetti, E., McCrickard, D. S., & Booker, J. E. (2004). Automating a design reuse facility with critical parameters: Lessons learned in developing the LINK-UP system.

In *Proceedings of the 2004 International Conference on Computer Aided Design of User Interfaces* (CADUI 2004, pp. 236–247), Island of Mediera, Portugal.

Cutrell, E., Czerwinski, M., & Horvitz, E. (2001). Notification, disruption, and memory: Effects of messaging interruptions on memory and performance. In *Proceedings of the IFIP TC.13 International Conference on Human-Computer Interaction* (INTERACT 2001, pp. 263–269), Tokyo, Japan.

Dahley, A., Wisneski, C., & Ishii, H. (1998). Water lamp and pinwheels: Ambient projection of digital information into architectural space. In *Proceedings of the ACM Conference on Human Factors in Computing Systems* (CHI '98, pp. 269–270). Los Angeles, CA: ACM Press.

Duchnicky, R. L., & Kolers, P. A. (1983). Readability of text scrolled on visual display terminals as a function of window size. *Human Factors, 25*(6), 683–692.

Green, P. (1999). The 15-second rule for driver information systems. In *Proceedings of the ITS America Ninth Annual Meeting*. Washington, DC: CD–ROM.

Greenberg, S., & Fitchett, C. (2001). Phidgets: Easy development of physical interfaces through physical widgets. In *Proceedings of the ACM Conference on User Interface Software and Technology* (UIST '01, pp. 209–218), Orlando, FL.

Grudin, J. (2001). Partitioning digital worlds: Focal and peripheral awareness in multiple monitor use. In *Proceedings of the ACM Conference on Human Factors in Computing Systems* (CHI '01, pp. 458–465), Seattle, WA.

Harrison, B. L., Ishii, H., Vicente, K. J., & Buxton, W. A. S. (1995). Transparent layered user interfaces: An evaluation of a display design to enhance focused and divided attention. In *Proceedings of the ACM Conference on Human Factors in Computing Systems* (CHI '95, pp. 317–324). Denver, CO: ACM Press.

Healey, C. G., Booth, K. S., & Enns, J. T. (1996). High-speed visual estimation using preattentive processing. *ACM Transactions on Human Computer Interaction, 3*(2), 107–135.

Healey, C. G., & Enns, J. T. (1999). Large datasets at a glance: Combining textures and colors in scientific visualization. *IEEE Transactions on Visualization and Computer Graphics, 5*(2), 145–167.

Heiner, J. M., Hudson, S. E., & Tanaka, K. (1999). The information percolator: Ambient information display in a decorative object. In *Proceedings of the ACM Symposium on User Interface Software and Technology* (UIST '99, pp. 141–148), Asheville, NC.

Hix, D., & Hartson, H. R. (1993). *Developing user interfaces: Ensuring usability through product and process.* New York: Wiley.

Horvitz, E. (1999). Principles of mixed-initiative user interfaces. In *Proceedings of the ACM Conference on Human Factors in Computing Systems* (CHI '99, pp. 159–166), Pittsburgh, PA.

Horvitz, E., Jacobs, A., & Hovel, D. (1999). Attention-sensitive alerting. In *Conference on Uncertainty and Artificial Intelligence* (UAI '99, pp. 305–313), Stockholm, Sweden.

Horvitz, E., Kadie, C., Paek, T., & Hovel, D. (2003). Models of attention in computing and communication: From principles to applications. *Communications of the ACM, 46*(3), 52–59.

Ishii, H., Wisneski, C., Brave, S., Dahley, A., Gorbet, M., Ullmer, B., & Yarin, P. (1998). ambientROOM: Integrating ambient media with architectural space. In *Proceedings of the ACM Conference on Human Factors in Computing Systems* (CHI '98, pp. 173–174). Los Angeles, CA: ACM Press.

Jackson, M. (2003). *Position paper: A science of software design?* Position paper for the NSF Invitational Workshsop on Science of Design: Software-Intensive Systems, Airlie Center, VA.

John, B. E. (2003). *Position statement of Bonnie E. John for Science of Design: Software-Intensive Systems.* Position paper for the NSF Invitational Workshop on Science of Design: Software-Intensive Systems, Airlie Center, VA.

Kang, T. J., & Muter, P. (1989). Reading dynamically displayed text. *Behaviour and Information Technology, 8*(1), 33–42.

Kieras, D. E., Wood, S. D., & Meyer, D. E. (1997). Predictive engineering models based on the EPIC architecture for a multimodal high-performance human computer interaction task. *ACM Transactions on Human Computer Interaction, 4*(3), 230–275.

Lewis, R. L. (1999). Cognitive modeling, symbolic. In R. Wilson & F. Keil (Eds.), *The MIT Encyclopedia of the Cognitive Sciences* (pp. 525–527). Cambridge, MA: MIT Press.

MacIntyre, B., Mynatt, E. D., Voida, S., Hansen, K. M., Tullio, J., & Corso, G. M. (2001). Support for multitasking and background awareness using interactive peripheral displays. In *Proceedings of the 14th Annual ACM Symposium on User Interface Software and Technology* (UIST '01, pp. 41–50). Orlando, FL: ACM Press.

Maglio, P. P., & Campbell, C. S. (2000). Tradeoffs in displaying peripheral information. In *Proceedings of the ACM Conference on Human Factors in Computing Systems* (CHI 2000, pp. 241–248), The Hague, The Netherlands.

Mamykina, L., Mynatt, E. D., & Terry, M. A. (2001). Time aura: Interfaces for pacing. In *Proceedings of the ACM Conference on Human Factors in Computing Systems* (CHI '01, pp. 144–151). Seattle, WA: ACM Press.

Mankoff, J., Dey, A., Hsieh, G., Kientz, J., Lederer, S., & Ames, M. (2003). Heuristic evaluation of ambient displays. In *Proceedings of the ACM Conference on Human Factors in Computing Systems* (CHI '03, pp. 167–176). Fort Lauderdale, FL: ACM Press.

McCrickard, D. S. (1999). Maintaining information awareness with Irwin. In *Proceedings of the World Conference on Educational Multimedia/Hypermedia and Educational Telecommunications* (ED-MEDIA '99), Seattle, WA.

McCrickard, D. S., Catrambone, R., Chewar, C. M., & Stasko, J. T. (2003). Establishing tradeoffs that leverage attention for utility: Empirically evaluating information display in notification systems. *International Journal of Human-Computer Studies, 8*(5), 547–582.

McCrickard, D. S., & Chewar, C. M. (2003). Attuning notification design to user goals and attention costs. *Communications of the ACM, 46*(3), 67–72.

McCrickard, D. S., Chewar, C. M., Somervell, J. P., & Ndiwalana, A. (2003). A model for notification systems evaluation—Assessing user goals for multitasking activity. *ACM Transactions on Computer-Human Interaction (TOCHI), 10*(4), 312–338.

McCrickard, D. S., Czerwinski, M., & Bartram, L. (2003). Introduction: Design and evaluation of notification user interfaces. *International Journal of Human-Computer Studies, 8*(5), 509–514.

McFarlane, D. C. (1998). *Interruption of people in human-computer interaction.* Unpublished doctoral dissertation, George Washington University, Washington DC.

McFarlane, D. C. (2002). Comparison of four primary methods for coordinating the interruption of people in human-computer interaction. *Human Computer Interaction, 17*(3).

Newman, W. M. (1994). A preliminary analysis of the products of research, using pro forma abstracts. In *Proceedings of the ACM Conference on Human Factors in Computing Systems* (CHI '94, pp. 278–284). Boston, MA: ACM Press.

Newman, W. M. (1997). Better or just different? On the benefits of designing interactive systems in terms of critical parameters. In *Proceedings of the Conference on Designing Interactive Systems: Processes, Practices, Methods, and Techniques* (DIS '97, pp. 237–245). New York: ACM Press.

Newman, W. M., Taylor, A. S., Dance, C. R., & Taylor, S. A. (2000). Performance targets, models and innovation in interactive systems design. In *Proceedings of the Conference on Designing Interactive Systems: Processes, Practices, Methods, and Techniques* (DIS '00, pp. 381–387). New York: ACM Press.

Nielsen, J. (2003). *Getting the science of design used.* Position paper for the NSF Invitational on Science of Design: Software-Intensive Systems, Airlie Center, VA.

Norman, D. A. (1986). Cognitive engineering. In D. A. Norman & S. W. Draper (Eds.), *User centered system design: New perspectives on human computer interaction* (pp. 31–62). Hillsdale, NJ: Lawrence Erlbaum Associates.

Payne, C., Allgood, C. F., Chewar, C. M., Holbrook, C., & McCrickard, D. S. (2003). Generalizing interface design knowledge: Lessons learned from developing a claims library. In *Proceedings of the 2003 IEEE International Conference on Information Reuse and Integration* (IRI 2003, pp. 362–267), Las Vegas NV.

Peck, V. A., & John, B. E. (1992). Browser-Soar: A computational model of a highly interactive task. In *Proceedings of the Conference of Human Factors in Computing Systems (*CHI 1992, pp. 165–172), Monterey CA.

Potts, C. (2003). *Policy modularity: Toward a science of socially-embedded system design.* Position paper for the NSF Invitational Workshop on Science of Design: Software-Intensive Systems, Airlie Center, VA.

Redström, J., Skog, T., & Hallnäs, L. (2000). Informative art: Using amplified artworks as information displays. In *Proceedings of Designing Augmented Reality Environments* (DARE 2000, pp. 103–114). New York: ACM Press.

Rhodes, B., & Maes, P. (2000). Just-in-time information retrieval agents. *IBM Systems Journal, 39*(3–4), 685–704.

Salvucci, D. D. (2001). Predicting the effects of in-car interface use on driver performance: An integrated model approach. *International Journal of Human-Computer Studies, 55*, 85–107.

Shaw, M. (2003). *Research questions for foundations of complex software design.* Position paper for the NSF Invitational Workshop on Science of Design: Software-Intensive Systems, Airlie Center, VA.

Somervell, J., Chewar, C. M., McCrickard, D. S., & Ndiwalana, A. (2003). Enlarging usability for ubiquitous displays. In *Proceedings of the 41st Annual ACM Southeast Conference* (ACM-SE 2003, pp. 24–29). Savannah, GA: AMC Press.

Somervell, J., Wahid, S., & McCrickard, D. S. (2003). Usability heuristics for large screen information exhibits. In *Proceedings of the IFIP TC.13 Conference on Human-Computer Interaction* (INTERACT 2001, pp. 904–907), Zurich, Switzerland.

Sutcliffe, A. (2000). On the effective use and reuse of HCI knowledge. *ACM Transactions on Computer-Human Interaction, 7*(2), 197–221.

Sutcliffe, A. (2002). *The domain theory: Patterns for knowledge and software reuse.* Mahwah, NJ: Lawrence Erlbaum Associates.

Sutcliffe, A. G., & Carroll, J. M. (1999). Designing claims for reuse in interactive systems design. *International Journal of Human-Computer Studies 50*(3), 213–241.

Turnbull, D. G., Chewar, C. M., & McCrickard, D. S. (2003). Are cognitive architectures mature enough to evaluate notification systems? In *Proceedings of the International Conference on Software Engineering Research and Practice* (SERP '03). Las Vegas, NV, 5 pages (CD-ROM).

Tufano, D., Knee, H., & Spelt, P. (1996). In-vehicle signing functions and systems concepts. In *Proceedings of the 29th International Symposium on Automotive Technology and Automation (ISATA) Dedicated Conference on Global Deployment of Advanced Transportation Telematics/ITS* (pp. 97–104). Florence Italy.

van Dantzich, M., Robbins, D., Horvitz, E., & Czerwinski, M. (2002). Scope: Providing awareness of multiple notifications at a glance. In *Proceedings of the 6th International Working Conference on Advanced Visual Interfaces* (AVI '02). Trento, Italy: ACM Press.

Vertegaal, R., Velichkovsky, B., & van der Veer, G. (1997). Catching the eye: Management of joint attention in cooperative work. *SIGCHI Bulletin, 29*, 4.

Wahid, S., Allgood, C. F., Chewar, C. M., & McCrickard, D. S. (2004). Entering the heart of design: Relationships for tracing claim evolution. In *Proceedings of the 16th International*

Conference on Software Engineering and Knowledge Engineering (SEKE 2004, pp. 167–172), Banff, Alberta, Canada.

Weiser, M., & Brown, J. S. (1996). Designing calm technology. *PowerGrid Journal, 1,* 1.

Whittaker, S., Terveen, L., & Nardi, B. A. (2000). Let's stop pushing the envelope and start addressing it: A reference task agenda for HCI. *Human-Computer Interaction, 15,* 75–106.

Wickens, C. D., & Hollands, J. G. (2000). *Engineering psychology and human performance* (3rd ed.). Upper Saddle River, NJ: Prentice-Hall.

CHAPTER FOUR

The Technological Relevance of Natural Language Pragmatics

Michael A. Covington
The University of Georgia

Communication pervades modern technology; because of this, linguistics, especially pragmatics, is relevant to engineering. We build machines that exchange not only energy, but also information. Control signals are no longer simple things. An automobile has as many as two dozen microprocessors, all communicating. Even a Nikon autofocus camera has four or more CPUs in a local-area network. Meanwhile, the Internet is enabling our machines to communicate with each other globally. Pragmatics, the newest major area of linguistics, is as relevant to machines as it is to human speech. *Pragmatics* is defined as the relation of language to context and purpose. That is, phonology tells you how to pronounce things, syntax tells you how to put words together, semantics tells you what the utterances mean, and pragmatics tells you what you should say, to whom, when, and why.

In what follows, I explore some applications of human-language pragmatics to the world of machines, describing their communications with each other and with their human users.

KEY CONCEPTS OF PRAGMATICS

Pragmatics Defined

Pragmatics is the study of how language is used in specific situations to achieve specific goals. The term *pragmatics* goes back to Morris (1938), who offered these definitions, applicable to any system of communication:

Syntax	describes the relationships of signs to	*each other*
Semantics	describes the relationships of signs to	*what they denote*
Pragmatics	describes the relationships of signs to	*those who use them.*

Pragmatics is the newest major area of linguistics, first widely studied in the 1970s, and new applications are still being discovered. Some important areas of pragmatics include discourse structure, the use of language in social context, and speech act theory. I concentrate on the third of these.

Speech Act Theory

Speech act theory is the study of *what we do when we talk:* stating facts, asking questions, making requests, expressing feelings, and so forth. An important three-way distinction was introduced by Austin (1962):

Locution	is	*what you say.*
Illocution	is	*what you intend to accomplish by saying it.*
Perlocution	is	*what you actually accomplish by saying it.*

Crucially, the three need not match. You do not have to swallow what people say to you. You do not even have to succeed in decoding their intentions. Consider a situation in which you ask someone, "Can you open the door?", intending it as a polite request. Here the locution (a question) and the illocution (a request) are already mismatched, making it an indirect speech act. Yet a sufficiently perverse hearer could decode it as a stupid question, resulting in an entirely unforeseen perlocution (an insult).

Searle (1969) was the first to make a detailed study of illocutions, which he called *speech acts.* Besides the obvious types (statements, questions, requests, and promises), he found many others. Some linguists today recognize dozens of kinds (Bach & Harnish, 1979). Some, such as christening a ship, are possible only in special circumstances.

The key claim of speech act theory is that every utterance is wrapped in an illocution. You cannot simply express a fact; you have to perform a speech act. More formally, every utterance consists of an illocutionary force F applied to a proposition P. This is called the $F(P)$ *hypothesis*, and Moore (1998) summed it up thus: "The outermost [logical] operator of every utterance (everything we could possibly say) is not Boolean, not temporal, not even defeasible—it is an illocutionary force" (p. 215).

Putting this another way, we do not perform "Vulcan mind melds." That is, unlike Mr. Spock on *Star Trek,* we cannot simply place information into another person's mind. All we can do is *offer* the information, wrapped in a suitable illocution, and hope that the hearer takes it appropriately. Computers *do* perform "Vulcan mind melds," receiving data and instructions willy-nilly from other computers, and that is why we have viruses and other malicious software.

TECHNOLOGICAL RELEVANCE

Windows Message Boxes

Lets us look now at the pragmatics of some simple computer–human communication. The exact examples in Figs. 4.1 to 4.3 are fictitious, but realistic.

Figure 4.1 shows a straightforward, direct speech act performed by a computer (or its software). The computer is offering a piece of information as a statement of fact, together with a request for acknowledgment. But the recipient of the message is expected to make an inference—that the printout should be picked up, not just known about. In this sense, even the simplest speech act, if worth receiving, is partly indirect. It calls for inference and action.

The speech act in Fig. 4.2 may be clearer (except that it is puzzling whether "Cancel" is any different from "No"). The computer is stating a fact and asking permission to proceed, in the light of this fact. The human being who receives the message is expected to figure out what the answer should be, answer honestly, and remain committed to the answer (because it may not be possible to cancel later).

Figure 4.3 shows something that is all too much a part of modern life. The message is utterly cryptic, but it demands a response. The recipient is

FIG. 4.1. A speech act that requires decoding, acknowledgment, and response.

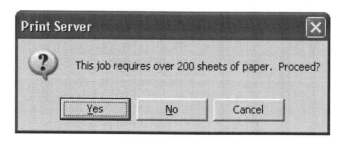

FIG. 4.2. A speech act that expects a commitment ("speak now or forever hold your peace").

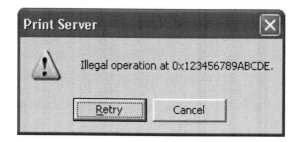

FIG. 4.3. An obscure speech act that demands a response.

required to act, but not *qualified* to act. Things like this teach people to ignore error messages.

Network Protocols

The relevance of pragmatics is more generally appreciated in network protocols, which often provide an elaborate set of illocutions. Consider, for example, the Extended SMTP protocol for delivering e-mail. What follows is a possible dialogue between the sender and recipient, both of which are machines, although the messages are designed to be human readable for troubleshooting purposes. To discourage hackers, all the machines and addresses in this dialogue are fictional.

In what follows, the sender's output is in italics, and the recipient's output is in upright type. First, the sender establishes a connection, and the recipient identifies itself:

(establishes connection)
220 wumpus.ai.uga.edu ESMTP Sendmail 8.8.8/8.8.8

This is actually a whole volley of illocutions: "I am wumpus.ai.uga.edu, I am running Sendmail 8.8.8, and I hereby offer to accept e-mail messages from you." Next, the sender identifies itself and is greeted:

EHLO possum.ai.uga.edu

250 wumpus.ai.uga.edu Hello possum.ai.uga.edu . . .

Crucially, this EHLO (Extended Hello) message may be insincere. It is common for e-mail systems to misidentify themselves. The main reason we have so much spam today is that e-mail systems are gullible; they accept anything a computer says by way of identification.

The 250 message here is an invitation: "Start sending me e-mail commands and I'll execute them for you." One thing the other computer can do is ask a question:

EXPN logicians

250 Donald Nute <dnute@wumpus.ai.uga.edu>

250 Don Potter <potter@wumpus.uga.edu>

That is: "Who is on the list called 'logicians'?" The reply gives the names and addresses, one per line, and invites further commands.

But the sender can do more than just ask questions. Here is how a piece of mail is actually delivered:

MAIL FROM: mc@xyzzy.ai.uga.edu RET=HDRS

250 mc@uga.edu: sender OK

RCPT TO: mac@xyz.com NOTIFY=SUCCESS

250 mac@xyz.com: recipient OK

DATA

354 Enter mail, end with. on a line by itself

Greetings from sunny Santa Fe!

Got your voicemail; will reply later.

.

250 Message accepted for delivery

Pragmatically, what is going on is that the sender announces that a piece of mail is ready to be sent from mc@xyzzy.ai.uga.edu; the recipient (of the announcement) indicates willingness to handle it; the destination, mac@xyz.com, is approved in the same way; the message is transmitted, and from there the recipient machine has to honor its promise to deliver it (or reply indicating why it could not be delivered). In accepting a piece of e-mail, a computer makes a promise to another. The high reliability of e-mail shows how trustworthy these machines have become.

Electronic Commerce

Pragmatics is also important for electronic commerce, as I have noted in other articles (Covington, 1997, 1998). By electronic commerce, I mean machine–machine negotiations, where a computer asks other computers about availability of products and then actually places orders.

The original electronic commerce standards, ANSI X.12 and EDIFACT, include little or no explicit pragmatics (or even semantics). There is a separate "form" for each kind of transaction, and computers simply fill in the data and deliver the filled-out forms to each other digitally. This is only a small step up from the "Vulcan mind meld." The forms seem to assume that the computer will just accept whatever is sent to it. In reality, some pragmatic inference takes place, but the system does not provide for it explicitly.

Much better is Knowledge Query Manipulation Language (KQML; Labrou & Finin, 1997). KQML wraps every utterance in an illocution and recognizes many illocution types, such as *tell, deny, untell* (retract), *insert* (into a database), *delete, ask-if, ask-about, ask-one* (requesting one of a series of answers), *ask-all*, and responses such as *error* ("I can't understand you"), *sorry* ("I can't do it"), and *eos* ("end of stream," i.e., end of the requested series of statements).

Extensible Markup Language (XML), by the way, is far less powerful than KQML and should not be confused with it. XML is gaining wide acceptance as a language for encoding all types of data files. Unlike KQML, XML hardly addresses pragmatics at all. XML is a universal syntax for data, with some minimal indications of semantics.

Operating System Calls

Even a computer program talking to the operating system has a repertoire of speech act types. Moore (1998) found a variety of illocutionary acts in MacOS AppleEvents. More generally, a computer program can:

- State facts to the OS
- Ask questions of the OS
- Give commands to the OS
- Make requests of the OS (which the OS can turn down)
- Make promises to the OS (by providing a callback method)

The last of these was the nemesis of early Windows programmers: To put a window on the screen, a program had to promise to handle events pertaining to it. Newer programming methodologies are *contract-free*, meaning the program need not make any promises; the underlying application framework ensures that all obligations are met.

More generally, operating systems could benefit from a clearer distinction between requests that the operating system can turn down and commands that it cannot. The concept of *success, error code,* or *error level* is often vague. Several operating systems have tried to make it into something systematic, but the concept has never been fully developed.

What to Do Next

What I have just given you is not a state-of-the-art report, but rather an indication of where to explore. Awareness of pragmatics provides a new perspective, a new set of questions to ask, when confronting any kind of communication between agents, be they human or mechanical. This does not mean that all machines are intelligent agents, of course. Yet even when no intentionality is involved, pragmatics provides a way to describe communication.

The simplest machines defy the $F(P)$ hypothesis and simply force information into each other. A turn of a steering wheel, for example, is not a request; it is a physical cause, and we probably wouldn't trust cars if they didn't work this way. As soon as computing power becomes available, speech acts come into play, and pragmatics becomes applicable. (The crucial distinction is whether the recipient of the signal has the ability to make decisions about it and perhaps even refuse it.) From linguistics, engineers can borrow a systematic view of things that, until now, they have only been doing in an ad hoc manner.

REFERENCES

Austin, J. L. (1962). *How to do things with words.* Oxford: Clarendon.
Bach, K., & Harnish, R. M. (1979). *Linguistic communication and speech acts.* Cambridge, MA: MIT Press.
Covington, M. A. (1997). On designing a language for electronic commerce. *International Journal of Electronic Commerce, 1,* 31–47.
Covington, M. A. (1998). Speech acts, electronic commerce, and KQML. *Decision Support Systems, 22,* 203–211.
Labrou, Y., & Finin, T. (1997). *A proposal for a new KQML specification* (Technical Report CS-97-03). Baltimore: Computer Science and Electrical Engineering Department, University of Maryland–Baltimore County.

Moore, S. A. (1998). Categorizing automated messages. *Decision Support Systems, 22,* 213–241.

Morris, C. W. (1938). *Foundations of the theory of signs: Vol. 1, No. 2. International encyclopedia of unified science.* Chicago: University of Chicago Press.

Searle, J. R. (1969). *Speech acts.* Cambridge: Cambridge University Press.

CHAPTER FIVE

Augmented Cognition

Chris Forsythe
Sandia National Laboratories

Amy Kruse
Strategic Analysis

Dylan Schmorrow
*Defense Advanced Research Projects Agency
and Office of Naval Research*

In the development of complex systems, it is tempting to assume human performance will be constant across time and conditions. Both practical experience and a wealth of scientific research clearly illustrate that human performance declines under the stress of excessive workload, heightened emotions, fatigue, and other conditions. As a result, system failure may follow from the failure of humans to perform within acceptable boundaries, and catastrophic failure may occur as the consequences of human failures propagate through a system. It is a noteworthy development that, over the past decades, consideration of human factors has generally become a customary component of the engineering design process. Valuable steps have been taken with respect to human–machine interface design, training and support, and procedures and policies. However, these are relatively modest measures. They largely achieve their success through administrative constraints, standardization, and accommodation of the masses. Gains in human performance capabilities beyond those attainable with current measures will require a more dynamic human–machine interaction, in which the machine has an awareness of the cognitive state of the operator and actively adapts to the operator. Such systems are the subject of this chapter and represent a next step in the transition from today's human–machine interfaces to cognitive systems that do more than avoid impediments to operator cognitive processes, but augment those cognitive processes producing enhanced human performance under stress.

For the most part, the ideas and technologies discussed in this chapter are the product of or have been influenced by the Defense Advanced Research Projects Agency (DARPA) investment in the field of Augmented Cognition, through the "Improving Warfighter information Intake Under Stress" program. The goal of this program has been to create a new generation of technologies that adapt in real time to the cognitive state of the operator(s).

Augmented cognition has a precedent, although no direct lineage, at DARPA in the Biocybernetics program that the Advanced Research Projects Agency (ARPA) funded from 1973 into the 1980s. The objective of this program was to augment the human–computer interface through novel human–computer communication channels, primarily psychophysiological signals. It was recognized that "any attempt to involve computers in the enhancement of human activity requires the development of techniques for machine monitoring of individuals and groups to continuously assess, momentary states of such attributes and functions as vigilance, fatigue, emotional state, decision making and general cognitive ability" (Donchin, 2004, p. 7). Projects funded through the Biocybernetics program sought to detect EEG signals associated with thinking specific words, explored the control of cursor movements through steady-state event-related potentials (ERPs), and demonstrated ERP-based real-time assessments of workload while piloting an aircraft.

A guiding belief of the augmented cognition research community is that most human–computer interface technologies have failed to address core limitations of the human. There has been a failure to account for variability in workload, stress, attention, or individual differences in knowledge or cognitive capabilities. In operational systems, the fit between the required and actual functional state of the operator is a continuous process that sometimes breaks down. As Donchin (2004) stated, "Within the complexity of contemporary control boards, there is an overload of information to the operator and poverty of information about the operator" (p. 7). Furthermore, systems do not take advantage of information that is often readily available concerning the cognitive state of the operator. As noted in a recent NATA Report from the Operational Functional State Assessment Task Group (NATO RTO HFM-056/TG-008), "Other system components (are) monitored for their status and if deficiencies are found, corrective actions are taken" (p. 7). Similar closed-loop adaptations are rarely found in which the system adjusts in response to the cognitive state of the operator. Unfortunately, when system adaptations to the operator are found, they are often contextually or otherwise inappropriate (e.g., Clippy). Raley et al. (2004) commented that a capability for machines to merely make discriminations concerning whether the operator is thinking or not thinking, or the operator is busy or not busy, would be an improvement.

Technologies being advanced through current Department of Defense investments emphasize closed-loop systems in which neurophysiological and other sensors (i.e., gauges) assess the state of the operator in real time, enabling the system to anticipate, predict, and initiate contextually appropriate measures to maximize the performance potential of the operator. Validation is based partly on the ability for gauges to accurately assess cognitive state. More important, system validation requires that gauges accurately drive system adaptations to the operator in a manner that produces superior operator performance. Ultimately, validation comes through the operational benefits derived from enhanced operational effectiveness.

The military impact of the "Improving Warfighter Information Intake Under Stress" program is being demonstrated through projects cofunded by the service agencies and undertaken by industry-led teams to create and evaluate prototype systems for four operational platforms (see Fig. 5.1):

- Dismounted Soldier—led by Honeywell Laboratories.
- Unmanned Vehicle Interface—led by Boeing Phantom Works.
- Ship-Based Command and Control Workstation—led by Lockheed Martin Advanced Technology Laboratories.
- Vehicular Command and Control Environment—led by DaimlerChrysler.

FIG. 5.1. Industry-led teams in conjunction with partners representing each branch of the U.S. military are validating augmented cognition systems for four operational platforms: Dismounted Soldier, Unmanned Vehicle Interface, Ship-Based Command and Control Workstation, Vehicular Command and Control.

The development of augmented cognition systems within the program is occurring through a phased development process with increasing involvement and investment by the sponsoring service agencies. During Phase 1, the primary objective was the real-time assessment of warfighter status. This phase extended for 18 months, ending in mid-2003. Several key accomplishments of Phase 1 are listed here:

- Detected cognitive state shift (verbal to spatial) in less than 1 minute using EEG: real-time, online processing, and characterization of brain function based on incoming cognitive state data.
- Demonstrated real-time spatial and temporal imaging of brain activity with one technology (noninvasive functional near infrared imaging) to measure and monitor cognitive state in real time.
- Improved encoding, storage, and retrieval of information through a cognitively designed information system with a 131% improvement in memory.
- Demonstrated >3x reduction in stress and increased task completion in a complex task environment using an intelligent interruption and negotiation strategy.
- Real-time EEG analysis (event-related negativity) improved human–machine performance by reducing errors 23% without interrupting the pace of the main task.
- Demonstrated real-time machine inference of an operator's ongoing interpretation of situations with an accuracy of 87%.
- Conducted a Technical Integration Experiment—utilizing and validating multiple sensors across a shared operationally based task.

Based on the successful Phase 1, Phase 2 of the program was initiated in 2003. In Phase 2, the overall objective has been the real-time maximization of warfighter potential based on real-time cognitive state sensing. To meet this objective, it has been required that systems assess the status of a warfighter in less than 2 seconds with a 90% classification accuracy and, in response, adapt information-processing strategies in less than 1 minute. Adaptations to improve human performance have focused on four cognitive information bottlenecks (see Fig. 5.2) based on the following targets, with no accompanying degradation to performance:

- 500% increase in working memory throughput measured by successful task completion.
- 100% improvement in executive function measured by recall and time to reinstate context.

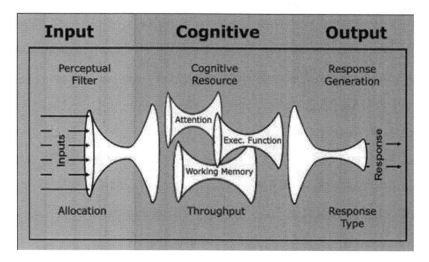

FIG. 5.2. Emphasis on mitigation strategies has centered on four cognitive information bottlenecks that limit and constrain the information throughput achievable by a warfighter. These bottlenecks are associated with sensory input, attention, working memory and executive function.

- 100% increase in sensory input measured by functions performed simultaneously.
- 100% improvement in attention measured by task completion within a critical time period.

Phase 2 ended in December 2004, and all metrics associated with this phase have been accomplished. In addition to the metrics highlighted earlier, Phase 2 also featured multiple concept validation experiments (CVE) based on the four operational platforms identified previously. These are discussed in more detail in subsequent sections.

Phase 3 began in 2005. The objective is to demonstrate closed-loop adaptation based on cognitive state to support warfighter performance under operational and stressful conditions. Systems in this phase are not permitted to exhibit any catastrophic failures and are expected to be early prototypes suitable for demonstration to service components. Then in 2006, the program concludes with Phase 4, which is focused on operational demonstrations and testing under realistic battlefield conditions for eventual handoff and transition to service partners.

Through these activities, the DARPA Improving Warfighter Information Intake Under Stress program lays the foundation for a breadth of augmented cognition technologies in which closed-loop computational systems adapt in real-time to the cognitive state of an operator(s) through specifically targeted data presentation that does not interrupt or otherwise disrupt ongoing functions. The result is an unprecedented human–machine symbiosis with the potential to redefine basic conceptions of human–machine systems. The resulting augmented warfighter should be capable of handling an order of magnitude greater cognitive demand than today's warfighters.

The remainder of this chapter describes in more detail the accomplishments of researchers working in the field of augmented cognition, focusing on specific efforts and organizations that make up the community that has been spawned through this specific investment.

AUGMENTED COGNITION SYSTEMS

The following sections describe vital components of an augmented cognition system as conceptualized through the "Improving Warfighter Information Intake Under Stress" program (see Fig. 5.3 for a conceptual diagram of the proposed architecture for an augmented cognition system).

Cognitive State Detection

Central to the augmented cognition systems developed through this program is the use of various sensors to infer the cognitive state of an operator(s). As illustrated in Table 5.1, a wide variety of physiological and behavioral phenomenon may serve this function.

A prominent concept has been that of a gauge in which one or more of the measures listed in Table 5.1 are combined to provide an assessment along a common scale of the commitment of resources to cognitive functions, including attention, verbal working memory, spatial working memory, memory encoding, error detection, and autonomic activity. Through the activities of individual investigators and the coordinated activities of teams of investigators, each gauge has been assessed with respect to the correlation between its indication of cognitive load and lab-based tasks designed to manipulate cognitive load. Through the combination of gauges, ensembles have been created to provide a greater range of temporal and spatial fidelity. All totaled, the product has been gauges tailored to each of the information-processing bottlenecks described earlier, enabling the real-time detection of shifts in resource utilization (e.g., verbal to spatial).

In the following sections, several specific examples of cognitive state gauges are described to illustrate the capabilities demonstrated to date.

Auditory P300 as a Gauge for Differential Attention. Researchers at Columbia University and the City College of New York have successfully demonstrated utilization of auditory P300 magnitude as an indication of the resource demands associated with ongoing activities

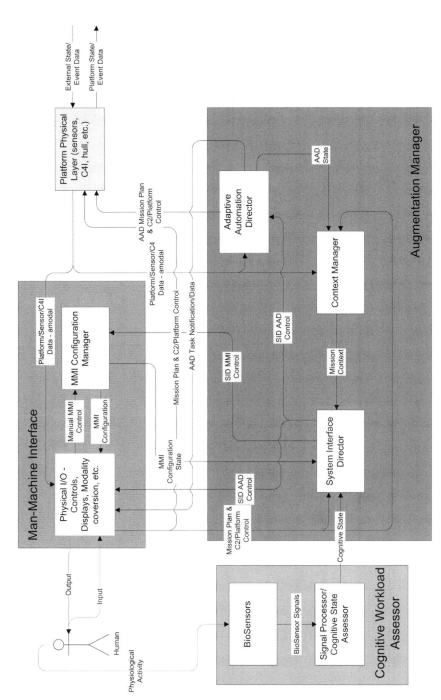

FIG. 5.3. Conceptual architecture for an augmented cognition system.

105

TABLE 5.1
Behavioral and Physiological Measures Postulated
as Indexes of Operator Cognitive State

• Cortical blood oxygenation	• Respiration rate
• Cortical blood volume	• Galvanic skin response
• Event related optical signal	• Postural position and adjustments
• Neuronal patterns	• Eye fixation duration
• Neuronal firing signatures	• Eye gaze location
• Frequency of neuronal population firing (e.g., alpha, beta, theta)	• Pupil dilation
• Synchronization/desynchronization among neuronal structures	• Mouse pressure
• Error-related negativity	• Rate of task completion
• EEG P300	• Error rate
• Heart rate, interbeat interval	

(Sajda, 2004). The P300 component of the ERP following an auditory stimulus has been well documented, as well as the differential effect of task environments on the magnitude (i.e., amplitude) of the P300 (see Rugg & Coles, 1995, for review). In general, the size of the P300 should vary with the level of attention demand, such that a larger P300 should correspond to distributed attention and a smaller P300 should correspond to focused attention. However, the approach taken here does not merely assess amplitude, but uses a linear discrimination to compute the spatial weighting that maximally discriminates between different conditions. Consequently, the assessments generated by the gauge reflect the differential localization and coupling of hypothetical sources, giving rise to the P300 for the different conditions for which the gauge may discriminate (i.e., conditions utilized in training to discriminant function).

The Auditory P300 gauge was assessed within the context of the Honeywell CVE (Ververs, 2004). Here subjects operating in a simulated Military Operations in Urban Terrain (MOUT) environment were presented auditory (i.e., radio) messages that required a differential response by the subjects. Auditory probes were presented immediately before each auditory message to assess the level of commitment of attentional resources. The auditory P300 was 90% accurate in predicting attention to the auditory probe, with there being significant differences between attended and ignored conditions (see Fig. 5.4).

EEG-Based Differentiation of Resource Utilization. Techniques were developed by researchers from Electrical Geodesics Inc. to utilize real-time dense-array EEG to gauge patterns of activation corresponding

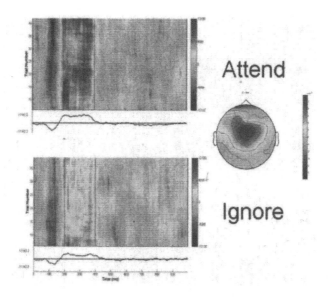

FIG. 5.4. Utilizing the P300 in response to and auditory probe presented immediately prior to an auditory message, conditions in which subjects subsequently attended to or ignored the auditory message could be differentiated (Sajda, 2004).

to the differential utilization of verbal and spatial resources. Input consisted of 128 channels of EEG filtered for activity in the theta (4–7 Hz) bandwidth. This provided estimates for the activity of 20 brain regions that served as the basis to obtain a discriminant function for each subject. This function corresponded to the individualized pattern of activity exhibited by subjects as they coped with shifting resource demands through the reorganization of cortical networks (see Fig. 5.5).

During the Lockheed Martin CVE, subjects performing a simulated Aegis operator task received either verbal or spatial alerts (Tucker et al., 2004). As Table 5.2 illustrates, on a subject-by-subject basis, a reasonably high level of accuracy was obtained for differentiating which type of alert a subject was processing for any given stimulus presentation.

EEG-Based Determination of Overall Workload.   To assess overall workload, researchers from Advanced Brain Monitoring utilized an approach in which for each second of EEG recordings, a ratio was computed that reflected the relative power associated with each 1 Hz bin for frequencies ranging from 3 to 40 Hz. These ratios were then incorporated into a model combining variables representing activity in each of the conventional EEG frequency bands (i.e., alpha, theta, and beta).

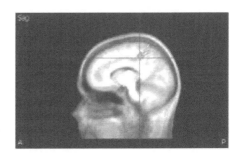

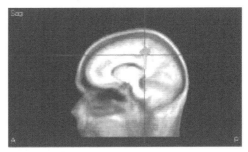

FIG. 5.5. These figures from Tucker et al., (2004) illustrate the differential activation observed at 388 msec post-stimulus in response to congruous (top), as opposed to incongruous (bottom), stimulus conditions (i.e., N400 incongruity effect). These same differential patterns of activity have been used to discriminate between conditions involving verbal and spatial alerts.

TABLE 5.2
Accuracy Observed for the Classification of Conditions Involving
Either Verbal or Spatial Alerts Based on Theta Activity Observed
Through Dense-Array EEG (Tucker et al., 2004)

Variable	Subject 1	Subject 2	Subject 3	Subject 4	Subject 5	Subject 6
Verbal	73%	71%	88%	91%	82%	83%
Spatial	73%	91%	72%	87%	83%	88%

Evaluations conducted as part of the TIE found an $r > 0.85$ for the correlation between the workload gauge and subject performance in easy, moderate, and hard task difficulty conditions (Berka et al., 2004). Within the context of the Lockheed Martin CVE for the primary task, the workload gauge was 95% accurate in recognizing the high-workload condition, with a 5% incidence of false positives. Additionally, a relationship was observed

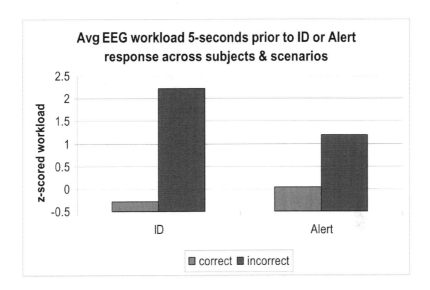

FIG. 5.6. Utilizing an EEG-based gauge of workload, subjects were monitored as they performed a simulated Aegis task. A relationship was observed
in which workload five seconds prior to an event was a predictor of errors
associated with that event (Berka et al., 2004).

where the workload index 5 seconds prior to an event was predictive of
the occurrence of errors related to the event (see Fig. 5.6).

Similarly, Human Bionics developed the eXecutive Load Index (XLI),
which takes EEG from FCZ and CPZ in the delta, theta, and alpha band-
widths to calculate an indicator of the ongoing demand on attentional resources (DuRousseau & Fraser, 2004). For their calculation, a weighted ratio was found for the peak frequency difference in the delta, theta, and
alpha bands for 2-second samples relative to a 20-second running average.
The gauge then utilized the sum of the differential power for delta and
theta, divided by the differential power for alpha. Within the context of the
Honeywell CVE, the resulting gauge successfully discriminated between
the high- and low-workload conditions.

Arousal Meter.   Researchers at Clemson University measured high-
frequency fluctuations in heart rate variability to gauge autonomic nervous system (ANS) arousal (Hoover, 2004; Hoover & Muth, 2004). The
arousal meter monitors the R-wave component of the electrocardiogram
to obtain the interbeat interval. As shown in Fig. 5.7, this requires error
correction to compensate for situations in which beats are missed due to a
low R-wave or the interval between R-waves is confused due to a high P-
wave. Once normalized for a given individual, the relative frequency over

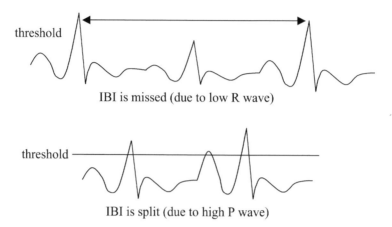

FIG. 5.7. The Arousal Meter indicates the relative activation of the para-sympathetic nervous system based on fluctuations in the inter-beat interval of the electrocardiogram (Hoover, 2004). To advance this capability, it has been necessary to develop error correction mechanisms to compensate for conditions involving either a low R wave or high P wave.

time may be used to identify frequency shifts indicative of parasympathetic nervous system activity.

For subjects undergoing sleep deprivation, a correspondence has been demonstrated between the relative level of arousal as indicated by the fluctuation in interbeat interval and performance in a dual-task paradigm that combined primary tracking tasks with secondary spatial and short-term memory tasks. Additionally, assessed through the Honeywell CVE, conditions involving high, low, and baseline levels of cognitive load were successfully differentiated on the basis of the arousal meter.

Index of Cognitive Activity.   Work conducted by EyeTracking, Inc. has utilized real-time measurement of changes in the diameter of the pupils of the eyes to gauge cognitive load (Marshall, 2004). For these measurements, miniature cameras record images of each eye at a rate of 250 images per second while a third camera compensates for head movement. With this configuration, changes in pupil diameter may be measured with 0.01 mm degree of accuracy.

It has been observed that, in contrast to the reflexive response of the pupils to light in which there is a constriction of the pupil, a dilation of the pupil occurs in response to cognitive load (see Fig. 5.8). By measuring the relative pupil size, an index may be obtained that corresponds to the ongoing level of cognitive load. This index has been shown to correlate

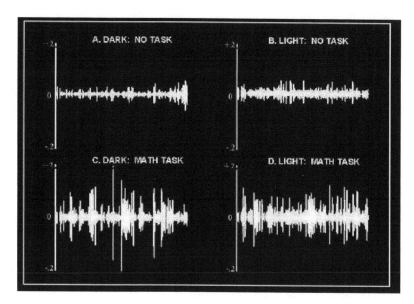

FIG. 5.8. This figure illustrates a wavelet analysis of ongoing measures of pupil diameter observed for baseline conditions relative to conditions in which subjects were presented with a math task (Marshall, 2004).

with task difficulty for studies involving effortful information processing during reading, stimulus search, and problem solving (Marshall, 2004). Furthermore, during the TIE, this index was shown to be a reliable means of differentiating among high, medium, and low levels of task load (St. John et al., 2004).

Postural Control. Researchers at the University of Pittsburgh and Naval Research Laboratory have developed indicators of cognitive load that utilize data concerning the postural load and adjustments of an individual performing a task (Balaban et al., 2004). It is observed that postural control is the product of the context-dependent integration of visual, vestibular, proprioceptive, haptic, and auditory information. Postural adjustments may be either reactive or reflexive and reflect the voluntary trade-off between voluntary movement and postural maintenance.

For inferences concerning cognitive load, the operator's seat and seat back is equipped with an array of capacitive pressure sensors. Additionally, an ultrasonic head tracking system provides the orientation of the head. A real-time dynamic analysis of the resulting data allows detection of task-related voluntary movements, including spontaneous movements such as fidgeting. Likewise, there is detection of automatic postural adjustments that occur as a reactive response to dynamic events or predictive adjustments that occur in anticipation of upcoming events.

Postural control measures have been assessed in two contexts. First, through the Lockheed Martin CVE (Balaban, 2004a), for subjects performing the simulated Aegis task, behavioral templates were developed to detect postural sway (i.e., spontaneous anterior/posterior and lateral weight shifts) and anticipatory shifts (i.e., orienting movements and leaning relative to the computer display). Results reveal a linear association between head position and seat COP (Center of Pressure) relative to the screen and the number of tracks being engaged with 50% of the variance in these measures accounted for by the number of tracks in a given engagement (see Fig. 5.9). Furthermore, these measures were predictive of user actions within the next 5 seconds (61% probability of an action within 2 seconds of a postural shift, 76% within 3 seconds, 86% within 4 seconds, and 94% within 5 seconds).

The second assessment occurred through the DaimlerChrysler CVE (Balaban, 2004b). Data have been collected for automobile drivers under highway conditions and postural adjustments correlated with driving events. For these measures, the time derivatives of the seat and seat back were calculated for the left and right sides of the body. This allowed development of a gauge reflecting the body COP torsion (i.e., angle of the body

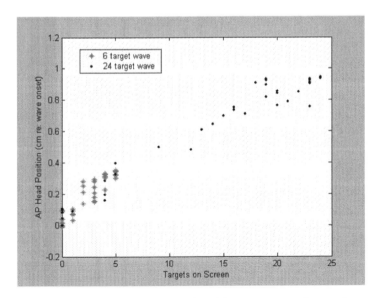

FIG. 5.9. A linear association was found between postural control reflected in the head position relative to the screen and the number of tracks that appeared on the screen for a simulated Aegis task (Balaban, 2004a).

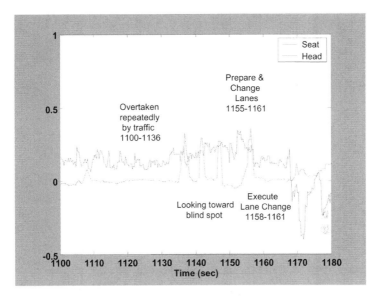

FIG. 5.10. For a driver operating an automobile under highway conditions, a correspondence was found between shifts in the front-back COP (Center of Pressure) recorded from seat and seat back pressure sensors and driving events (Balaban, 2004b).

in the seat relative to a global center) and postural stability based on the RMS (Root Mean Square) of derivatives within a time window. Results show that 98% of the variability in postural data was explained by shifts in the front-back COP recorded on the left and right sides of the seat, with no significant contribution from lateral shifts in the COP. As shown in Fig. 5.10, these front-back shifts in COP were found to be indicative of orienting responses to vehicles, highway signs, and other situations requiring vigilance (e.g., being overtaken by vehicles, lane changes, and passing large vehicles). Additionally, postural control sensors indicated relative quiescent periods with lower vigilance demands.

Emotional State. Advanced Interfaces represent one group that is currently developing systems that utilize various sensors for the detection of emotional state (Sharma, 2004). The system being developed by Advanced Interfaces utilizes a combination of intrusive (pupil dilation, blood pressure, and chemosignals) and nonintrusive (facial expression, facial perspiration, facial blood flow, speech prosody, and head/hand gestures) indicators. Currently, the system utilizes a video camera focused on the face, a video camera for tracking hand gestures, a directional microphone, and thermal cameras with different spectral properties. The system responds to facial indicators that include expression, perspiration pattern, and temperature distribution.

A two-stage classification uses the dynamic optical flow in these data to first assess the specific pattern of motion between two images and then the specific temporal pattern across a sequence of images. At the frame scale, motions of the face are classified with respect to expressions of emotion based on k-nearest neighbor. Then at the level of temporal sequences, it is verified that the temporal signature corresponds with expression of a given emotion utilizing hidden Markov models.

The ability to detect facial expressions of emotion has been assessed for three sets of data: the Cohn-Kanade facial expression database, a collection of TV sequences featuring facial expressions of emotion, and records obtained from emotion-elicitation experiments. Results indicate 90% accurate classification of emotional expressions relative to expert ratings. For specific emotions, there was 100% accuracy for surprise, 96% for happiness, 96% for sadness, 76% for fear, 100% for anger, and 62% for disgust.

Classification of Cognitive State

Augmented cognition systems often require specialized algorithms for the interpretation of sensor data with respect to cognitive states. Based on the output of cognitive state classification algorithms, the system may adapt to the operator through appropriate mitigation strategies. For instance, when a high level of cognitive load is detected, the system may delay nonessential communications until cognitive load has diminished to a level that the communications are unlikely to negatively impact performance. The following sections provide illustrative descriptions of four approaches to the classification of cognitive state.

Cognitive State Classification Using a Linear Discrimination Function. In the cognitive cockpit developed by researchers at QinetiQ, a cognitive state classifier provides an ongoing assessment of executive load (Belyavin, 2004; Dickson, 2004; Pleydell-Pearce et al., 2003). For this classifier, input is utilized from a 32-channel EEG. For each subject, data are collected for a standard set of tasks designed to provide a controlled manipulation with multiple levels of cognitive workload. After removing artifacts, a large set of measures is created based on various derivatives of the EEG data. Multiple regression is then utilized to select the subset of EEG measures that best predict cognitive load with respect to the controlled manipulation of load for the standard tasks. This then provides the basis for a linear discrimination function that operates as the classifier. In practice, at 1-second intervals, the classifier provides an indication of executive load indicating that the operator's load is either acceptable or unacceptable.

Classification of Cognitive State Using Independent Components Analysis.

In conjunction with DaimlerChrysler, the Fraunhofer Institute has utilized independent components analysis as a basis for classification of the cognitive state of automobile drivers (Müller, 2004). Development of the classifier began with collection of EEG data through a field experiment in which subjects performed tasks selected to create either a high visual (visual discrimination), auditory (auditory oddball), or attentional (mental arithmetic) load while driving under a variety of roadway conditions.

Based on the experimental data, a feature space is created in which dimensions correspond to the μV measurement at each electrode site. Using a binary linear classification, a hyperplane is created dividing the feature space. Then a projection line is derived that best describes the discriminating function. A Regularized Fischer Distribution (Mika, Raisch, & Muller, 2000) maximizes the difference between the means of the resulting classes and minimizes the intraclass variance. The resulting classifiers implemented in a real-time automotive platform enable the ongoing cognitive state of the driver to be distinguished on the basis of high and low visual, auditory, and attentional load.

Cognitive State Classification Using Blind Source Separation.

A team consisting of the University of New Mexico, Drexel University, and Integrated Management Services utilized blind source separation for cognitive state classification with respect to the anticipated performance of an operator (Chang, 2004). Performance prediction has been demonstrated for a visual search and target identification task based on 128-channel EEG input. In this task, subjects identified a target consisting of a line in a field of distracters, with the level of difficulty differed by varying the degree to which the target was off-angle relative to the distracters.

Training sets were created that consisted of either correct or incorrect trials. The objective was to identify differential sources of brain activity that could be described spatially and temporally and would allow the performance on a given trial to be predicted. Sources were described using a second-order blind identification (SOBI) approach. With this approach, the EEG signal is decomposed into separate components allowing development of spatial filters that respond to activity within specific brain regions. Based on training data, templates are constructed using wavelet and temporal representations for each of the conditions to be classified

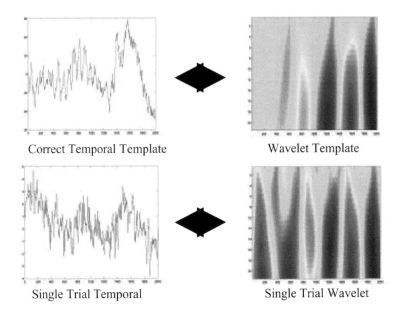

Correct Temporal Template   Wavelet Template

Single Trial Temporal   Single Trial Wavelet

FIG. 5.11.   Based on separate EEG sources, a temporal and wavelet template is created for the conditions to be classified (Chang, 2004). In the example shown here, the template corresponds to correct performance on a
visual target search and identification task. Through comparison of single
trial performance to templates, it has been demonstrated that performance
on a given trial may be predicted with an accuracy of 90% or greater.

(see Fig. 5.11). For the target search and identification task, templates
classified conditions as either correct or incorrect with a 91% accuracy.

A similar approach has been used to differentiate conditions involving
high and low levels of load for visual processing and executive function
with the Warship Commander task utilized in the TIE. In this case, single
events were classified as either high or low cognitive load with a 90% or
greater accuracy.

Functional Near-Infrared Brain Imaging (fNIR)

Although the technology and practical application of fNIR as a means to
image brain activation is not as mature as other technologies, there has
been great interest in the development of fNIR as a sensor for the real-time
detection of cognitive state. This interest has been motivated by the relative noninvasiveness of the sensors, as well as affordability, portability,
and compatibility with other sensors.

With fNIR, an array of LED light sources is affixed to the subject's head, and near-infrared light capable of readily passing through the skull is directed at the brain. Reflected light is then captured by silicon detectors. By assessing the differential absorption of light, inferences may be made concerning metabolic activity associated with brain activation. A variety of phenomena may be measured with fNIR, including fast neuronal responses (EROS) and slower hemodynamic responses. Activation of brain regions may be mapped with a spatial resolution of less than 1 cm and a temporal resolution in the ms range for fast neuronal responses and the sec range for slower hemodynamic responses (Fabiani & Gratton, 2004; Gratton & Fabiani, 2004).

Gratton and colleagues at the University of Illinois have assessed the use of fNIR as a means to differentiate between the utilization of cognitive resources (Fabiani & Gratton, 2004; Gratton & Fabiani, 2004). The EROS was recorded from subjects during experimental conditions that involved either an auditory oddball paradigm and a Sternberg memory paradigm alone or in combination. A typical pattern of results was found, in which accuracy was better for the oddball task alone, compared with the dual-task condition, and reaction time for the Sternberg task was better with two as opposed to four letters. For these different experimental conditions, brain areas approximately 1.5 cm apart in the right middle frontal gyrus showed an activation-inhibition response reciprocity that varied in accordance with the cognitive processes engaged during each task condition. Based on a relatively small number of trials (i.e., 50 or less), encoding could be distinguished from retrieval in the Sternberg task, conditions involving either task alone could be distinguished, and, in the dual-task condition, the Sternberg task with a set size of 2 could be distinguished from the same task with a set size of 4.

Technology Integration Experiment (TIE)

From March 3 to March 6, 2003, the TIE brought together 20 psychophysiological measures of cognitive state from 11 different research organizations for assessment using a common test environment (St. John et al., 2003). For this evaluation, the developers of psychophysiological measures or gauges of cognitive state were organized into four teams to create four separate suites of individually compatible gauges. Through this integration, the TIE demonstrated the ability to combine multiple sensors and collect real-time data in a semi-realistic task environment.

For the TIE, the Warship Commander task was developed to provide a common test environment that introduced controlled variations in the level of task load. As shown in Fig. 5.12, the Warship Commander offers an analogue to a Navy air warfare task. Users monitor some number of air-

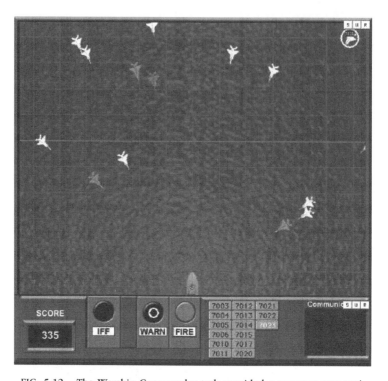

FIG. 5.12. The Warship Commander task provided a common test environment for gauges of cognitive load assessed through the TIE (St. John et al., 2003). Incoming tracks require the subject identify the track and engage hostile tracks following explicit rules of engagement. Cognitive load was manipulated through varying the number of tracks, proportion of tracks that were potentially hostile and requiring subjects perform a secondary auditory task.

craft (i.e., tracks), determine when it is appropriate to warn tracks, and engage hostile tracks on the basis of explicit rules of engagement. The task was designed to manipulate different aspects of cognition, including perception, motor, memory, attention, and decision making. Task load was manipulated in three ways: (a) number of tracks constituting each wave of tracks, (b) track difficulty manipulated by varying the proportion of potentially threatening tracks, and (c) presence or absence of a secondary concurrent auditory verbal memory task (i.e., ship status task).

As shown in Table 5.3, 11 of the gauges successfully identified changes in one or more of the task load factors. Five additional gauges showed promise for detecting changes in task load sufficient to warrant further research and development. Where positive results were found, gauges responded to certain task attributes, and it was inferred that the same gauges would be successful with other tasks that involve the same task at-

TABLE 5.3

This Table Identifies the Sensors for Which Associated Gauges Were
Successful in Detecting Differential Cognitive Load Due to Manipulation
of One of the Cognitive Load Factors in the Warship Commander Task

Number of Tracks Per Wave	Track Difficulty	Secondary Verbal Task
Functional Near-Infrared, left and right activation	Mouse click-based perceptual-motor load	EEG-ERP, loss perception (Event-related negativity)
Continuous EEG, high and low vigilance, and executive load	Mouse pressure-based cognitive difficulty	EEG-ERP, synched anterior-posterior
EEG-ERP, Ocular-Frontal Source		Pupil dilation-based index of cognitive load
Mouse click-based perceptual-motor load		
Mouse pressure-based cognitive difficulty		

tributes. This is particularly true for tasks that involve detection, identification, and memory recall, such as fast-paced, computer-based command and control.

In the conclusions drawn from the TIE, it was emphasized that many of the gauges were prototypes with little previous testing. Consequently, negative results do not necessarily indicate a failure, but could be a product of a noisy data-collection environment, small sample size, or failure of the Warship Commander task to impose demands on the cognitive resources for which a given gauge was most sensitive. Although two of the gauges were consistent for all subjects (i.e., mouse-based gauges and QinetiQ EEG-based gauges), the majority were sensitive with some participants, but not for others. Finally, the most common difficulty arose from the limited headspace for sensors of brain activity and the time required for attachment and verification of sensors.

Awareness of Current Context

With an augmented cognition system, based on operator cognitive state, the system may initiate various adaptations to enable the system to better accommodate the operator's cognitive demands and resource availability. However, in deploying system adaptations or mitigations, there is a risk that if adaptations are contextually inappropriate, the adaptations may worsen the situation for the operator. For example, to reduce the incoming flow of information to the operator, the system may block or mask information vital to the operator's ongoing situation awareness. Therefore, it is vital to augmented cognition systems that there are mechanisms to provide an ongoing awareness of the operator's context so that adaptations may be initiated in a contextually appropriate manner.

As described in an earlier chapter, researchers at Sandia National Laboratories developed technology that utilizes a real-time user cognitive model to infer context as the basis for the context manager of an augmented cognition system. Initially, context awareness was demonstrated for a simulated AWACS operator's workstation (Forsythe et al., 2003), but currently the same technology is being used by DaimlerChrysler and is a component of the system evaluated in the CVE. For this application, the context manager receives input from automobile data sources (e.g., steering wheel angle, relative rotation of the wheels, etc.), an ultrasonic head position sensor, and postural control sensors located in the seat and seatback, described in an earlier section of this chapter. Over 20 separate driving contexts were identified, for which readily available data would allow their recognition. These included entering a high-speed roadway, waiting at an intersection, preparing and executing a lane change, being overtaken by another vehicle, and so on.

Development of the context manager for the DaimlerChrysler augmented cognition prototype system began with collection of data from field tests in which drivers traveled a designated route under actual driving conditions. Utilizing video records, the data were tagged with respect to the occurrence of each of the identified driving contexts. Then optimization routines were utilized to train a cognitive model to recognize each context utilizing single and derivative data sources. Currently, the context manager recognizes each context with an accuracy of 97%, with a threshold function allowing the direction of errors to be shifted between a preference for false positives or false negatives.

In the prototype system being developed by DaimlerChrysler, EEG-based gauges provide an ongoing indication of the driver's cognitive load. When an excessive level of cognitive load is detected, the automotive system may adapt by either blocking or delaying information presented to the driver, switching the modality for information presentation, or initiating automated driver assistance. An augmentation manager initiates specific adaptations. The context manager provides input to this augmentation manager, which determines the appropriate augmentation based on the current driving context. For example, if the driver is engaged in a relatively difficult maneuver, such as entering high-speed traffic, the augmentation manager may block information presentation as opposed to merely switching the modality for information presentation to accommodate the high visual load detected through the EEG sensors. Additional details concerning the DaimlerChrysler prototype augmented cognition system appear in a separate chapter devoted to this particular illustration of a cognitive system.

System Adaptation and Mitigation

The mechanisms for adaptation to a user and the appropriate implementation of these mechanisms are probably the least understood component of an augmented cognition system. A number of approaches by which a system might adapt to an operator have been proposed. However, the CVEs have offered the first opportunity to observe these adaptations in operation within a closed-loop system. Significant improvements in human performance have been found in some cases. However, it is apparent that there remains much to be learned with regard to the appropriate mechanisms for system adaptation to operator cognitive load. In particular, as is discussed by Radvansky and colleagues in a separate chapter, preliminary studies conducted as part of Phase 1 of the DARPA program have shown that adaptations intended to aid the operator may have no effect or, in some cases, may have a deleterious effect on operator performance. Thus, it is important for there to be continuous testing and assessment of potential mitigation strategies in as close to the actual operational conditions as possible.

The selection of system adaptations has been partly driven by the emphasis placed on the four information-processing bottlenecks described earlier. Table 5.4 summarizes alternative approaches that are being explored to mitigate the effects of cognitive load on these bottlenecks.

With this chapter, attention has been focused primarily on conditions in which human performance suffers due to an excessive cognitive load. Performance may also be degraded in conditions in which an operator does not receive sufficient stimulation (i.e., "underload"). Currently, underload conditions are a topic of interest in the automotive domain, given that drivers often face extended periods of monotony (Heisterkamp, 2004). In these cases, the low situational demand decreases the attention level (i.e., immediately available resources) of the operator so that sudden increases in situational demand cause an immediate overload condition. Proposed approaches for overcoming conditions of underload include presentation of unexpected perceptual events (e.g., haptic or auditory stimuli) and the introduction of appropriate spoken dialogue.

PROTOTYPE SYSTEMS

As noted earlier, for Phase 2 of the program, teams formed to develop and validate prototype augmented cognition systems targeting specific military operational domains. Each team included a government sponsor, an industry lead, and some combination of organizations to provide cognitive state gauges and other supporting components to be combined into

TABLE 5.4

This Table Summarizes Various Approaches to System Adaptation That Are Being Explored Through the DARPA Augmented Cognition Program Relative to the Four Information-Processing Bottlenecks

Sensory Processing	Attention	Working Memory	Executive Function
Modality switching—when there is evidence that a given modality (e.g., vision) is loaded, information is presented through an alternative modality (e.g., auditory).	**Attention monitoring**—the system may monitor the operator to ascertain whether specific information was processed.	**Intelligent interruption and negotiation**—the system may coordinate the presentation of information so as to avoid disruptions in ongoing tasks.	**Cued retrieval strategy**—the system may provide cues to facilitate memory recall and minimize the resources that would otherwise be committed to memory recall processes.
Modality multiplexing—information may be simultaneously displayed to multiple modalities (e.g., visual and auditory).	**Directed attention**—the system may take measures to increase the salience of information that is of high priority or the operator has failed to process.	**Context switching support**—when the operator must switch between contexts (e.g., display screens), measures may be taken to preserve the context and facilitate reacquiring contexts.	**Automated message delivery**—through scheduling the delivery of information, demands associated with information requests are lessened.
Automated sensory processing—sensors may be deployed to detect significant events that an operator may fail to detect due to other task demands (e.g., automotive lane departure and dead angle sensors).			**Automated prioritization of tasks**—executive functions associated with scheduling may be off-loaded.
Message delay and blocking—in high load conditions, nonessential messages may be delayed or blocked avoiding additional load on sensory channels.			**Task Offloading**—task management demands may be lessened through the automated delegation and offloading of tasks to other people and to automated systems.

an integrated system by the industry lead. At the time this chapter was written, each team had developed an initial prototype sufficient to conduct concept validation experiments. The following sections describe three of these efforts in detail, while summarizing the fourth effort (i.e., the effort led by DaimlerChrysler), which is described in detail in a separate chapter of this book.

Unmanned Vehicle Interface (UVI)

This team is led by Boeing Phantom Works and has developed a prototype augmented cognition system to support the mission control station operator for a squadron of unmanned aerial vehicles. This is a challenging domain in that it requires operators to integrate multidimensional information to make decisions concerning the navigation and engagement of onboard weapon systems (Barker, 2004a, 2004b). In particular, human–machine interface technologies are needed to aid operators in maintaining their situation awareness as they move among different contexts.

Four specific shifts in context have been identified as problematic for Unmanned Aerial Vehicle (UAV) operators:

- shifting context between UAVs,
- shifting context between facets of information within a given display,
- shifting context between situation display and target imaging, and
- shifting context among situation display, target imaging, and vehicle health displays.

Four concept validation experiments were conducted from March to September 2004. In the CVEs, the goal was to evaluate the covariance among cognitive state gauges, facets of the UAV operator's task, and system adaptations to manipulate the operator's cognitive load. For the prototype augmented cognition system, the initial sensor suite utilized EEG, ECG, pupillometry, functional near infrared, and EOG. The four CVEs allowed an iterative assessment of the performance characteristics of each sensor.

UAVs were depicted as icons on the tactical display of the operator's console. Groups of UAVs formed flight packages that could attack targets within a specified corridor. Either a specific UAV could be directed to a target or the attack on a target could be distributed between the UAVs in a flight package. UAVs were autonomous with regard to flight planning and control of onboard systems, placing the operator in the role of mission manager, as opposed to remote pilot. The weapon load was not the same for all vehicles in a flight package and varied between test scenarios. One task for the subjects was to appropriately assign ordinances to different types of targets. The type of target could be identified by placing the cursor over the target, with some of the targets designated as time-critical.

A second targeting display was used to present Synthetic Aperture Radar (SAR) images and allowed a Direct Mean Point of Impact to be assigned to a target. Vehicle health alerts were presented that involved either Engine Fire or General Failure. In either case, the outline of a UAV's icon was changed to red, and by selecting the icon a dialogue box was displayed that provided additional information.

A Situation Assessment Support Module offered general mission status and provided recommended actions. Advice concerning the best course of action was provided based on the initial mission plan, the current allocation of tasks, and mission events.

A Tasking Interface Manager controlled the presentation of information on the basis of the operator's actions, the operator's cognitive state and the determination of overall context by the Situation Assessment Support Module. Through changes to the user interface, the system attempted to adapt in a manner that allowed the operator's cognitive load to remain within acceptable ranges. These modifications include switching between sensory modalities (e.g., a pop-up window as opposed to a synthesized voice to announce a failure), changing the amount of information displayed (e.g., declutter to remove information not relevant to a current task), and advisories (i.e., blinking icon to indicate the next critical task).

Specific mitigations employed during the CVEs and the targeted cognitive bottlenecks are summarized in Table 5.5. As discussed next, these mitigations have been shown to provide performance benefits for tasks that place demands on their respective cognitive bottlenecks.

The assessment of executive function utilized scenarios in which the operator had accessed either the Targeting Display or the Vehicle Health Status display. In these cases, the operator was required to switch context to the Tactical Situation display to respond to a target. This was a forced-pace task, in which the level of load was manipulated by increasing the number of strike packages and airspeed of the UAVs.

Performance was assessed on the basis of the number of errors in assigning UAVs to targets where there was less than 30 seconds available for the assignment. Combining the four test subjects, there were only 8 errors with the mitigations, as opposed to 69 in the absence of mitigations. However, a primary reason for there being fewer errors with augmented cognition was that operators tended to switch context more effectively and, as a result, there were fewer instances in which less than 30 seconds remained without the operator having taken action (i.e., 10 instances with mitigation and 70 instances without mitigation).

TABLE 5.5
Mitigations Utilized for the Boeing Concept Validation Experiments
and the Cognitive Bottlenecks Targeted by These Mitigations

Mitigation	Cognitive Bottleneck		
	Sensory Input	Working Memory	Response Generation
Map declutter	X		
Earcons	X		
Vehicle health tones	X		
Time-critical target voice	X		
Bookmark	X		
Unified bookmark	X		
Alert manager	X	X	
UAV menu tokens	X		X

Note. Mitigations may be summarized as follows: (a) Map declutter involved placing a fog over the map that obscured map details and UAV flight paths that were not relevant to immediate activities; (b) "Earcons" provided distinct sounds accompanying user actions (e.g., a camera click occurred when the user called for a SAR image); (c) Vehicle Health Tones consisted of a distinct tone to distinguish which flight package had a UAV that was experiencing problems; (d) Time-Critical Voice alerts used a synthesized voice to indicate that a time-critical target was present; (e and f) Bookmarks provided operators with a visual symbol to indicate the next action that would be most expedient; (g) Alert Manager consisted of a dialog box which placed active alerts within a single list. Once the operator successfully handled one alert, the Alert Manager automatically brought up the next alert; and (h) UAV Menu tokens consisted of icons placed over UAVs that allowed operators to directly initiate the capture of a SAR image or execution of an attack.

The evaluation of attention presented operators with time-critical targets in which there were only seconds to respond with the lead vehicle before that UAV had flown over the target. Again combining subjects, there were 15 successful attacks with mitigation compared with only 2 without mitigation. Furthermore, there were 11 errors in assigning UAVs to targets without mitigation and only 1 with mitigation.

For working memory, subjects were taught a series of correct solutions for 15 different vehicle health problems. Then during testing, when presented with a vehicle health problem, it was necessary that the subject recall and carry out the correct solution. Without mitigation, combined, subjects failed to correctly respond to 35 problems, compared with only 9 incorrect responses with mitigation.

Sensory processing was assessed in conditions in which there was a joint occurrence of two high-priority events: a vehicle health task (i.e., engine fire) and tactical situation display task (time-critical target). With mitigation, subjects successfully resolved both tasks on 17 occasions, whereas there were only 6 successful resolutions of both tasks without mitigation.

Conditions in which targets required subjects to both take an SAR image and then initiate an attack allowed consideration of response generation. Failure to perform either action resulted in an error. With mitigation, there was only 1 error, with there being 19 errors without mitigation.

Ship-Based Command and Control Workstation

This team is being led by Lockheed Martin Advanced Technology Laboratory and has utilized a command and control environment emphasizing target tracking and retargeting. The objective has been to improve working memory throughput by detecting when the demands on verbal working memory are high relative to capacity and intelligently scheduling tasks to alleviate demands on verbal working memory.

The task environment features a Tactical Strike Coordinator (TSC) who must monitor and adjust missile strikes. In such a strike, there is a set of missiles that must be individually followed and adjusted in response to events to hit their targets. Particular attention was placed on specific responsibilities of the TSC, including reassigning missiles to emergent targets, tracking the coverage of already launched missiles, and maintaining overall situation awareness with respect to the current strike. Performance measures were based on the ability of subjects to optimally reallocate missiles while maintaining sufficient overall situation awareness to answer questions to simulated queries that might be received from a commanding officer.

In a Location task, subjects were required to perform a coverage zone assessment. Subjects were allowed to study a 10-minute coverage zone for each missile for 15 seconds. Then following a 45-second interval, the subject was asked to recall whether targets were covered by any of the missiles. An Alert task presented subjects with questions (e.g., Which targets require or prefer more than one missile?), and subjects were required to answer by either clicking on the missile or entering the corresponding number in a response box. With the Retarget task, during a missile strike, emergent targets would appear. In response, subjects were required to redirect missiles to emergent targets under the presumption that they were generally a high priority. Subjects were allowed 90 seconds to target as many emergent targets as achievable while maintaining coverage for medium- and low-priority targets.

Mitigation consisted of intelligent sequencing, whereby alerts were only presented during conditions believed to involve relatively low demands on verbal working memory (e.g., during the largely spatial Location task). This mitigation was based on findings illustrating that the verbal task of Alerting interfered with the competing verbal task of Retargeting, but not with the spatial Location task. In addition, cognitive state assessment was utilized to make inferences concerning the subjects' allocation of resources to specific tasks.

Sensors incorporated into the prototype include EEG, EKG, GSR, heart rate variability (HRV), posture control, fNIR, and pupillometry. Each sensor provided input to a neural network, with the output being a set of values for cognitive state gauges corresponding to the relative load imposed on verbal and spatial working memory.

Performance was measured in two respects. First, an interference cost was determined, which reflected the degradation to performance associated with interfering verbal tasks, compared with performing a verbal task with the spatial Location task. Second, Scheduling Benefit assessed the gains in performance associated with mitigation.

Using these measures, results averaged across subjects show a 622% reduction in the effects of interference on task performance. Accordingly, averaged across subjects, there was a 642% benefit associated with the mitigation.

Dismounted Soldier

This team is being led by Honeywell Laboratories and has focused on developing a prototype augmented cognition system for the dismounted soldier that is wireless and wearable, detects attentional state, and selects appropriate system adaptations to optimize cognitive throughput.

The prototype is implemented in a simulated Military Operations in Urban Terrain (MOUT) environment in which subjects must use a keyboard and mouse to navigate to an objective and engage enemy forces. Additionally, subjects managed the communications flow between team members and commanders and carried out procedures such as calling for a medevac (Medical Evacuation). Communications involved sending and receiving reports, issuing and receiving commands, providing and requesting status updates and information, and coordinating friendly forces.

Cognitive state gauges included a stress gauge based on a composite of EMG, ECG, EDR, and pupil size; an arousal gauge based on heart rate variability; an EEG-based gauge that uses the P300 to assess whether there has been attention to stimuli; an EEG-based executive load index; and an EEG-based engagement index.

Four mitigation strategies were implemented: (a) task scheduling, (b) task offloading, (c) task sharing, and (d) modality management. Table 5.6 illustrates how each strategy was deployed for the three conditions. The communications scheduler classified messages as either high priority (i.e., mission-critical and time-critical), medium priority (i.e., mission-critical only), and low priority (i.e., not critical). Then based on the cognitive state assessment, which provided an indication of workload and message com-

TABLE 5.6
Mitigation Strategies Employed for the
Honeywell Concept Validation Experiment

Mitigation Strategy	Scenario 1 Divided Attention	Scenario 2 Divided Attention	Scenario 3 Sustained Attention
Task Scheduling	Communications scheduler		
Task Offloading		Medevac negotiation	
Task Sharing			Mixed-initiative target identification
Modality Management	Communications scheduler	Tactile navigation cueing	

prehension, the message priority, and the contextual relevance of the message, the communications scheduler did one of the following:

- allowed messages to pass through immediately,
- deferred and rescheduled nonrelevant or low-priority messages,
- diverted attention to incoming high-priority messages (i.e., alerting tones of differing salience),
- escalated high-priority messages that were not attended to (i.e., repeated message and increased salience of alerting tone),
- changed the modality of message presentation (i.e., audio or text), or
- deleted expired or obsolete messages.

The tactile navigation cueing system provided tactile cues directing subjects in accordance with the correct route. Without mitigation, subjects received no support in determining and navigating a route. The Medevac Negotiation Agent facilitated coordination of medical evacuations by organizing the needed information into an interactive form and, where possible, automatically filling in information. Additionally, it allowed the coordination of the medevac to be delegated to other personnel. For surveillance, the Mixed Initiative Target Identification System highlighted suspected targets on surveillance photos. This system provided an accuracy rate of only 68%; however, as vigilance decrements develop, human accuracy for the same task falls to 40%. Thus, use of the aide was focused on conditions in which the human exhibited low attentional states.

During the first study, subjects were presented with different scenarios that placed different demands on their cognitive resources. The first scenario emphasized divided attention and centered on a mission that may be characterized as "Raid an Objective," with emphasis on the task elements of Navigate to Objective, Identify Friend or Foe, and Manage Communications. Subjects were presented with an extremely high volume of radio traffic. Within this traffic, there were three high-priority messages (e.g., "Hold at the bus stop and await further order"). One performance measure concerned message comprehension and was based on the subject behaving in a manner consistent with these high-priority messages. Situation Awareness was assessed on the basis of the subject's ability to correctly answer questions concerning mission-critical details of the scenario that had been relayed through communications.

In this scenario, subjects correctly responded to 79.7% of messages with mitigation, but only 39.9% without mitigation. Similarly, subjects correctly answered 58.9% of the situation awareness questions with mitigation, compared with 26.2% without mitigation. Measures of time to complete missions and success in enemy engagements were not informative because the mitigation allowed subjects to operate in a manner that required longer time periods, but also allowed them to avoid enemy engagements.

In a second condition emphasizing divided attention, the scenario required subjects to utilize an electronic map to select and navigate a route through unfamiliar urban terrain.

In accomplishing this objective, it was also required that subjects coordinate a medevac, which is a lengthy and communications- and information-intensive operation. With mitigation subjects required, on average, 20% less time to navigate to the objective. However, in the unmitigated condition, subjects encountered four times as many ambushes as the mitigated condition (19 instances vs. 5, with 12 subjects in each condition). Thus, as might be expected, subjects with mitigation also took fewer hits from enemy forces than those without mitigation.

With respect to the coordination of medical evacuations, subjects with mitigation answered 100% of the questions correctly, compared with 51% without mitigation, with 98 questions in each condition. Furthermore, the medical evacuation was completed more quickly in the condition with mitigation.

A third scenario focused on sustained attention and required subjects to conduct continuous surveillance to identify enemy targets. This surveillance was based on observation of photos presented at regularly occurring intervals (i.e., every 2 seconds). It was observed that the experimental conditions did not produce the expected vigilance decrement. However, performance with the mitigation (85%) was superior to either the human without mitigation (66.2%) or the Mixed Initiative Target Identification System alone (68%).

Mobile Command and Control Vehicle

This team is led by DaimlerChrysler and has developed an augmented cognition system for automotive applications consistent with the needs of military noncombat vehicles as well as nonmilitary vehicles. Kincses (chap. 10, this volume) provides a detailed account of these activities, therefore the current section only offers a brief summary.

An S-class Mercedes Benz is being used for the Phase 2 prototype. The vehicle has been equipped to allow data to be collected during normal driving conditions from EEG and posture control sensors. In addition, the prototype system uses a wide range of data from various standard and nonstandard electronic systems. Nonstandard electronic systems include an infrared-based lane departure sensor, active cruise control based on GHz radar, and a video-based dead angle/blind spot detector. Standard electronic systems include electronic stability program (ESP) and active cruise control based on GHz radar (Distronic).

Based on EEG measures, the driver's cognitive state is classified as high or low for the visual and auditory modality and attention working memory. Augmentation involves the delay of nonessential information during high-load conditions and switching the modality of information delivery and warnings (e.g., lane departure) and automated safety systems (i.e., distronic).

APPLICATION OF AUGMENTED
COGNITION TECHNOLOGIES

The preceding sections have described the fundamental research and development that is now underway to make augmented cognition systems a reality. It should not be a surprise that for every success there remains an equal or greater number of questions to be answered. However, development is on a trajectory to obtain the answers to these questions, enabling the transition of augmented cognition systems from the laboratory to operational systems. Once augmented cognition systems are ready to take the next step moving into operational systems, a new set of issues arises, some of which are unique to augmented cognition systems and others which are common to advanced technologies being transitioned into operational systems. The NATO RTO (NATO RTO HFM-056/TG-008) has identified many of these issues. Table 5.7 summarizes the issues discussed in the NATA RTO report and others.

Due to the reliance on cognitive state gauges that utilize direct skin contact sensors to detect physiological signals (e.g., EEG, ECG), one issue that is particularly pertinent to augmented cognition systems concerns the

TABLE 5.7

This Table Summarizes Issues Affecting the Transition
of Augmented Cognition Systems From the Prototype
Demonstration Stage of Development to Implementation
in Operational Systems (NATO RTO HFM-056/TG-008)

- Discomfort and annoyances due to the use of sensors that require direct skin contact.
- Equipment weight and volume, including cabling and connectors.
- Provision of power, total power consumption, cooling requirements, and electrical interference.
- Additional tasks associated with preparing and maintaining equipment.
- Restrictions on user activities including head and body movements and interference with the user's ability to carry out tasks.
- Data storage and encryption.
- Loss of privacy.
- Trust in automation including the willingness to accept forcible control, associated changes in how tasks are accomplishments, and potential reductions in situation awareness.
- Robustness to operational environments including the reliability and system dependence on specific sensors, ability to withstand environmental extremes, and adaptations to system degradation.
- Minimal impact on communications bandwidth available for operational requirements.
- Sensitivity of sensors and the ability to provide required levels of accuracy despite artifacts associated with the muscle activity of chewing, talking and swallowing, eye movements, electromagnetic interference and characteristics of electrodes (e.g., instability in the electrode/electrolyte half-cell potential disturbing the electrode-electrolyte equilibrium due to sweating, gels drying, and skin hydration).
- System operational limitations with respect to the latencies that would occur within the closed-loop system.
- Cost–benefit relationship relative to other potential system components proposed for upgrades to existing systems or as components in new systems.

wearability and operational usefulness of these sensors. In addition, there is the encumbrance and limitations on mobility caused by the attached wiring, as well as the time needed to place and verify sensors. A possible solution to this issue may arise from research and development underway at Quasar (Mathews, 2004). They have demonstrated the detection of cardiac signals from noncontact electrodes and are currently working to adapt this capability to EEG electrodes. Likewise, the adaptation of wireless technologies to create nontethered sensor suites will minimize the encumbrance and restrictions to mobility (e.g., Downs & Downs, 2004). These advances may culminate in augmented cognition systems similar to the objective system described by Boeing, in which a wireless harness and softcap integrate a suite of miniaturized, noncontact electrodes into the existing communications headset (Tollar, 2004). Additionally, off-head eye-tracking systems are under development to enable the pupillometric measures typically found with on-head systems. Throughout the program, concurrent investments have been made, through Small Business Innovation Research contracts and industry team involvement, to push the development of the most advanced, rugged, wearable, and reliable sensors.

Finally, there exists the potential that users will behave differently due to their knowledge that their physiological processes are being measured and recorded, and the variation from their normal behavior may be deleterious to task performance. However, accompanying the downside to the data collection afforded by augmented cognition systems, there is also the opportunity to mine these data in various ways to gain insight to the optimal design of equipment and tasks, as well as basic brain functions while carrying out real-world operations.

CONCLUSION

Although the bulk of this chapter has focused on the technological advances achieved through DARPA's technology development, the most significant achievement may be less tangible. In particular, through the coordinated efforts of a large number of researchers, the basic concepts underlying augmented cognition have progressed from a collection of ideas being advanced by a few individuals to a coherent construct being adopted and adapted by a growing community. This book is partly a product of the program. Augmented Cognition serves as the topic for a special issue of the *International Journal of Human-Computer Interaction*. Finally, and perhaps most significant, in the summer of 2005, the First Annual Augmented Cognition International Conference will be held in Las Vegas. Through these and other activities occurring within the augmented cognition community, it is becoming increasingly probable that there will be a real impact on the future of technology and, in particular, the future of human–machine systems long after the DARPA Augmented Cognition program has reached its completion.

ACKNOWLEDGMENTS

This work was performed at Sandia National Laboratories. Sandia is a multiprogram laboratory operated by Sandia Corporation, a Lockheed-Martin Company, for the U.S. Department of Energy under Contract DE-AC04-94AL85000.

REFERENCES

Balaban, C. D. (2004a, January 6–8). *Context-dependent postural control: Gauges for cognitive state detection*. Presented at the Augmented Cognition: Improving Warfighter Information Intake Under Stress Conference, Orlando, FL.

Balaban, C. D. (2004b, June 29–July 1). *Trade-offs between automatic postural adjustments and orienting responses as indices of cognitive engagement.* Presented at Cognitive Systems Workshop, Santa Fe, NM.

Balaban, C. D., Cohn, J., Redfern, M. S., Pinkey, J., Stripling, R., & Hoffer, M. (2004). Postural control as a probe for cognitive state: Exploiting human information processing to enhance performance. *International Journal of Human-Computer Interaction, 17*(2), 275–285.

Barker, R. (2004a, January 6–8). *UAV: Update and plans.* Presented at the Augmented Cognition: Improving Warfighter Information Intake Under Stress Conference, Orlando, FL.

Barker, R. (2004b, January 6–8). *UAV: Executive function bottleneck mitigation.* Presented at the Augmented Cognition: Improving Warfighter Information Intake Under Stress Conference, Orlando, FL.

Belyavin, A. (2004, January 6–8). *Discrimination of current state—The Cognitive Cockpit approach.* Presented at the Augmented Cognition: Improving Warfighter Information Intake Under Stress Conference, Orlando, FL.

Berka, C., Levendowski, D. J., Davis, G., Lumicao, M. N., Ramsey, C., Olmstead, R. E., Cvetinovic, M., Zivkovic, V., Petrovic, M. M., & Radovic, S. (2004, January 6–8). *Predicting performance in complex cognitive tasks with EEG indices of workload.* Presented at the Augmented Cognition: Improving Warfighter Information Intake Under Stress Conference, Orlando, FL.

Chang, K. C. (2004, January 6–8). *Performance prediction with EEG/fNIR sensor.* Presented at the Augmented Cognition: Improving Warfighter Information Intake Under Stress Conference, Orlando, FL.

Dickson, B. (2004, January 6–8). *UAV: Identifying, understanding and minimizing artifact in operational environments.* Presented at the Augmented Cognition: Improving Warfighter Information Intake Under Stress Conference, Orlando, FL.

Donchin, E. (2004, January 6–8). *Biocybernetics and ERPs as a tool in the study of cognition.* Presented at the Augmented Cognition: Improving Warfighter Information Intake Under Stress Conference, Orlando, FL.

Downs, H., & Downs, T. (2004, January 6–8). *Planes, trains and brains: Mobile brain sensing.* Presented at the Augmented Cognition: Improving Warfighter Information Intake Under Stress Conference, Orlando, FL.

DuRousseau, D., & Fraser, E. (2004, January 6–8). *Spatial frequency EEG as an index of executive load.* Presented at the Augmented Cognition: Improving Warfighter Information Intake Under Stress Conference, Orlando, FL.

Fabiani, M., & Gratton, G. (2004, January 6–8). *EROS measures of functional connectivity: A new type of cognitive gauge.* Presented at the Augmented Cognition: Improving Warfighter Information Intake Under Stress Conference, Orlando, FL.

Forsythe, C., Bernard, M., Xavier, P., Abbott, R., Speed, A., & Brannon, N. (2003). Using psychologically plausible cognitive models to enhance operator performance. *Proceedings of the 47th Annual Meeting of the Human Factors and Ergonomics Society* (pp. 302–306), Denver, CO.

Gratton, G., & Fabiani, M. (2004, January 6–8). *Applications of fNIR methods to the analysis of cognitive states: Rationale and examples.* Presented at the Augmented Cognition: Improving Warfighter Information Intake Under Stress Conference, Orlando, FL.

Heisterkamp, P. (2004, January 6–8). *In-vehicle mitigation of cognitive overload and underload conditions.* Presented at the Augmented Cognition: Improving Warfighter Information Intake Under Stress Conference, Orlando, FL.

Hoover, A. (2004, January 6–8). *Arousal meter: Improvements, integration and testing.* Presented at the Augmented Cognition: Improving Warfighter Information Intake Under Stress Conference, Orlando, FL.

Hoover, A., & Muth, E. (2004). A real-time index of vagal activity. *International Journal of Human-Computer Interaction, 17*(2), 197–210.

Marshall, S. P. (2004, January 6–8). *The Index of Cognitive Activity: Recent developments in measuring and interpreting pupil response.* Presented at the Augmented Cognition: Improving Warfighter Information Intake Under Stress Conference, Orlando, FL.

Mathews, R. (2004, January 6–8). *First steps towards the invisible electrode.* Presented at the Augmented Cognition: Improving Warfighter Information Intake Under Stress Conference, Orlando, FL.

Mika, S., Raisch, G., & Muller, K. R. (2000, November 27–December 2). *A mathematical programming approach to the Kernel Fisher algorithm.* Presented at 14th Annual Neural Information Processing Systems Conference, CO.

Müller, K. R. (2004, January 6–8). *Some remarks on classification of EEG.* Presented at the Augmented Cognition: Improving Warfighter Information Intake Under Stress Conference, Orlando, FL.

Pleydell-Pearce, C. W., Whitecross, S. E., & Dickson, B. T. (2003, January 6–9). *Multivariate analysis of EEG: Predicting cognition on the basis of frequency decomposition, inter-electrode correlation, coherence, cross phase and cross power.* Presented at 36th Annual Hawaii International Conference on System Sciences, Big Island, HI.

Raley, C., Stripling, R., Kruse, A., Schmorrow, D., & Patrey, J. (2004, September 20–24). *Augmented cognition overview: Improving information intake under stress.* Proceedings of the 48th annual meeting of the Human Factors and Ergonomics Society, New Orleans, LA.

Rugg, M. D., & Coles, M. G. H. (1995). *Electrophysiology of mind: Event-related potentials and cognition.* New York: Oxford University Press.

Sajda, P. (2004, January 6–8). *Supervised and unsupervised linear methods for recovering task-relevant activity in EEG.* Presented at the Augmented Cognition: Improving Warfighter Information Intake Under Stress Conference, Orlando, FL.

Sharma, R. (2004, January 6–8). *Toward non-intrusive multi-modal emotional state monitoring.* Presented at the Augmented Cognition: Improving Warfighter Information Intake Under Stress Conference, Orlando, FL.

St. John, M., Kobus, D. A., & Morrison, J. G. (2003). *DARPA Augmented Cognition Technical Integration Experiment (TIE).* Technical Report 1905, SPAWARS Systems Center, San Diego, CA.

St. John, M., Kobus, D. A., Morrison, J. G., & Schmorrow, D. (2004). Overview of the DARPA Augmented Cognition Technical Integration Experiment. *International Journal of Human-Computer Interaction, 17*(2), 131–150.

Tollar, J. (2004, January 6–8). *UAV: Evolution of an integrated sensor suite in response to issues of technology, ergonomics and fieldability.* Presented at the Augmented Cognition: Improving Warfighter Information Intake Under Stress Conference, Orlando, FL.

Tucker, D., Luu, P., & Renner, T. (2004, January 6–8). *Validating verbal and spatial memory gauges.* Presented at the Augmented Cognition: Improving Warfighter Information Intake Under Stress Conference, Orlando, FL.

Ververs, T. (2004, January 6–8). *Honeywell AugCog Phase 2A CVE.* Presented at the Augmented Cognition: Improving Warfighter Information Intake Under Stress Conference, Orlando, FL.

PART THREE

ILLUSTRATIONS OF COGNITIVE SYSTEMS

Engaging Innate Human Cognitive Capabilities to Coordinate Human Interruption: The HAIL System

Daniel C. McFarlane
Lockheed Martin Advanced Technology Laboratories

Most modern work environments require humans to juggle several concurrent responsibilities. A human's level of success is largely dependent on how well they manage their cognitive resources to handle their responsibilities in a timely manner. Although tasks compete for time and attention, complete failure to fulfill any responsibility is unacceptable. To be considered successful, humans must succeed, at least minimally, in all tasks. Interruption of one task by competing tasks is inevitable in this environment. Time-critical information must be disseminated, requests must be made, reminders must be delivered, and interactions must be initiated. In technology-rich work environments, interruptions are often presented on a computer screen by user-interface (UI) applications. The design challenge for UIs is to deliver balanced support for the powerful information access humans need to succeed while avoiding disruptive interruptions that degrade overall task performance. This is a great application for a cognitive system.

Forsythe and Xavier (chap. 1, this volume) say that humans are the most prototypical cognitive system, and the most compelling application for a computer-based cognitive system is to facilitate human–computer interaction (HCI). *Cognitive* in the name *cognitive system* means that the referent human or computer has the capability to be knowledgeable and aware of their/its environment in a way that can facilitate coordination, collaboration, and cooperation between their/itself and one or more other cognitive systems.

What cognition capabilities can be captured in a computer-based cognitive system and at a reasonable cost to best deliver a dramatic increase in HCI capability? Human cognition is heterogeneous, and humans with remarkably different cognitive talents often work successfully together. The U.S. TV show "M.A.S.H." is a useful analogy of how to design cognitive models: The characters have extreme differences, but they work effectively together. It is the differences among the characters that make them an effective team. M.A.S.H. is a Mobile Army Surgical Hospital. The commanding officer, Colonel Henry Blake, relies on personal assistant, Corporal Walter "Radar" O'Reilly, for the information he needs to make command decisions. To create a computer-based cognitive system to replace Radar would require a cognitive model exactly opposite of Blake's model. Blake has a talent for leading medical people, but a poor memory for detail and an inability to understand military processes. Radar is not a leader, but understands detail, remembers military processes, and arranges logistics.

The Human Alerting and Interruption Logistics (HAIL) system is a cognitive system that increases human capability to handle high rates of alert-related interruptions while accomplishing other activities. Like Radar, HAIL delivers the inverse cognitive capability of its human users. Experiments with humans at the Naval Research Laboratory in Washington, DC, found that humans have natural cognitive strengths to negotiate when and how they will deal with interruptions (McFarlane, 1998, 1999, 2002). Humans maintain a potentially fragile awareness of their work objectives, current status, and their own interruptability. Under specific conditions, they can coordinate effectively with the interruptor to best deal with the interruption and minimize its negative impact on their other activities. The HAIL research also found that humans have cognitive weaknesses, and interruptions can degrade human performance and cause them to make errors. The HAIL system delivers the required cognitive capabilities to mitigate human weaknesses through an interactive design that leverages a human's cognitive strengths.

BACKGROUND

The design of notification UI systems can focus primarily on creating technologies that will improve the content of the notifications, so that necessary information is presented clearly, accurately, and efficiently. Equally important is the strategy for how and when the notifications are delivered to the recipient. Notification mechanisms must maximize the likelihood that a human will attend to necessary information while minimizing the detrimental effects of interrupting progress on a task. This chapter describes methods to accomplish these goals by extending the mechanisms that humans use in their interactions with others to control the interruption processes in notification UI systems.

Humans possess limited attentional cognitive resources and have developed vast resources to compensate for these limitations in almost everything they do (Cypher, 1986; Miyata & Norman, 1986). Raby and Wickens (1991) noted that aircraft pilots naturally manage their own attentional resources for maximal effect (see also Adams & Pew, 1990). They say, "Humans are not passive role-players, they do play an active role in the monitoring of both their performance and perceived level of workload" (pp. 1130–1135). Researchers have observed human ability to manage their attentional resources to successfully perform multiple tasks simultaneously (Cherry, 1953; Spelke, Hirst, & Neisser, 1976) and have found that they can multitask better when they use different perception channels (Liu & Wickens, 1988; Treisman & Davies, 1973).

Humans normally and routinely use subtle mechanisms to influence the state of their information environment to maximize success and minimize the degree of workload needed for their limited, attentional, cognitive resources. People also have natural abilities to manage large numbers of dependencies between tasks in information environments (Malone & Crowston, 1994). They use preattentive processing capabilities to process huge quantities of peripheral information in parallel and maximize the use of their limited attentional resources (Woods, 1995). They use subtle messages in human–human communication to signal turn taking (Duncan, 1972) and for signaling their dynamically changing degree of interruptibility (Bannon, 1986). They create common ground in human–human conversations (McCarthy & Monk, 1994), which minimizes the need for attention by off-loading some of the cognitive workload to contexts of joint activities. For example, Galdes, Smith, and Smith (1991) found that human tutors use several subtle, context-sensitive cues to determine when to interrupt students to minimize the required workload on their students' attentional cognitive resources.

Modern information technologies deliver ever more powerful information products, but with mixed results. They increase the volume of important information delivered to decision makers, but they also increase the frequency of interruptions and, therefore, degrade the decision maker's capacity to manage. This is the key design goal for any notification UI. Unlike most design problems, use of a UI is not tied to a specific task, but to the crossroads between multiple tasks that a human might process concurrently. This is a goal not easily reached because it is difficult to interrupt humans without interfering with the meta-task coordination strategies they are exploiting in their work. To succeed in this highly dynamic and stressful information environment, humans must divide their attention across a wide variety of tasks while still focusing tightly on the tasks of most immediate concern.

To succeed, humans must concurrently perform multiple tasks, each requiring a commitment of their single source of limited cognitive capacities. These commitments require them to (a) broadly distribute their attention and to be constantly aware of their changing information environment, (b) apply this constant awareness to generate foresight, but (c) simultaneously narrow their attention to make decisions on specific tasks, (d) carry out, and (e) dynamically monitor and evaluate the progress of several decided activities (Cooper & Franks, 1993; McFarlane & Latorella, 2002). See Table 6.1 for a full breakdown of these requirements.

The paradox of requiring humans to simultaneously divide and focus their attention in information work environments has five basic solutions: (a) training, (b) incentives, (c) personnel selection, (d) automation, and (e) integration with better UI technology. Although each solution has its place, the UI solution has the most potential for improving overall per-

TABLE 6.1
Concurrent Work Responsibilities and Their Associated Requirements

Concurrent Work-Role Responsibilities	Cognitive Activities Required to Succeed	Human Cognitive Resources Required for Success
Awareness	Observation: Unrelenting active vigilance and pursuit of status information	Distributed attention, memories for directing preattentive processing, and perceptive resources for vigilance
Foresight	Analysis: Constantly apply status information to dynamically infer potential consequences of observed changes relative to work goals	Distributed and focused attention, memories for work goals, and inferential cognitive capabilities
Focus	Hypothesis: Continually re-invent a plausible "best" approach solution to integrate goals, observations, and predictions	Focused attention; memories for objectives, awareness, and foresight; and decision-making cognitive capabilities
Plan	Synthesis: Construct and maintain a plan that implements the current hypothesis	Focused attention, memories of plan strategies, and cognitive capacities for planning
Act	Experiment: Act to implement the current plan	Focused attention, memories for plan execution, motor control resources for action
Monitor	Evaluation: Constantly determine the degree of effectiveness of current actions to achieve work goals	Distributed and focused attention, memories for evaluation strategies, and cognitive and meta-cognitive capacities for monitoring

formance. It preserves human accountability for success, and it is not tied to their unchanging, basic, cognitive capacities (McFarlane & Latorella, 2002; Morrison, Kelly, Moore, & Hutchins, 1998).

The design of modern UI technologies has often facilitated the expeditious completion of single, specific tasks. This design philosophy is like an assembly line, in which indistinguishable components arrive singularly in front of the assembler, each to be handled in its own turn. For typical notification UIs, each task set before the human is treated as a singular, remote instance, and the average throughput of tasks is the measure of overall success.

This assembly-line design generally worsens the attentional paradox by (a) delivering more volume of information to users and widening their domain of responsibility, which requires accurate foresight; and (b) increasing the importance of human decisions because of enhanced power in system actuators. Humans adopt these technologies and tolerate their usability paradoxes because these tools increase the potential for success. However, to realize this potential, humans will have to exponentially increase their cognitive effort as the power of information technologies improves. With modern information technologies, humans typically reach their unaided, cognitive, attentional capacities and a wall bounding their potential overall success. There are several example domains where this usability paradox leads to performance problems and requirements for innovative, future UI solutions. These include modern aircraft cockpits (Adams, Tenney, & Pew, 1995; Thompson, 1980), office environments (Rouncefield, Hughes, Rodden, & Viller, 1994; Speier, Valacich, & Vessey, 1997), and Naval command-and-control systems (Osga, 2000).

To truly succeed, we postulate that a cognitive system must model the human's cognitive weaknesses—relative to interruption—and deliver these capabilities through a human cognitive strength. The UI must better model and support the way humans naturally handle interruptions. Humans have invented a vast array of negotiation techniques to coordinate how and when they will permit themselves to be interrupted. As humans grow from children to adults, they receive almost constant training and practice in the use of these interruption-negotiation techniques. A normal adult will have learned this subtle art over years of heavy practice and can execute complicated negotiations for interruption without conscious thought about the process. Indeed we might say that an individual's social success could depend on him or her having some basic level of proficiency with this process of negotiating interruption.

Consider this example in the physical work environment. You are at your desk, engaged in a writing task with a quickly approaching deadline. Jim comes to your office with a question. As this interruption progresses, the following steps might occur:

1. *Priming:* You hear the sound of someone approaching your office, signaling that someone may be coming to see you. Jim knocks on your door and asks if he can speak with you for a moment, confirming the visit as a potential interruption to your task.

2. *Assessment:* You notice that Jim is carrying an agenda for a meeting you are planning together, but a few minor details remain. Based on this observation, you surmise that the issue may just be a quick question about one of those details.

3. *Decision (and Negotiation):* You ask Jim if the question will take much time, and he replies that he just wants to confirm a time change he has made. The question should not take much time, and you agree to address it. Alternatively, you might determine that the issue is too complex and negotiate with Jim to address it after your deadline.

4. *Execution:* Jim describes the change. You ask a few questions for clarification and eventually agree to his proposal. Jim leaves your office.

5. *Recovery:* You return to your task. You have forgotten exactly what you were doing before Jim's interruption, so you read the last few sentences of the paragraph that you were writing and consult the open notes beside your keyboard before starting to write again.

Note the characteristics of this interaction. You have at your disposal several mechanisms to ease the context switch that inevitably accompanies an interruption. Before the interruption is even proposed, you can observe physical cues that indicate a potential need to switch tasks. These warning signals help mentally prepare you to decide whether to switch task contexts.

Once it becomes clear that the warning signals accurately signal an impending request, you can gather information about the likely topic of the interruption based on the artifacts that surround the request delivery: Who is delivering it? What artifacts are associated with it? What tone is used to present it? These cues allow for you to assess the priority of the interruption in relation to the task which it will interfere. Jim can help them in this task by making these cues as apparent as possible.

You are then able to decide whether to defer your current task and attend to the interruption. In this interactive setting, you can negotiate with the person requesting your time to support this decision. If you decide that the interruption must be immediately attended to, then you can stop what you are doing and deal with the interruption. If you decide that the interruption should wait until you are finished with your higher priority task, then you can ask Jim to return later.

TABLE 6.2
Concurrent Work Responsibilities Mapped
to the Human-Interruption Process

Concurrent Work-Role Responsibilities	Cognitive Activities Required to Succeed	Human Interruption Process States
Awareness	Observation	Priming assessment
Foresight	Analysis	
Focus	Hypothesis	Decision/negotiation
Plan	Synthesis	
Act	Experiment	Execution
		Recovery
Monitor	Evaluation	Recovery

After dealing with the interruption, you must recover your understanding of what you were doing before you switched contexts. You can use visual cues to support recall: What file is open on my computer screen? Where is my cursor positioned in the file? How are my notes organized when I stopped working?

Designers must consider each of these components of the interruption process—priming, assessment, decision/negotiation, execution, and recovery—when creating UIs to support interruption. For each stage in the process, the design should also consider what information can be supplied to the user to support established human mechanisms for managing interruptions. This is where the *assembly line* metaphor breaks down. It only considers the execution component of the interruption process. It robs the user of the rich landscape of contextual cues that would be available in a UI that more closely modeled the human-interruption process, and it fails to support the user in most of that person's responsibilities in managing concurrent tasks. Table 6.2 shows a UI that more closely follows the methods humans use to manage interruptions and provides much broader coverage of these responsibilities.

HUMAN COGNITIVE MODELS AND DESIGN

There are risks associated with humans performing more than one activity at a time because of vulnerability to error during multitasking. For important tasks, it would be much safer to limit activity to a single foregrounded activity, but most work roles do not limit responsibility in this way. Humans make mistakes while multitasking (Schneider & Detweiler, 1988; Spelke et al., 1976). The Federal Aviation Administration (FAA) concluded that most errors made by air traffic controllers resulted from their failure to maintain situational awareness (Redding, 1992).

Theoretical Tools

When humans multitask with computers, they do not simultaneously do everything. Miyata and Norman (1986) provided a useful theory-based classification of the different ways humans manage the individual HCI activities of their multitasks (see also Cypher, 1986). They discussed activities in terms of human cognition and described the current state of action for each activity in a human's multitasks. The important questions for describing the current state of action for an activity are: (a) Is the activity currently being acted on? (b) If the activity is current, then is it under the human's conscious control? and (c) If the activity is current but not under the human's conscious control, then is the human acting on it subconsciously or is some other entity acting on it? Designers can use these questions to describe individual HCI activities to reveal the inherent timing dependencies of multitasks and human strategies for concurrently coordinating and accomplishing a set of individual activities.

The Taxonomy of Human Interruption (McFarlane, 1997) is a practical tool for understanding the dimensions of human cognition that relate to the interruption phenomenon. Using this taxonomy, system designers can identify specific areas of interest in which better design strategies are likely to improve a human's ability to manage interruptions in an HCI environment. The taxonomy identifies the most useful dimensions of the problem. These dimensions or factors each describe a crucial aspect of the human-interruption phenomenon that can stand alone and serve as a handle for working the design problem from a useful perspective. The taxonomy of human interruption is a highly concentrated summary of the set of theoretical constructs. Each factor of the taxonomy represents an independent perspective for looking at the problem from a theoretical foundation of existing work (Table 6.3).

Latorella (1996, 1998) proposed the Interruption Management Stage Model (IMSM), a theoretically based and empirically supported model of human interruption in complex systems (see also McFarlane & Latorella, 2002). The model captures the human-interruption process from a human's information-processing perspective. The IMSM can be used as a design tool to analyze human cognitive requirements for negotiation UIs. McFarlane and Latorella reviewed the IMSM and the taxonomy of human interruption and showed how the two address different aspects of the design problem. The taxonomy of human interruption is an attempt to map the total design space and identify a broad array of potential influences of human performance with ties to relevant design literature for addressing

TABLE 6.3
Taxonomy of Human Interruption (see McFarlane, 1997)

Descriptive Dimension of Interruption	Example Values
Source of Interruption	Self [human]; another person; computer; other animate object; inanimate object
Individual Characteristic of Person Receiving Interruption	State and limitations of personal resource (perceptual, cognitive, and motor processors; memories; focus of consciousness; and processing streams); sex; goals (personal, public, joint); state of satisfaction of face-wants; context relative to source of interruption (common ground, activity roles, willingness to be interrupted, and ability to be interrupted)
Method of Coordination	Immediate interruption (no coordination); negotiated interruption; mediated interruption; scheduled interruption (by explicit agreement for a one-time interruption, or by convention for a recurring interruption event)
Meaning of Interruption	Alert; stop; distribute attention; regulate dialogue (meta-dialogue); supervise agent; propose entry or exit of a joint activity; remind; communicate information (illocution); attack; no meaning (accident)
Method of Expression	Physical expression (verbal, paralinguistic, kinesic); expression for effect on face-wants (politeness); signaling type (by purpose, availability, and effort); meta-level expressions to guide the process; adaptive expression of chains of basic operators; intermixed expression; expression to afford control
Channel of Conveyance	Face-to-face; other direct communication channel; mediated by a person; mediated by a machine; meditated by other animate object
Human Activity Changed by Interruption	Internal or external; conscious or subconscious; asynchronous parallelism; individual activities; joint activities (between various kinds of human and nonhuman participants); facilitation activities (language use, meta-activities, use of mediators)
Effect of Interruption	Change in human activity (the worth of this change is relative to the person's goals); change in the salience of memories; change in awareness (meta-information) about activity; change in focus of attention; loss of willful control over activity; change in social relationships; transition between stages of a joint activity

these factors. The IMSM focuses on revealing the process structure for guiding UI design for improving process performance. The common ground between the two tools is applicability for guiding design of coordination support for negotiation UIs.

The IMSM describes the process stages of interruption management. These stages are detection of the interruption annunciation, interpretation of the annunciation, integration of the interruption into the ongoing task set, and resumption of the ongoing task set. Table 6.4 integrates the

TABLE 6.4
IMSM Stages Incorporated Into the Mapping Between
Process and UI Support for Work-Role Responsibilities

Concurrent Work-Role Responsibilities	Cognitive Activities Required to Succeed	Human Interruption Process States	IMSM [Interruption Management Stage Model (Latorella)]
Awareness	Observation	Priming assessment	Detect Interpret
Foresight	Analysis		Integration
Focus	Hypothesis	Decision/negotia-tion	
Plan	Synthesis		
Act	Experiment	Execution recovery	
Monitor	Evaluation	Recovery	Resumption

IMSM stages into the mapping between process and the UI support for work-role responsibilities. This is intended to be a design aid for transitioning between process analyses and product design.

Cognitive Models of Human Interruption for System Design

McFarlane (2002) presented guidelines for the design of the HCI for human interruption in notification UIs. These guidelines are supported by empirical evidence from experiments with human subjects. The basic finding from this research is that negotiation-based, UI-design solutions for human interruption result in overall better user performance, except where small differences in the timeliness of beginning the interruption task are critical, and then the immediacy-based solution is best. Table 6.5 summarizes the pros and cons of each coordination solution. The external validity should be strong, but has not been fully explored.

There are two basic generalizations from this research: (a) Giving humans negotiation support to control the timing of interruptions allows them to perform very well; however, the presence of this kind of control may sometimes cause them to not handle interruptions in a timely way; and (b) UI designs that force humans to immediately handle interruptions to get timely responses to notifications cause more mistakes and are less effective overall. Table 6.6 summarizes the best and worst means of interruptions for various design goals. In cases where there are two best or worst solutions, both are listed.

McFarlane (2002) also included additional guidelines for UI design to support individuals. The guidelines in Table 6.7 are based on observed

TABLE 6.5
Comparison of the Coordination Solutions
Presented in McFarlane (2002)

UI Coordination Solution	Pros	Cons
Immediate	Minimizes delay in human beginning interruption task; ensures that human deals with every interruption	Causes relatively more overall errors and worst performance in resuming the primary task after interruption. Also, humans ranked it least in overall preference
Negotiated	Maximizes quality of decisions on primary and interruption tasks; maximizes efficiency and minimizes degree of human effort. Humans ranked it best in overall preference	Can cause small delays in starting interruption tasks. If interruption tasks have time deadlines, then these small delays can cause them to be skipped
Mediated	Slightly better performance on timeliness and completeness than negotiated	More disruptive on main task performance than negotiated
Scheduled	Minimizes frequency of task switching, and causes slightly better efficiency on handling interruption task than immediate	Most disruptive on main task

TABLE 6.6
Overall Best and Worst: Tentative Design Guidelines (McFarlane, 2002)

Design Goal	Best	Worst
Accuracy on continuous task	Neg*	Sch
Efficiency on continuous task	Neg/Med	Imm/Sch
Fewest task switches	Sch	Imm
Accuracy on intermittent task	Not Imm	Imm
Completeness on intermittent task	Imm/Med	Sch/Neg
Promptness on intermittent task	Imm	Sch/Neg
Efficiency on intermittent task	Neg/Sch	Imm
Keying accuracy	Neg/Sch	Imm
User preference	Neg/Med	Imm/Sch
User perception of his or her own accuracy on continuous task	Not Imm	Not Neg
User perception of least interruptive	Neg/Med	Imm/Sch
User perception of most predictable	Sch/Neg	Imm/Med
User perception of complexity of continuous task when interrupted	Neg/Med	Imm/Sch

Imm—Immediate; Neg—Negotiated; Med—Mediated; Sch—Scheduled.

TABLE 6.7
Relative Best and Worst: Tentative Design Guidelines,
Reproduced (McFarlane, 2002)

Individual's Subjective Value	*Individual's Performance Level*
Best preferred	Best effectiveness and efficiency on the continuous task, best efficiency on intermittent task, and best overall keying accuracy
Best ease of use	Best accuracy on intermittent task
Worst interruptive	Worst effectiveness and efficiency on the continuous task, worst efficiency on intermittent task, and worst overall keying accuracy
Worst distractive	Worst effectiveness on the continuous task, and worst accuracy and efficiency on intermittent task
Best predictability of interruptions	Best efficiency on intermittent task, and best overall keying accuracy; however, also worst completeness and timeliness on intermittent task
Best timing of onset of interruptions to occur when continuous task is not difficult	Best effectiveness and efficiency on the continuous task, and best efficiency on the intermittent task

correlations between human subjective experience and actual performance. If information is available about humans' relative subjective perceptions of their performance levels for the four interruption coordination solutions, then the UI could use that information. The UI could automatically adjust the default HCI predictive support to maximize perception or performance.

DESIGN OF THE HAIL COGNITIVE SYSTEM

The principles described earlier were implemented as a software realization of the HAIL cognitive system. A combined analysis of research results, and point-application requirements indicated the need for four blocks of software capabilities. Table 6.8 shows how the IMSM relates to the HAIL design. The HAIL cognitive system delivers these capabilities through a negotiation-based, mixed-initiative, interaction solution that leverages human cognitive talent for coordinating their own interruptions. This functional analysis lends itself directly to an architecture design.

Support for overall human awareness of incoming information flow is enacted through Information-Alert Management. This function is responsible for gathering and localizing changes in information over time, as well as managing the presentation of the current information state to the user. Information alerts—alerts that inform the human without necessarily re-

TABLE 6.8
How the IMSM Relates to the HAIL Design

Concurrent Work-Role Responsibilities	IMSM (Interruption Management Stage Model, Latorella)	Human Cognitive Limitations	HAIL Cognitive System Capabilities
Awareness	Detect Interpret	Distributed attention and perception	Information Alert Management
Foresight	Integration	Memory and inference	Automation Management
Focus		Focused attention and reasoning	Action-Alert Management
Plan		Planning	
Act		Concentration and motor control	
Monitor	Resumption	Meta-cognition	Recovery Management

quiring immediate action in response—tend to be produced rapidly in large numbers, thus making them ephemeral in nature.

Management of alert-related human tasks is supported by Action Alert Management. Action alerts are the greatest source of human interruption within software systems. Support for alert priming and negotiation are key features of this functional block.

Resumption of interrupted tasks is the domain addressed by Recovery Management. Humans can take advantage of a large amount of contextual information to guide themselves in resuming a task, but only if that context is provided to them. Recovery Management encompasses functions related to the identification of context information, proper indexing of that context, and timely recall and presentation of contextual information when appropriate.

Supporting these capabilities is a suite of assessment functions contained within the Automation Management functional block. Automation Management includes functions for assessing the critical alerts toward which to focus human attention. Automation Management also provides alert filtering, combining, and synthesis functions to modify the stream of alerts to be presented to the human.

The functional architecture translates directly to a software design for the HAIL software framework (see Fig. 6.1). The HAIL framework supports the construction of computer interfaces that follow the principles of the HAIL cognitive system described earlier. Each major capability is realized by a software manager governed by a central-administrator function. HAIL is integrated with legacy interface systems through an integration layer

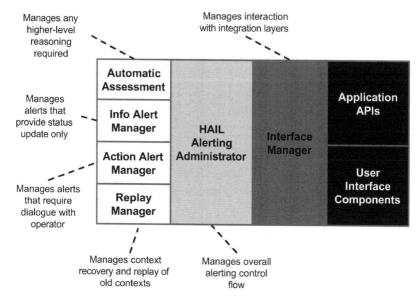

FIG. 6.1.   HAIL performances in Aegis application.

that provides directed interaction among HAIL, underlying information system(s), and human-interface components. The HAIL framework currently supports integration with legacy systems in C, C++, and Java.

ACKNOWLEDGMENTS

Our gratitude goes to the members of the HAIL-SS team and the Office of Naval Research, Knowledge Superiority and Assurance, Future Naval Capabilities Program (contract number N00014-02-C-0014). Some additions to software functionality were constructed under the Office of Naval Research, Autonomous Operations, Future Naval Capabilities Program (contract number N0014-03-C-0181). Parts of this research were conducted at the Navy Center for Applied Research in Artificial Intelligence at the Naval Research Laboratory.

REFERENCES

Adams, M. J., & Pew, R. W. (1990). Situational awareness in the commercial aircraft cockpit: A cognitive perspective. *IEEE/AIAA/NASA 9th Digital Avionics Systems Conference*.

Adams, M. J., Tenney, Y. J., & Pew, R. W. (1995). Situation awareness and the cognitive management of complex systems. *Human Factors, 37*(1), 85–104.

Bannon, L. J. (1986). Computer-mediated communication. In D. A. Norman & S. W. Draper (Eds.), *User centered system design* (pp. 433–452). Hillsdale, NJ: Lawrence Erlbaum Associates.

Cherry, E. C. (1953). Some experiments on the recognition of speech with one or two ears. *Journal of the Acoustical Society of America, 25*(5), 975–979.

Cooper, R., & Franks, B. (1993, February 1). Interruptibility as a constraint on hybrid systems. *Minds & Machines, 3,* 73–96.

Cypher, A. (1986). The structure of user's activities. In D. A. Norman & S. W. Draper (Eds.), *User centered system design* (pp. 243–263). Hillsdale, NJ: Lawrence Erlbaum Associates.

Duncan, S., Jr. (1972). Some signals and rules for taking speaking turns in conversations. *Journal of Personality and Social Psychology, 23*(2), 283–293.

Galdes, D. K., Smith, P. J., & Smith, J. W., Jr. (1991). Factors determining when to interrupt and what to say: An empirical study of the case-method tutoring approach. *International Conference on the Learning Sciences, Association for the Advancement of Computing in Education* (pp. 194–202), Evanston, IL.

Latorella, K. A. (1996). *Investigating interruptions: Implications for flightdeck performance.* Unpublished doctoral dissertation, State University of New York at Buffalo. (Also published in 1999 as NASA Technical Memorandum 209707, National Aeronautics & Space Administration, Washington, DC.)

Latorella, K. A. (1998). Effects of modality on interrupted flightdeck performance: Implications for data link. *Proceedings of the 42nd annual meeting of the Human Factors and Ergonomics Society* (pp. 87–91). Santa Monica, CA: Human Factors and Ergonomics Society.

Liu, Y., & Wickens, C. D. (1988). Patterns of task interference when human functions as a controller or a monitor. *Proceedings of the 1988 IEEE International conference on Systems, Man, and Cybernetics* (pp. 864–867), Beijing and Shenyang, China, Institute of Electrical and Electronics Engineers, Piscataway, NJ.

Malone, T. W., & Crowston, K. (1994). The interdisciplinary study of coordination. *ACM Computing Surveys, 26*(1), 87–119.

McCarthy, J. C., & Monk, A. F. (1994). Channels, conversation, cooperation and relevance: All you wanted to know about communication but were afraid to ask. *Collaborative Computing, 1,* 35–60.

McFarlane, D. C. (1997). Interruption of people in human–computer interaction: A general unifying definition of human interruption and taxonomy *(NRL Formal Report NRL/FR/5510-97-9870)*. Washington, DC: Naval Research Laboratory.

McFarlane, D. C. (1998). *Interruption of people in human–computer interaction.* Unpublished doctoral dissertation, George Washington University, Washington, DC.

McFarlane, D. C. (1999). Coordinating the interruption of people in human–computer interaction. In M. A. Sasse & C. Johnson (Eds.), *Human-computer interaction - INTERACT'99* (pp. 295–303). The Netherlands: IOS Press.

McFarlane, D. C. (2002). Comparison of four primary methods for coordinating the interruption of people in human–computer interaction. *Human-Computer Interaction, 17*(3), 63–139.

McFarlane, D. C., & Latorella, K. A. (2002). The scope and importance of human interruption in HCI design. *Human-Computer Interaction, 17*(3), 1–62.

Miyata, Y., & Norman, D. A. (1986). Psychological issues in support of multiple activities. In D. A. Norman & S. W. Draper (Eds.), *User centered system design* (pp. 265–284). Hillsdale, NJ: Lawrence Erlbaum Associates.

Morrison, J. G., Kelly, R. T., Moore, R. A., & Hutchins, S. G. (1998). Implications of decision making research for decision support and displays. In J. A. Cannon-Bowers & E. Salas (Eds.), *Making decisions under stress: Implications for individual and team training* (pp. 375–406). Washington, DC: American Psychology Association.

Osga, G. A. (2000). 21st century workstations—active partners in accomplishing task goals. *Proceedings of the Human Factors and Ergonomics Society 44th Annual Meeting.*

Raby, M., & Wickens, C. D. (1991). Strategic behaviour in flight workload management. *Proceedings of the Sixth International Symposium on Aviation Psychology* (pp. 1130–1135).

Redding, R. E. (1992). Analysis of operational errors and workload in air traffic control. *Proceedings of the Human Factors Society 36th Annual Meeting.*

Rouncefield, M., Hughes, J. A., Rodden, T., & Viller, S. (1994). Working with "constant interruption": CSCW and the small office. *Proceedings of the conference on Computer-Supported Cooperative Work (CSCW '94)* (pp. 275–286). New York: Association of Computing Machinery.

Schneider, W., & Detweiler, M. (1988). The role of practice in dual-task performance: Toward workload modeling in a connectionist/control architecture. *Human Factors, 30*(5), 539–566.

Speier, C., Valacich, J. S., & Vessey, I. (1997). The effects of task interruption and information presentation on individual decision making. *Proceedings of the 18th International Conference on Information Systems* (pp. 21–36). New York: Association for Computing Machinery.

Spelke, E., Hirst, W., & Neisser, U. (1976). Skills of divided attention. *Cognition, 4,* 215–230.

Thompson, D. A. (1980). Commercial air crew detection of system failures: State of the art and future trends. In J. Rasmussen & W. B. Rouse (Eds.), *Human detection and diagnosis of system failures* (pp. 37–48). New York: Plenum.

Treisman, A. M., & Davies, A. (1973). Divided attention to ear and eye. In S. Kornblum (Ed.), *Attention and performance IV* (pp. 101–117). New York: Academic Press.

Woods, D. D. (1995). The alarm problem and directed attention in dynamic fault management. *Ergonomics, 38*(11), 2371–2393.

CHAPTER SEVEN

Text Analysis and Dimensionality Reduction for Automatically Populating a Cognitive Model Framework

Travis Bauer
Sandia National Laboratories

Darrell Laham
Knowledge Analysis Technologies

Zachary Benz
Sandia National Laboratories

Scott Dooley
Knowledge Analysis Technologies

Joseph Kimmel
Sandia National Laboratories

Rob Oberbrekling
Knowledge Analysis Technologies

At Sandia National Laboratories, the Cognitive and Exploratory Systems and Simulation group has created a cognitive model software framework. An integral part of this framework is the representation of key concepts, the relationships among those key concepts in a semantic memory, and collections of those concepts that represent various topical contexts.

In the past, this model has been populated through a manual knowledge-elicitation technique, in which a psychologist sits down with an expert and, through an interview process, derives this information. In this chapter, we discuss how a cognitive model can be automatically generated through the use of textual analysis.

OVERVIEW

The cognitive model framework being developed at Sandia National Laboratories has already been discussed in detail in chapter 1. A discussion of the model is left to that chapter. Here we discuss the automated creation of semantic memory through text analysis.

In previous work, we have manually populated the cognitive model framework. In this manual process, one of our psychologists works with an expert in a particular field to build a model of that expert's understanding of their field. Through a series of interviews, key concepts for that person are identified, as well as the strengths of associations among those concepts. This information can then be used to populate the model framework.

Three difficulties make this manual process infeasible in the long run. First, the process is very time-consuming for both the expert and the psychologist. If one wants to build a model of all the experts in a large organization, this would require taking them away from their jobs, disrupting the functioning of the organization. Second, people change over time. This means that, depending on the application, the models would have to be updated periodically to stay synchronized with the actual people modeled. This updating process would require continuous attention from psychologists just to keep the models valid. Third, one might not always have access to the individuals being modeled.

Fortunately, experts in many fields make extensive use of desktop computers in the course of their work. Their interaction with the computer—the kinds of transactions they perform and the kinds of text they produce and access—are a reflection of their expertise and modus operandi. By capturing and analyzing this information, we hope to create plausible models that give us insight into how they think about their subject matter by uncovering key concepts and their interrelations.

We recognize that a person's computer interactions are only a subset of their professional work. We do not have the technology to acquire unconstrained spoken conversations, phone conversations, and access of noncomputerized written text (like printed trade journals). However, we have shown that we can successfully capture a substantial amount of data, and that the analysis of these data provides qualitatively pleasing results. We also report results showing that, given enough data, the system begins to discover the same relationships that people would have themselves, given access to the same data.

We show how we can use a log entropy-based statistical analysis on the contents of documents to compute the relationships among concepts. We then show how this analysis can be further refined through latent semantic analysis (LSA; Deerwester et al., 1990).

SOFTWARE APPLICATIONS

We are currently building and developing multiple applications and proof-of-concept demonstrations around these technologies for automatically building models of individuals from text. These technologies allow individual users to create models of either themselves or others, explore that model, and export it into a format that can be understood by our cognitive model framework.

The entire automated textual elicitation system is built in an extensible and reusable library known as the Sandia Text ANaLysis Extensible library (STANLEY). This object-oriented library, written in .NET, implements our ideas for automated knowledge elicitation through text. The library is written in such a way as to allow multiple applications to be built around it. We describe two such applications—the Sandia Cognitive Aide and the Semantic Space Analyst—in the upcoming sections. STANLEY is optionally able to interact with a server built by Knowledge Analysis Technology to perform LSA when useful.

Sandia Cognitive Aide

The Sandia Cognitive Aide (hereafter referred to as the Aide) is a tool for automatically creating a model of an individual while that person is using a personal computer. The software runs in the background during computer use, collecting information both automatically and via manual input. For automatic knowledge elicitation, the application observes Microsoft Word, PowerPoint, Outlook, and Internet Explorer, recording Web pages visited, documents accessed, and various operations performed on those documents. The transaction information such as "document opened," "document closed," and "Web page accessed" is recorded to a log file, generating a record of how and when a person used particular documents. We are currently in the process of building methods for mining this information to enhance the cognitive profile of the user. The other type of information automatically collected is the text of the documents. This information is added to an indexing engine, which is fundamental to the generation of the individual's profile. This index is kept continuously up to date as the documents are added. We can optionally use LSA to enhance the quality of the profile depending on the application requirements.

The other facility for collecting information about the user is the "manual scan" interface (see Fig. 7.1). Here the user opens a window and is able to drag and drop files and file folders from Explorer as well as folders from Outlook onto the window. The system then analyzes all these documents to enhance the model. This allows the user to easily create an initial model from the documents available on his or her desktop. It also allows

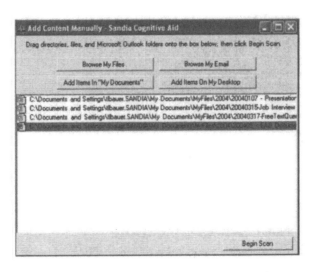

FIG. 7.1.   Sandia Cognitive Aide manual scan window.

the user to choose what files get put into their model, especially if they do not feel comfortable with the system automatically collecting data while they work.

In addition to indexing the documents while creating/updating the profile of the user, the system keeps a list of the user's potential key concepts through a variety of means. The user is able to utilize this collected information in multiple ways. One of the most basic ways is to search through the documents that have been collected (see Fig. 7.2). Additionally, a collection of visualization tools is available for exploring the relationships among key concepts or among documents.

Semantic Space Analyst

The Aide is a tool for creating a model of an individual through watching that individual work, whereas the Semantic Space Analyst (hereafter referred to as the Analyst) is a tool for creating models of multiple cognitive profiles based on the documents a person chooses.

One primary visualization of the semantic space is a two-dimensional map showing the concepts and their relationships to one another (see Fig. 7.3). This visualization has a number of different features. In addition to displaying key concepts, one can see lists of terms related to each key concept. One can also look at the paragraphs where each term occurs in the documents analyzed. Single clicking on a term highlights the links between that term and all those to which it is connected, showing the

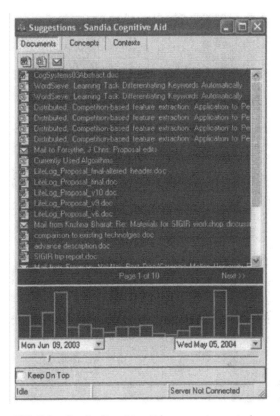

FIG. 7.2.   Sandia Cognitive Aide suggestions window.

weights of the strengths of the relationship. Right clicking on a link shows all the paragraphs where those two terms co-occur.

When the visualization is first created, the terms are laid out randomly. Clicking *Perform Layout* causes a forced layout algorithm to place the nodes on the screen according to the strength of their relative connections to one another. As can be seen earlier, these terms often cluster, suggesting higher ordered contexts within which these terms are used.

These abilities support the main goal of our research group—augmented cognition. The goal is not to replace people, but rather to help them quickly focus on the part of a data set that would be of the most use.

Context Cruiser

The Context Cruiser application provides a graphical interface to our first implementation of automated context recognition from text sources and integrates the data analysis with the cognitive model software. It uses a combination of statistical analyses at the level of individual concepts and

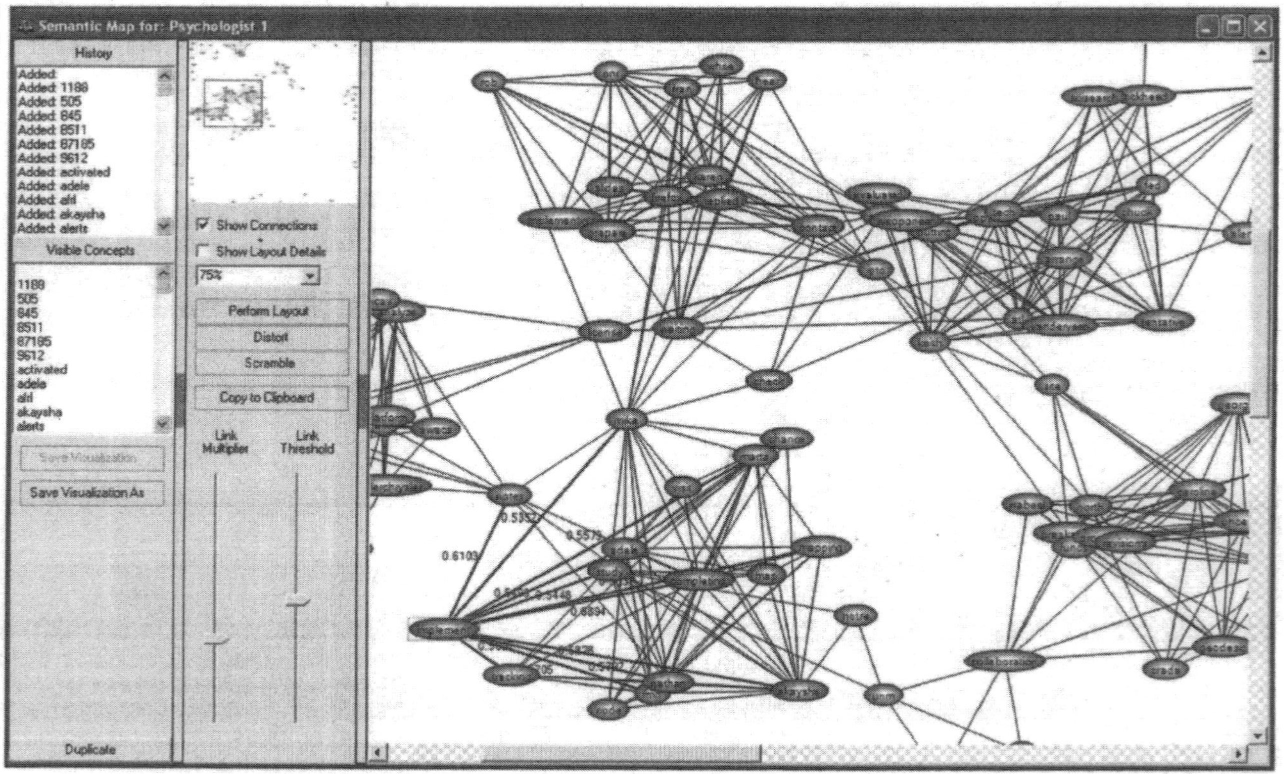

FIG. 7.3. Sample semantic memory space.

clustering at the level of whole documents to generate topical contexts from the documents provided to the system. This information can be uploaded into the cognitive model software.

The screenshot shown in Fig. 7.4 illustrates the results of an analysis of the writings of philosopher Immanuel Kant. Each individual document is split into smaller chunks. These chunks are analyzed to generate topical context knowledge on top of the semantic memory. This analysis discovered the contexts shown in the window in the left of Fig. 7.4. As we might expect, "Pure Reason," which is activated in this screenshot, was a discovered context, corresponding to one of Kant's (1929) seminal volumes, the *Critique of Pure Reason*.

This information is uploaded into the cognitive model framework. The Context Cruiser can then read a document, mimicking per-word fixation times as described in the experimental record (Boff & Lincoln, 1986; Breznitz & Berman, 2003; Just et al., 1982; Rayner, 1998, 2003). As the cruiser reads each word, it checks whether that word has been identified as a key concept, sending words that are to the cognitive model.

The cognitive model activates the concept as described by Forsythe and Xavier (chap. 1, this volume). Any relevant context is activated via a bottom–up process, receiving their excitatory inputs from the active concepts. The earlier visualization shows the contexts in the black squares and the concepts in the blue squares. The context cruiser is reading the introduction to the *Critique of Pure Reason*. It correctly identifies pure reason as the context of the text being read.

The STANLEY library lies at the heart of each of the applications described in the previous sections. At its core, the library performs text analysis to conduct automated knowledge elicitation. The following sections describe the low-level functionality of the library in providing these services.

DATA ANALYSIS

This section describes the basics of indexing via the bag of words approach. This approach is well documented in other literature, and for a more complete explanation such literature should be consulted (Baeza-Yates & Ribeiro-Neto, 1999; Berry & Browne, 1999; Salton et al., 1975). This section gives an overview of the main concepts for generating indexes for documents and how that translates into generating an index for terms that allows us to generate a semantic memory model.

The system indexes documents of multiple types, converting all documents to a common internal format so they can be compared to one an-

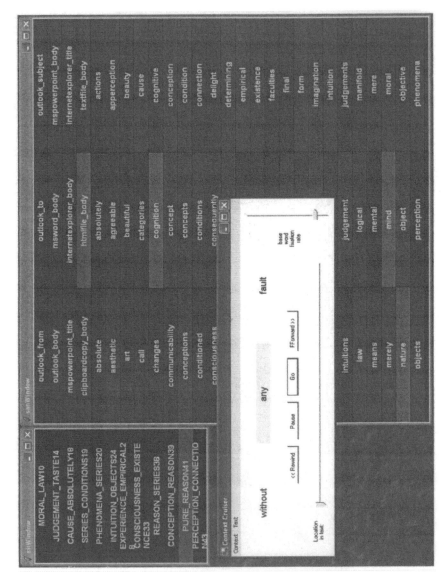

FIG. 7.4. Context Cruiser reading text into a cognitive model.

160

other and analyzed by the same internal processes. This original content is processed before indexing using the following steps:

1. All extraneous document specific information (such as HTML tags or e-mail headers) is removed.
2. All punctuation and nonalphanumeric information is removed.
3. All terms of three or smaller letters are dropped as well as all terms greater than 19 characters.
4. All terms that are combinations of letters and numbers, such as SBN456A8, are dropped.
5. All the text is converted to lowercase.
6. Finally, all the stop words are dropped. Stop words include terms like *because* or *therefore*.

Clearly, this type of processing drops out the syntactical cues needed to interpret the meaning of the sentence and leave behind only the terms most likely to indicate the key concepts in a text. This way of processing text is called the *Bag of Words* representation of a document. No syntactical processing is done. In fact an effort is made to remove it so that we only deal with the semantically meaningful terms. In the Bag of Words methodology, a document is seen as a big collection of words. Their order is not important (although the number of times they occur is). This is the most common methodology used in Information Retrieval (IR) currently for indexing and computing relationships.

We are building software to analyze the syntax and part of speech processing to improve performance. This ability will help eliminate terms that are not semantically meaningful and also to identify noun phrases as potential concepts. In the next generation of the software, for example, *cognitive model* is identified as a single concept rather than *cognitive* and *model* as two separate concepts. Additionally, research is currently underway to investigate the usefulness of word sense disambiguation methods in an attempt to better identify canonical concepts within text.

Document Index Generation

Having extracted indexable text from documents, we then generate indexes for each document. We do this using the Vector space method, where a multidimensional feature space is created and each term corresponds to a dimension. Documents are placed inside this space (see Fig. 7.5).

Documents are indexed by assigning values along dimensions in a multidimensional space. These dimensions correspond to terms (this is not true with LSA, as discussed in a later section, but even with LSA one starts

Software

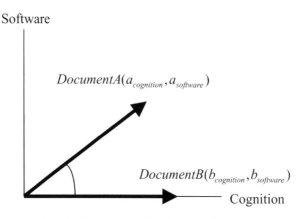

FIG. 7.5.   Documents plotted in two dimensions.

by going through this step). So imagine that there are two terms in your multidimensional space—cognition and software. The space could be visualized as follows.

In this space, there is a dimension for each of the two terms, and we can see two documents placed within that space. Document B, with a vector passing through point ($b_{cognition}$, $b_{software}$), has a relatively high weighting along the cognition dimension and zero weighting along the software dimension. This means that the term *cognition* is relevant for Document a and the term *software* is irrelevant. Document A, with a vector passing through point ($a_{cognition}$, $a_{software}$), in contrast, is weighted along both dimensions, indicating that both terms are relevant to that particular document.

We can compute the similarity between Documents a and b by computing the size of the angle between the two vectors. We use the cosine similarity metric to do this. Given the vectors for Documents A and B, where a_i and b_i represent the weight along Dimension i (i.e., for Term i) in an m-dimensional space, cosine similarity is defined as:

$$\cos \Theta = \frac{\sum_{i=1}^{m} a_i b_i}{\sqrt{\sum_{i=1}^{m} a_i^2}\ \sqrt{\sum_{i=1}^{m} b_i^2}}$$

This measure provides a number between 0 and 1 indicating how similar the documents are. As is shown later, once one has enough documents, the same method can be applied to determining the similarities among the different dimensions (i.e., we can compare the terms to one another in addition to the documents).

The relevant mathematics scale to an arbitrary number of dimensions. Therefore, we can compute a weight for every document along dimensions representing every term that occurs in the document set. Obviously, for any given document, a relatively small number of terms will have non-zero weights. We now turn our attention to how these weights are computed.

Global and Local Weights

The determination of the weight for a given document a along a given dimension i is determined by two factors: the global and local weights of the given term. *Global weight* refers to how good an indexing term is for all the documents that are to be indexed. *Local weight* refers to how relevant the indexing term is for the given document. The weight for document a in dimension i is the product of the global and local weights.

$$a_i = G_i \times L_{ai}$$

where G_i is the global weight of term i and L_{ai} is the local weight of term i for document a.

Intuitively, we want to give each document a large weight along dimensions that both correspond to good indexing terms and are relevant to the document. So, if a particular term is relevant to a specific document, but is not a good indexing term, we want to give it a small weight. Also (and more intuitively), if a term is a good indexing term, but is simply not relevant to a given document, then we do not want to give it a high weight along that dimension. We now look at two computations that are done to compute the global and local weights.

TFIDF

TFIDF stands for Term Frequency, Inverse Document Frequency. The Term Frequency (TF) component refers to the local weight. The Inverse Document Frequency (IDF) refers to the global weight.

TF is simply the number of times the term occurs in the document. This simple measure says that the relevance of a particular term to a given document is a function of the number of times the term occurs in that document. Stop words like *the* and *and* are probably the most frequent terms in most documents. However, as described in an earlier section, we drop those terms early on so that they are not taken into consideration.

IDF, intuitively, says that if a term occurs in only a few documents, it helps differentiate those documents from the rest. So given a large set of news stories from CNN, the terms *CNN* and *news* occur in almost every document, and thus do not help differentiate documents. The term *Iraq* only occurs in a subset of the documents, differentiating some documents from the others. Thus, it makes a good indexing term. IDF is defined mathematically as:

$$\log\left(\frac{n}{\sum_j g(f_{ij})}\right)$$

where n is the number of documents being indexed, f_{ij} is the number of times (the frequency of) term i in document j. The function g is 1 if f_{ij} is greater than 0. It is 0 otherwise. This function is in the software and is available for use, but is not the preferred algorithm. At the time of this writing, we are using the next algorithm, log entropy, and preparing to use LSA.

One problem with IDF is that it does not fully take into consideration the distribution of a term across the set of documents. Let us consider two corpora, each with 100 documents and some term X. In the first corpus, X occurs twice in each of the last 50 documents. In the second corpus, X occurs twice in each of 25 documents and 50 times in each of another 25 documents. This is summarized in Table 7.1.

IDF does not really capture all the information regarding how good a differentiator X is in this case. Remember that $g(f_{ij})$ in the earlier equation is either zero or one depending on whether the term occurs at all. Thus, it cannot take into account the fact that the term's occurrences are relatively concentrated in Documents 75 to 100 in the second corpus and spread out evenly across Documents 50 to 100 in the first corpus. This information is lost, and the IDF is exactly the same for both corpora. To account for this information, we have to take entropy into account.

TABLE 7.1
Sample Composition of Two Corpora

Documents	First Corpus	Second Corpus
Numbers 1–50	Term X occurs 0 times	Term X occurs 0 times
Numbers 50–75	Term X occurs 2 times in each document	Term X occurs 2 times in each document
Numbers 75–100	Term X occurs 2 times in each document	Term X occurs 50 times in each document

Log Entropy

Log entropy is another indexing algorithm that specifies how the global and local weights are computed. *Log* refers to the local weight, and *entropy* refers to the global weight. The local weight using this algorithm is just a slightly modified version of TF used in TFIDF. It is defined mathematically as:

$$\log(1 + f_{ij}),$$

where, as before, f_{ij} is the number of times term i occurs in document j. This gives a nonlinear change in local weight as the frequency of a given term decreases. Essentially this makes the system give favor to terms that occur frequently.

Entropy is a somewhat more complicated measure. Entropy is a measure of the distribution of the term across the document set. If all of the occurrences of the term are bound up in a few documents, the entropy is low. If the occurrences of the term are spread across all the documents, the entropy is high. We want to give a high global weight to terms that have low entropy. Mathematically, this is defined as:

$$1 + \left(\frac{\sum_{j} (p_{ij} \log(p_{ij}))}{\log n} \right)$$

where

$$p_{ij} = \frac{f_{ij}}{g_i}$$

As before, f_{ij} is the number of times term i occurs in document j, and g_i is the number of documents in which term i occurs. Since p_{ij} does not throw away the number of times the term occurs in each document, as g_{ij} did in the IDF calculation, it is able to better deal with situations such as that given in the last section, where some term X is a better differentiator in one corpus than another.

Document Term Matrix

Up to this point, we have discussed how indexes for individual documents can be computed and how documents can be compared to one another. However, for cognitive modeling, the goal is not to compare documents

TABLE 7.2
Sample Sparse Matrix

	Doc 1	Doc 2	Doc 3	Doc 4	Doc 5	Doc 6	Doc 7	Doc 8
Model	0.57	0.76	0.23	0.23	0.89			
Cognitive	0.12	0.84	0.43	0.14	0.79			
Psychology	0.32	0.91	0.75					
Software				0.76	0.43	0.12	0.74	0.87
UMBRA						0.65	0.12	0.99
Debug						0.23	0.21	0.78

to each other, but to develop a way of comparing terms. We have not explained how terms can be compared to one another or how large sets of vectors are represented. The standard way to represent groups of documents is the "document term matrix." In a document term matrix, each column contains a vector for a single document, and each row corresponds to a single dimension. Imagine a set of eight documents that are indexed by six terms. The document term matrix is illustrated in Table 7.2.

The specific numbers are not computed from actual documents, but rather are examples of numbers one might see. The blank cells are 0.0. Notice that only about half of the cells are nonzero. In an actual matrix, there would be many more terms and documents, and a much larger percentage of cells would be zero.

A casual survey of the matrix shows several things. First, Documents 1, 2, and 3 are probably about the same topic, psychology and cognitive models, whereas Documents 6, 7, and 8 are probably about debugging UMBRA software. Documents 4 and 5 are somewhat similar to both sets and especially similar to each other, being about cognitive modeling software. The cosine similarity between any two columns can be computed to estimate the similarity of the corresponding documents.

Likewise, we can compute the similarity between any two terms by thinking of each row as a vector and using the same similarity measure. This matrix shows a strong similarity between *cognitive* and *model*, but not between *model* and *debug*. Thus, having constructed the matrix, we can compare terms to one another and not just documents.

Latent Semantic Analysis

The matrix described earlier contains implicit information not accessible through cosine similarity. For example, the terms *cognitive* and *model* are somewhat related to *software*, and *software* is somewhat related to *UM-BRA*. This implies that the terms *cognitive* and *model* are somewhat re-

FIG. 7.6.   Matrixes produced through SVD.

lated to *UMBRA* as well. However, in the earlier matrix, the cosine similarity is zero between these terms and *UMBRA*.

Latent Semantic Analysis provides a way to draw out these implicit relationships using a technique from linear algebra known as Singular Value Decomposition (SVD). In SVD, the matrix is decomposed into three submatrixes and modified in a way that can be used to reduce the rank of the original matrix. The details of performing SVD are beyond the scope of this chapter, but a graphical view of the decomposition is shown in Fig. 7.6.

The original MxN matrix is decomposed into the three other matrixes shown. The middle matrix contains a single diagonal from the upper left corner, ordered from highest number to lowest. By setting the lower entries in the diagonal to zero and remultiplying the rest of the matrix, one can get a reduced rank matrix in which the implicit relationships are exposed.

Typically, the rank is reduced to around 300. Experiments, including those described in the Results section, show the greatest performance at approximately this value. Consider a simplified version of the matrix given previously, with every entry either 1.0 or 0.0 (see Table 7.3).

Table 7.4 provides the results when we use SVD to reduce this to a Rank 2 matrix. There are three main points that we would like to draw from this new matrix. First of all, LSA filled in the gaps. Notice that *cognitive, model,* and *psychology* usually occur together, implying that these three terms

TABLE 7.3
Sample Sparse Matrix With Only Ones and Zeros

	Doc 1	Doc 2	Doc 3	Doc 4	Doc 5	Doc 6	Doc 7	Doc 8
Model	1	1	1	1	1			
Cognitive	1	1	1	1	1			
Psychology	1	1	1					
Software				1	1	1	1	1
UMBRA						1	1	1
Debug						1	1	1

TABLE 7.4
Recomposed Matrix After Dimensionality Reduction

	Doc 1	Doc 2	Doc 3	Doc 4	Doc 5	Doc 6	Doc 7	Doc 8
Model	1.06	1.06	1.06	0.90	0.90	0.03	0.03	0.03
Cognitive	1.06	1.06	1.06	0.90	0.90	0.03	0.03	0.03
Psychology	0.71	0.71	0.71	0.53	0.53	−0.15	−0.15	−0.15
Software	0.21	0.21	0.21	0.63	0.63	1.10	1.10	1.10
UMBRA	−0.15	−0.15	−0.15	0.26	0.26	0.93	0.93	0.93
Debug	−0.15	−0.15	−0.15	0.26	0.26	0.93	0.93	0.93

are associated with one another. Yet in Documents 4 and 5, they do not. LSA effectively infers that, because *cognitive* and *model* occur in those documents, and those terms usually occur with the term *psychology*, it is reasonable to assume that those documents also have something to do with psychology, so it sets weightings for that term in those documents.

Second, LSA reduces noise. While the co-occurrence of *cognitive*, *model*, and *psychology* in Documents 1, 2, and 3 implies that they go together, it is also true that the absence of *psychology* in Documents 4 and 5 is evidence that they might not always go together. For this reason, you can see that the weight of *psychology* in Documents 1, 2, and 3 is reduced.

Third, LSA discovers new relationships among terms. Notice that in the first matrix, the cosine similarity between *cognitive*, *model*, and *UMBRA* is zero. That means that on a semantic map there is not a line drawn between them, and the cognitive model does not recognize this connection. However, *cognitive*, *model*, and *software* co-occur together in Documents 4 and 5. Also *software* co-occurs with *UMBRA*. Effectively, LSA infers a relationship between *cognitive*, *model*, and *UMBRA* because of this transitivity. Thus, in the rank-reduced matrix, the cosine similarity among these terms is greater than zero.

Another less obvious advantage is that it lets one reduce the space requirements of the matrix. The fully recomputed matrix contains the exact same number of values as the original. Because it contains relatively few zeros, it would take up substantially more space than the original (if the data storage format allows one to not store zero values). However, the matrix is often stored as the three decomposed matrixes, which requires much less space.

In the example given, we only used eight documents and six terms with obvious and simple relationships. We can eyeball the matrix and see the relationships. However, in a matrix with millions of documents and tens of thousands of terms, these relationships are not at all obvious and far more complex. SVD provides a convenient and straightforward computation to draw out this information.

The LSA functionality is being provided by Knowledge Analysis Technologies (KAT). We currently can run a preliminary version of the server and have the bridge between the server and our software functioning.

Results

Previous LSA work has established that the analysis of a large document set can be used to successfully compute the similarity among terms to pass synonym tests (Landauer & Dumais, 1997). However, such work has not shown how the size of the corpus used to compute the synonym values affects the quality of the results. This is a significant question because it can give us an indication of the number of documents we might need to build a model of an individual that captures commonsense knowledge.

In this experiment, we used the Metametrics corpus containing 3.6 million documents. This corpus was carefully chosen to span many topic areas and many different reading levels. Two types of tests were run. In the first, we looked at the performance of the system on the TOEFL synonym task using spaces built from different subsets of the Metametrics corpus. In this task, the system is shown a term and asked to choose the most similar term from four alternatives. We chose the term with the most similar semantic relationship as the system's answer. The second test was a categorization task, in which we measured how well the system could choose the correct category out of 14 possibilities given 10 exemplars from that category.

First, we look at a qualitative comparison between semantic spaces of two different sizes. Then we look at specific results for the different tests. The following two graphs (see Figs. 7.7 and 7.8) show subsets of semantic spaces built using four different subsets of the document set, allowing one to qualitatively view the similarities between two different spaces. Along the X and Y axes are terms clustered by topic. For example, different kinds of fruit (apple, peach, pear, and grape) are listed together as are different kinds of trees (oak, pine, elm, maple). The heights of the bars in the Z axis are the similarities between the two terms on the X and Y axes at that point (except that the bars on the diagonal representing the similarity between a term and itself are set to zero). The left and right triangular matrixes display the semantic relationships between two different spaces. Because the terms are clustered by category, we expect that in a well-developed semantic space there would be high bars along the diagonal, indicating that the system recognized strong semantic relationships among terms from the same category. Thus, the organization of each triangular matrix is a mirror of the other, but built using a different set of documents.

Figure 7.7 gives a qualitative comparison of the two spaces, each built using 10,000 randomly chosen documents from the metametrics corpus.

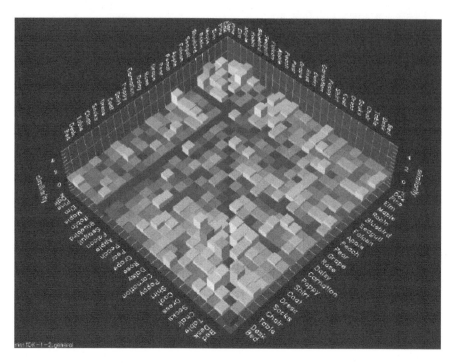

FIG. 7.7.   Two spaces built using 10,000 randomly chosen documents.

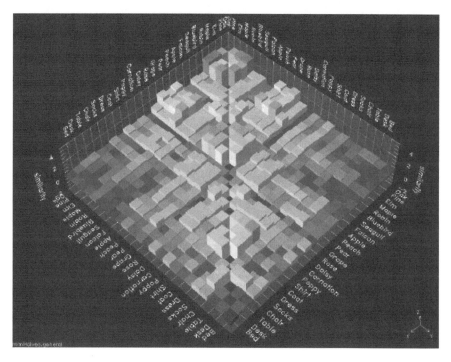

FIG. 7.8.   Spaces built using 1.8 million documents each.

170

We see that along the diagonal there are a few high bars in both spaces, particularly for the clothing and trees categories. However, most of the comparisons are relatively low, indicating that the system has not yet really discovered many of the different semantic relationships.

Figure 7.8 shows the same term relationships, but with two much larger semantic spaces, each built with two much larger subsets of the metametrics corpus. Each space displayed in Fig. 7.8 contained half of the corpus (1.8 million documents). There was no overlap in the documents of each space. The graph shows significantly higher relationships along the diagonal, indicating that the system is much more likely to specify high semantic relationships between terms in the same categories.

What is really striking about Fig. 7.8, however, is that both spaces are remarkably similar, although there is no overlap in the documents used to build the spaces. Both spaces are built from completely different document sets. Despite this, the term similarities are similar among the terms. The two sides are almost mirror images of one another.

Now this would not be likely to happen between two different subsets of just any randomly chosen documents. The metametrics corpus is carefully chosen to span different topics and reading levels. However, given such a document set, using completely different subsets of the documents yields similar semantic spaces.

For the quantitative comparisons, we build 106 spaces using the criteria listed in Table 7.5. The spaces are named based on the number of documents included in them or based on the fraction of the metametrics corpus used. Note that the "10K Special" space was built not from a random selection of documents like the others, but from a subset of documents that were topically focused. We believe this is somewhat more indicative of the kinds of documents that would be used to automatically build a person's semantic space for the cognitive model.

TABLE 7.5
Quantitative Comparisons Based on 105 Spaces

Space Name	Number of Documents	AVG Number of Terms	Number of Instances
Full	3,600,000	724,633	1
Half	1,800,000	508,366	2
Quarter	900,000	359,851	4
Eighth	450,000	257,756	8
Sixteenth	225,000	186,309	16
100K	100,000	119,776	15
10K Special	10,000	40,663	15
10K	10,000	44,735	15
5K	5,000	32,102	30

TOEFL Test

Figure 7.9 shows the results of testing each space against 80 items in the TOEFL synonym test. In this test, each space was tested across a range of ranks, ranging from 2 to 300. The performance tended to increase when reduced to a higher rank, with performance tapering off as the size reaches 300. Performance also tended to increase as the size of the corpus increased as well. This is consistent with other research in LSA showing that larger corpora yield better results and a rank around 300 tends to yield good results.

Figure 7.10 shows the variability within the same size corpus for different corpus sizes reduced to Rank 300. The three-dimensional graphs at the beginning of this section indicate that the performance is lower with a smaller number of documents and increases with a larger number. This graph shows that there is greater variability with a smaller corpus size. In other words, a larger number of documents is necessary to get consistent results from different subsets of a corpus.

Category Test

The other test we performed shows the ability of the system to correctly identify 1 of 14 categories given 10 exemplars from that category. Figure 7.11 shows the results of that test. As with the synonym test, the

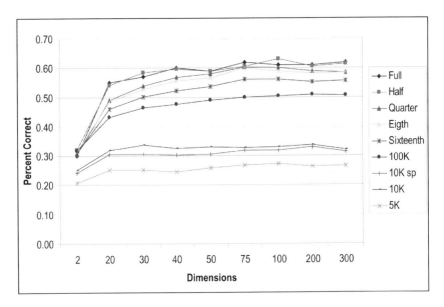

FIG. 7.9.   Results from 80-item TOEFL synonym test.

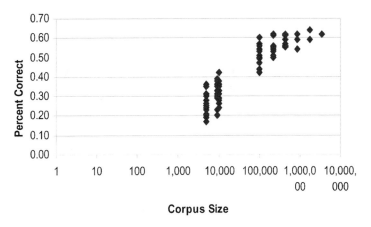

FIG. 7.10.   Results from 80-item TOEFL synonym test with 300 dimensions.

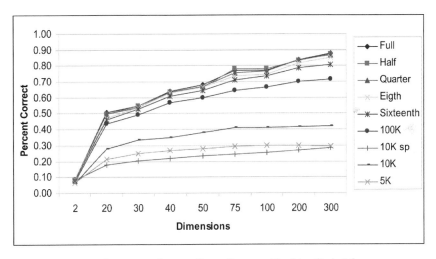

FIG. 7.11.   Concept to Superordinate Category Matching Task: 14 categories, 140 concepts.

performance varies with rank and corpus size. Performance is highest at rank 300 and with the largest corpus. Unlike the synonym test, however, the performance does not seem to taper off at rank 300 (our tests only go up to rank 300 on this test). The largest corpora have results around 90%.

These results suggest that using LSA is a viable way to produce a semantic space automatically from text, and that reduction to 300 is a good choice for the rank. These results also suggest that larger corpus sizes yield less variability in the semantic space given a homogeneous composition of document types, even if the documents are not exactly the same.

FUTURE WORK

Four deficiencies in our current identification of key concepts are:

- The inclusion of extraneous terms as key concepts, such as the terms *determining* and *absolutely* in the context cruiser earlier.
- The failure of the system to identify certain noun phrases such as *cognitive model* as single key concepts.
- The failure of the system to recognize that terms such as *concept* and *concepts* refer, in fact, to the same concept.
- The failure of the system to realize that sometimes the same term can refer to more than one concept, such as realizing that *rice* can refer to a food or a county.

Work is currently underway to deal with these problems. The first two can be dealt with through syntactic analysis of the documents using common natural language processing techniques. In particular, a current implementation of such analysis techniques employs the Transformation Based Learning methodology first proposed by Eric Brill. This deals with the first deficiency by allowing us to differentiate among different terms through the use of part of speech and noun phrase analysis. For example, we can decide to only use noun phrases as key concepts for the cognitive model. It deals with the second deficiency by allowing us to extract noun phrases from documents. The syntactic parsing will identify *cognitive model* as a single noun phrase that we can then treat as a single term in our computations.

The third deficiency can be dealt with through stemming. Stemming performs an operation roughly inverse to that of conjugation, to extract the root of each term. So *concepts* and *concept* would both get stemmed to *concept*.

The last deficiency can be solved, at least in part, through noun phrase chunking and word sense disambiguation. When rice is used as a county name, it tends to occur in the phrase *rice county*. Identifying the phrase effectively differentiates that term usage from other usages. Algorithms also exist to differentiate a term sense based on its co-occurrence with other terms, such as when rice is used with food terms. At the time of this writing, we have already implemented the transformation-based learning algorithm and the stemming algorithms, and we are in the process of incorporating them into the rest of the system.

SUMMARY AND CONCLUSION

This chapter presents ongoing work on automatically populating a cognitive model from text that an individual produces and reads. We have shown a range of applications and technologies being developed at Sandia National Laboratories for utilizing and visualizing such models. This is active, continuing research to build useful technologies utilizing automatically generated models for augmented cognition.

LSA is a viable method for building such models. Variability among spaces decreases as more documents are used (given a relatively homogeneous corpus). A rank reduction to 300 yields good results on both synonym and categorization tasks.

ACKNOWLEDGMENTS

This work was performed at Sandia National Laboratories. Sandia is a multiprogram laboratory operated by Sandia Corporation, a Lockheed-Martin Company, for the U.S. Department of Energy under Contract DE-AC04-94AL85000.

REFERENCES

Baeza-Yates, R., & Ribeiro-Neto, B. (1999). *Modern information retrieval.* New York: ACM Press.

Berry, M. W., & Browne, M. (1999). *Understanding search engines.* Philadelphia, PA: SIAM.

Boff, A. A., & Lincoln, M. R. L. (1986). *Engineering Data Compendium.* OH: Wright-Patterson AFB.

Breznitz, & Berman, (2003). The underlying factors of word reading rate. *Educational Psychology Review, 15*(3), 247–260.

Deerwester, S., Dumais, S. T., Furnas, G. W., Landauer, T. K., & Harshman, R. (1990). Indexing by Latent Semantic Analysis. *Journal of the American Society for Information Science, 41*, 391–407.

Just, Carpenter, & Woolley, (1982). Paradigms and processes in reading comprehension. *Journal of Experimental Psychology, 111*(2), 228–238.

Kant, I. (1929). *Critique of pure reason* (N. Kemp-Smith, Trans.). New York: Palgrave Macmillan. Available at: www.hkbu.edu.hk/~ppp/cpr/toc.hmtl

Landauer, T. K., & Dumais, S. T. (1997). A solution to Plato's problem: The Latent Semantic Analysis theory of the acquisition, induction, and representation of knowledge. *Psychological Review, 104*, 211–240.

Rayner, K. (1998). Eye movements in reading and information processing: 20 years of research. *Psychological Bulletin, 124*(3), 372–422.

Rayner, K. (2003). Reading disappearing text: Cognitive control of eye movements. *Psychological Science, 14*(4), 385–388.

Salton, G., Wong, A., & Yang, C. S. (1975). A vector space model for automatic indexing. *Communications of the ACM, 18*(11), 613–620.

CHAPTER EIGHT

AutoTutor: A Cognitive System That Simulates a Tutor Through Mixed-Initiative Dialogue

Arthur C. Graesser
Andrew Olney
Brian C. Haynes
Patrick Chipman
University of Memphis

AutoTutor is a complex cognitive system that simulates a human tutor, or an ideal tutor, by holding a conversation with the learner in natural language. AutoTutor qualifies as a cognitive system in two fundamental ways (see Forsythe & Xavier, chap. 1, this volume). First, its core architecture incorporates a humanlike model of knowledge, discourse, and cognitive processes. Second, AutoTutor recruits these psychological mechanisms to engage the learner cognitively and thereby promote learning. Therefore, AutoTutor both simulates cognitive mechanisms of human tutors and facilitates cognitive activities of human learners.

AutoTutor was developed by Graesser and colleagues in the interdisciplinary Institute for Intelligent Systems at the University of Memphis (Graesser et al., 2004; Graesser, Person, Harter, & Tutoring Research Group, 2001; Graesser, VanLehn, Rose, Jordan, & Harter, 2001; Graesser, K. Wiemer-Hastings, P. Wiemer-Hastings, Kreuz, & Tutoring Research Group, 1999). AutoTutor presents a series of challenging questions or problems that require approximately a paragraph (3–7 sentences) of information to answer correctly. An example question in conceptual physics is, "When a car without headrests on the seats is struck from behind, the passengers often suffer neck injuries. Why do passengers get neck injuries in this situation?" Although a perfect answer to this question is approximately 3 to 7 sentences in length, the initial answers by actual human learners are typically only 1 word to 2 sentences in length. This is where tutorial dialogue is particularly helpful, whether the dialogue is provided

by AutoTutor or a human tutor. AutoTutor assists the learner in the evolution of an improved answer that draws out more of the learner's knowledge that is relevant to the answer. The dialogue between AutoTutor and
the learner typically lasts 50 to 200 turns (i.e., the learner expresses something, then the tutor, then the learner, etc.). There is a mixed-initiative dialogue to the extent that each dialogue partner can ask questions and start
new topics of discussion. AutoTutor serves as a discourse prosthesis that
draws out more of what the learner knows and that adaptively improves
answers to questions through collaboration in natural language.

In this chapter, we hope to accomplish three goals. First, we describe
what AutoTutor does and clarify the scope of its functionality. Second, we
briefly review the evidence that AutoTutor both facilitates learning and
simulates a reasonably good conversation partner. Third, we describe the
architecture of AutoTutor's complex system.

WHAT DOES AUTOTUTOR DO?

Perhaps the best way to convey what AutoTutor is all about is through an
example conversational dialogue. The following conversation is one
with a student on the topic of conceptual physics. This depicts the true
output of AutoTutor, as opposed to serving as a hypothetical illustration
of what an ideal AutoTutor might do. The conversation begins with a
main question selected by AutoTutor from the repertoire of questions in
its curriculum.

AutoTutor-1:   The sun exerts a gravitational force on the earth as the
                earth moves in its orbit around the sun. Does the earth
                pull equally on the sun? Explain why.
Student-2:   I don't know.
AutoTutor-3: Could you at least try to give me an answer? That way
                we'll have something as a starting place to work from.
                How does Newton's third law of motion apply to this
                situation?
Student-4:   What?
AutoTutor-5: Once again, how does Newton's third law of motion ap-
                ply to this situation?
Student-6:   Does Newton's law apply to opposite forces?
AutoTutor-7: Yes, right! Hum. There's still something missing from
                your explanation. Newton's Third Law refers to the
                forces exerted by one body on another _____?
Student-8:   body.

AutoTutor-9: You're amazing! Bravo! Let's move on. What can you say about the magnitude of the force that the earth exerts on the sun?

Student-10: What is the difference between a force and a vector?

AutoTutor-11: Interesting question. Perhaps the following answer helps. Vector is an arrow drawn to scale used to represent a vector quantity. Does this answer help you in understanding the material?

Student-12: No.

AutoTutor-13: I might not have understood what you meant. Ask another conceptual physics question if you need more information.

Student-14: What is the difference between force and a vector?

AutoTutor-15: Force is any influence that tends to accelerate an object, a push or pull, measured in Newtons. Force is a vector quantity, and vector is an arrow whose length represents the magnitude of a quantity and whose direction represents the direction of the quantity. Okay, I bet you can get this! The sun experiences the same magnitude of gravitational pull from the earth as the earth does from the _____?

Student-16: sun.

AutoTutor-17: Yes, right! From the sun. What is going on in this situation between the earth and sun?

Student-18: The sun is pulling on the earth because it is bigger.

AutoTutor-19: Let's try this together. When two objects of different masses hit each other, which one exerts the greater force on the other, the heavy object, the light object, or are the forces equal?

Student-20: The heavy object.

AutoTutor-21: No. The forces are equal in magnitude. Um, well, for every force there is a reaction force, such that the two forces constitute an action reaction force pair. The two forces have opposite direction and equal magnitude. No matter how different the masses of the two objects are, they will exert reaction forces on each other in the same magnitude.

This example shows that AutoTutor can generate a reasonably smooth conversation. AutoTutor's answers are adaptive to what the student previously said and appear to be interpreting the student's speech acts. Obviously the dialogue is not perfect. One glitch of AutoTutor, for example, appears to be in Turn 7. It is not clear whether AutoTutor is answering the student's question asked in Turn 6 or is incorrectly interpreting Turn 6 as an assertion made by the student. However, for the most part, the conversation is reasonably smooth. It should be noted that the 21 turns in this example exchange do not completely answer the main question posed by AutoTutor in Turn 1. We have conducted experiments on over 1,000 students using AutoTutor, or roughly 2,000 to 3,000 hours of logged time of conversational dialogue. Some students require several hundreds of turns to answer a single main question posted by AutoTutor.

AutoTutor needs to accomplish a number of tasks to orchestrate a smooth and adaptive conversation. AutoTutor needs to classify and interpret the language expressed by the student. Students type in their input at present, but we do have a prototype version that incorporates speech recognition. AutoTutor needs to formulate one or more dialogue moves within each conversational turn in a fashion that is responsive to the student. Table 8.1 presents an analysis of the example dialogue by specifying the categorized dialogue moves of AutoTutor, the classified speech acts of the student, and comments to help the reader interpret what is going on. The content expressed by either AutoTutor or the student in Table 8.1 are signified in italics. Discourse categories of AutoTutor's dialogue moves have been added in capitals, whereas other information is added in normal font.

The example and analysis in Table 8.1 illustrate the mixed-initiative dialogue of AutoTutor. AutoTutor segments the student's turns into speech act units and then assigns these units into categories, such as Assertion, Short Answer, Metacognition, Metacommunication, Verification Question, and Comparison Question. There are approximately 20 categories of student speech acts; 16 of these are different categories of student questions. AutoTutor attempts to accommodate virtually any student question, assertion, comment, or extraneous speech act. This requires interpreting the student's speech acts by implementing modules developed in the field of computational linguistics (Allen, 1995; Covington, chap. 4, this volume; Jurafsky & Martin, 2000). AutoTutor needs to produce language in addition to comprehending language. Each turn of AutoTutor requires the generation of one or more dialogue moves that either adaptively respond to what the student just expressed or advance the conversation in a constructive fashion that answers the main question. The dialogue moves within a turn are connected by dialogue markers, as illustrated in Table 8.1. Some dialogue moves are responsive to the student's preceding turn, such as the short feedback (positive, neutral, vs. negative), the answers to student questions, and corrections of student misconceptions. Other dialogue moves push the dialogue forward in an attempt to cover the ex-

TABLE 8.1
Example AutoTutor–Student Dialogue With Classified Dialogue Moves
of AutoTutor, Classified Speech Acts of the Student, and Comments

Speaker	Dialogue
AutoTutor-1:	*The sun exerts a gravitational force on the earth as the earth moves in its orbit around the sun. Does the earth pull equally on the sun? Explain why.* (MAIN QUESTION. This is a main question selected from AutoTutor's curriculum script, which will take approximately 30–100 conversation turns to collaboratively answer.)
Student-2:	*I don't know.* (This expression by the student is classified as a metacognitive speech act because it conveys what the student knows about his or her own knowledge.)
AutoTutor-3:	*Could you at least try to give me an answer? That way we'll have something as a starting place to work from.* (PUMP. This dialogue move encourages the student to say more, but does not direct the student to express particular information.)
	How does Newton's third law of motion apply to this situation? (HINT. This dialogue move leads the student to articulate a particular sentence, clauses, or proposition.)
Student-4:	*What?* (This expression by the student is classified as a metacommunicative speech act because it addresses the communication channel between AutoTutor and student—in this case, a request for AutoTutor to repeat what was last said.)
AutoTutor-5:	*Once again, how does Newton's third law of motion apply to this situation?* (REPEAT. AutoTutor repeats its last dialogue move after signaling the function of the present move with the discourse marker *once again*.)
Student-6:	*Does Newton's law apply to opposite forces?* (This expression by the student is classified as a verification question, which calls for a yes/no answer.)
AutoTutor-7:	*Yes, right!* (ANSWER. AutoTutor answers the student's question.)
	Hum. (DISCOURSE MARKER. This is a discourse marker that connects different dialogue moves within a turn. Another good discourse marker is "Okay.")
	There's still something missing from your explanation. (DISCOURSE MARKER. AutoTutor lets the student know more is expected.)
	Newton's Third Law refers to the forces exerted by one body on another _____? (PROMPT. This dialogue move encourages the student to fill in a particular word or phrase of information, in this case the word *body*. Prompts are needed for students who are low verbal and to elicit a particular noun, verb, or adjective.)
Student-8:	*body* (short answer)
AutoTutor-9:	*You're amazing! Bravo!* (POSITIVE FEEDBACK. AutoTutor gives positive feedback on the answer the student just gave in the previous turn. There are five levels of feedback: positive, positive-neutral, neutral, negative-neutral, and negative.)
	Let's move on. (DISCOURSE MARKER)
	What can you say about the magnitude of the force that the earth exerts on the sun? (HINT)

(Continued)

TABLE 8.1
(Continued)

Speaker	Dialogue
Student-10:	*What is the difference between a force and a vector?* (This expression by the student is classified as a comparison question.)
AutoTutor-11:	*Interesting question. Perhaps the following answer helps.* (DISCOURSE MARKER. Notice that AutoTutor hedges on whether the subsequent answer is satisfying. Hedges are important when a computer lacks confidence.)
	Vector is an arrow drawn to scale used to represent a vector quantity. (ANSWER. This answer is fetched from a large textbook on physics rather than being canned. So AutoTutor performs information retrieval.)
	Does this answer help you in understanding the material? (ANSWER CONFIRMATION. AutoTutor seeks feedback on the quality of the answer it delivers.)
Student-12:	*No.* (Short answer. The student apparently was not satisfied with AutoTutor's answer to the student's question.)
AutoTutor-13:	*I might not have understood what you meant.* (DISCOURSE MARKER) *Ask another conceptual physics question if you need more information.* (QUESTION SOLICITATION. AutoTutor invites the student to ask a question. Question revisions are common in modern information retrieval facilities.)
Student-14:	*What is the difference between force and a vector?* (The student simply repeated the same question, but, as shown next, the answer will be different.)
AutoTutor-15:	*Force is any influence that tends to accelerate an object; a push or pull; measured in Newtons. Force is a vector quantity, and vector is an arrow whose length represents the magnitude of a quantity and whose direction represents the direction of the quantity.* (ANSWER. This answer is once again fetched from the textbook through information-retrieval methods.)
	Okay, I bet you can get this! (DISCOURSE MARKER)
	The sun experiences the same magnitude of gravitational pull from the earth as the earth does from the _____? (PROMPT)
Student-16:	*sun* (short answer)
AutoTutor-17:	*Yes, right!* (POSITIVE FEEDBACK)
	From the sun. (PROMPT COMPLETION. This is the correct answer to the prompt that was delivered in the previous AutoTutor turn.)
	Let's keep going. (DISCOURSE MARKER)
	What is going on in this situation between the earth and sun? (HINT)
Student-18:	*The sun is pulling on the earth because it is bigger.* (This expression by the student is classified as an assertion because it provides information that helps answer the main question. This answer is identified as a misconception because both bodies are pulling on each other.)
AutoTutor-19:	(No feedback is given to the student even though the student just expressed a misconception. AutoTutor sometimes refrains from negative feedback to avoid punishing the student when the student is starting to supply information.)

(Continued)

TABLE 8.1
(Continued)

Speaker	Dialogue
	Let's try this together: (DISCOURSE MARKER)
	When two objects of different masses hit each other, which one exerts the greater force on the other, the heavy object or the light object, or are the forces equal? (DIAGNOSTIC QUESTION. This question diagnostically verifies that the student really does have a misconception.)
Student-20:	*the heavy object.* (Short answer. This is classified as the student's answer to the diagnostic question, which is incorrect.)
AutoTutor-21:	*No.* (NEGATIVE FEEDBACK) *The forces are equal in magnitude. Um, well, for every force there is a reaction force, such that the two forces constitute an action reaction force pair. The two forces have opposite direction and equal magnitude. No matter how different the masses of the two objects are, they will exert reaction forces on each other in the same magnitude.* (CORRECTION. AutoTutor corrects the student's misconception.)

pected answer to the questions. These forward-directed dialogue moves include Pumps (e.g., *Tell me more, What else?*), Hints, Prompts for specific words or phrases, and Assertions. The responsive and forward-directed dialogue moves together provide a mixed-initiative dialogue in which both parties of the conversation exert an influence over the conversation. These are not scripted conversations, but rather are dynamically emerging exchanges.

AutoTutor delivers its dialogue moves with an animated conversational agent that has a text-to-speech engine, facial expressions, gestures, and pointing. Animated agents have become increasingly popular in learning environments on the Web, Internet, and desktop applications (Cassell & Thorisson, 1999; Johnson, Rickel, & Lester, 2000; Massaro & Cohen, 1995). Figure 8.1 shows the interface of one version of AutoTutor on the subject matter of Newtonian physics. The main question is presented in the top-right window. This major question (e.g., involving a boy dropping keys in a falling elevator) remains at the top of the Web page until it is finished being answered during a multiturn dialogue. The students use the bottom-right window to type in their contributions for each turn. The dialogue history between AutoTutor and student is shown in the bottom-left window. The animated conversational agent resides in the upper-left area. The agent uses a text-to-speech engine from either AT&T, SpeechWorks, or a Microsoft Agent (dependent on licensing agreements) to speak the content of AutoTutor's turns. Figure 8.2 shows a somewhat different interface that is used when tutoring computer literacy. This interface has a display area for diagrams, but no dialogue history window.

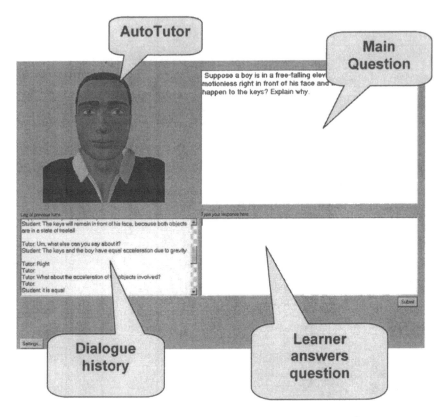

FIG. 8.1.   A computer screen of AutoTutor for the subject matter of conceptual physics.

AutoTutor With Interactive Three-Dimensional Simulation

One version of AutoTutor has an embedded, interactive three-dimensional simulation. Three-dimensional simulation provides an additional channel of communication to discuss conceptual physics with the learner. Each simulation is crafted to cover particular physics principles in an ideal answer or to help correct particular misconceptions about physics. For each of the physics problems, we developed an interactive simulation world in *3-d Studio Max*. This included the people, objects, and spatial setting associated with the problem. The student can manipulate parameters of the situation (e.g., mass of objects, speed of objects, distance between objects) and then ask the system to simulate what will happen. They can compare their expected simulated outcome with the actual outcome after the simulation is completed. Moreover, they describe what

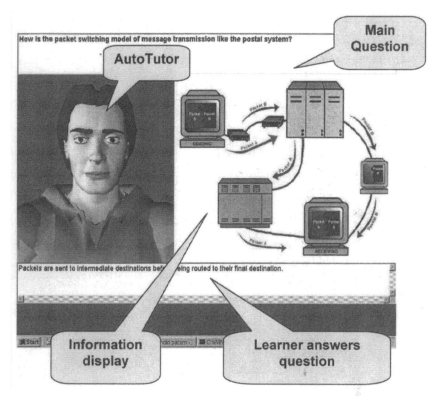

FIG. 8.2. A computer screen of AutoTutor for the subject matter of introductory computer literacy.

they see. Their actions and descriptions are evaluated with respect to covering the expected principles in an ideal answer. To manage the interactive simulation, AutoTutor gives hints and suggestions, once again scaffolding the learning process with dialogue. Thus, AutoTutor combines interactive simulation with mixed-initiative dialogue.

Figure 8.3 shows an example interface for the three-dimensional version of AutoTutor. The question is presented at the top of the screen—in this case, "When a car without headsets on the seats is struck from behind, the passengers often suffer neck injuries. Why do passengers get neck injuries in this situation?" Beneath the question are two windows that show the car and truck (middle window) and the driver in the car (right window). These components move whenever a simulation is run. Beneath the question on the left is the animated agent that guides the interaction with hints, suggestions, assertions, and other dialogue moves. These suggestions include having the student manipulate parameters, such as truck speed, mass of the car, and mass of the truck. The students also have a number of the binary

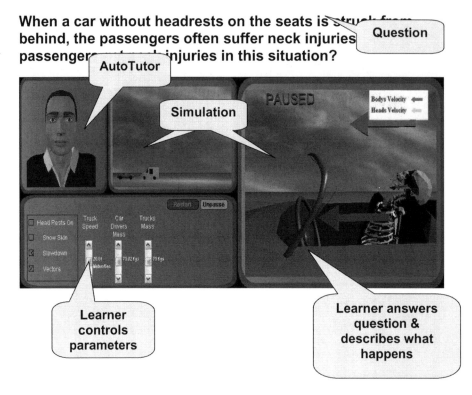

FIG. 8.3.   A computer screen of AutoTutor on conceptual physics with interactive
three-dimensional simulation.

options: Having the head rests in the car on, showing the skin on the driver,
slowing down the simulation, and vector arrows that depict forces. The student manipulates these parameters and options, as shown in the bottom
left, before a simulation is run. The activity of manipulating these inputs
and viewing the simulation is believed to provide a referentially grounded
and embodied representation of the problem, as well as a deeper understanding of physics (Bransford, Brown, & Cocking, 2000). However, empirical support for the pedagogical value of interactive simulation has not yet
been substantiated in the literature on cognition and instruction. The students can run as many simulations as they wish until they feel they understand the relationship between parameters and outcomes of simulations.
However, interacting with and viewing the simulations is not all there is.
The participants are also prompted to describe what they see and answer
the main question. Therefore, deep learning of physics is believed to
emerge from the combination of interactivity, perceptual simulation, feedback on the simulation, and explaining what happens.

Some previous systems have conversational agents that combined dialogue with interactive simulation. Some examples of these systems are Steve (Rickel & Johnson, 1999) and Mission Rehearsal (Gratch et al., 2002). However, AutoTutor is the only system that is available on the Internet, has systematically been tested on students, and has flexible tutorial dialogue that scaffolds interactive simulation.

Pedagogical Foundations of AutoTutor

The design of AutoTutor was inspired by three bodies of theoretical, empirical, and applied research. First, there are explanation-based constructivist theories of learning (Aleven & Koedinger, 2002; Chi, de Leeuw, Chiu, & LaVancher, 1994; VanLehn, Jones, & Chi, 1992). According to the explanation-based constructivist theories of learning, learning is more effective and deeper when the learner must actively generate explanations, justifications, and functional procedures than when merely given information to read (Bransford et al., 2000). Second, there are intelligent tutoring systems that adaptively respond to student knowledge (Anderson, Corbett, Koedinger, & Pelletier, 1995; VanLehn, Lynch et al., 2002). These tutors give immediate feedback to learners' actions and guide the learner on what to do next in a fashion that is sensitive to what the system believes the learner knows. Third, empirical research has documented the collaborative constructive activities that routinely occur during human tutoring (Chi, Siler, Jeong, Yamauchi, & Hausmann, 2001; Fox, 1993; Graesser, Person, & Magliano, 1995; Moore, 1995). The patterns of discourse uncovered in naturalistic tutoring are imported into the dialogue management facilities of AutoTutor.

One of AutoTutor's prominent dialogue patterns is called *expectation and misconception tailored dialogue* (EMT dialogue), which is known to be common in human tutoring. Both AutoTutor and human tutors typically have a list of anticipated good answers (called *expectations*) and a list of *misconceptions* associated with each main question or problem. One goal of the tutor is to coach the student in covering the list of expectations. Another goal is to correct misconceptions that are manifested in the student's talk and actions. Yet another goal is to give feedback and adaptively respond to the student. The expectations and misconceptions associated with a main question are stored in AutoTutor's *curriculum script*. AutoTutor provides *feedback* to the learner (positive, neutral, and negative feedback), *pumps* the learner for more information ("What else"), *prompts* the learner to fill in missing words, gives *hints*, fills in missing information with *assertions*, identifies and *corrects* bad answers, *answers* learners' questions, and *summarizes* answers. As the learner expresses information over many turns, the information in the 3 to 7 sentences of an expected answer is eventually covered and the question is answered. During the process of supplying the ideal answer, the learner periodically articulates misconceptions and false assertions. If these misconceptions have been anticipated in advance and incorporated into the program, AutoTutor provides the learner with information to correct the misconceptions. Therefore, as the learner expresses information over the turns, this information is compared to expectations and misconceptions, and AutoTutor formulates its dialogue moves in a fashion that is sensitive to the learner input.

AutoTutor does its best to handle questions posed by the learner. However, somewhat surprisingly, available research has revealed that students rarely ask questions in classrooms, human tutoring sessions, and Auto-Tutor sessions (Graesser & Olde, 2003; Graesser & Person, 1994). The rate of learner questions is 1 question per 6 to 7 hours in a classroom environment and 1 per 2 minutes in tutoring. This is disappointing news from the standpoint of a pedagogical theory that emphasizes curiosity and active inquiry. However, there is a silver lining. This characteristic of human–tutor interaction makes it easier to build a dialogue-based intelligent tutoring system such as AutoTutor. It is not computationally feasible to interpret any arbitrary input of the student from scratch and to construct a mental space that adequately captures what the learner has in mind. Instead the best that AutoTutor can do is perform conceptual pattern-matching operations that compare student input with expectations. Fortunately, the prevailing tutorial activities between humans is compatible with what currently can be handled computationally within AutoTutor.

AutoTutor uses Latent Semantic Analysis (LSA) as its primary conceptual pattern-matching algorithm when evaluating whether student input matches the expectations and misconceptions. LSA is a high-dimensional statistical technique that measures the conceptual similarity of any two pieces of text (Bauer et al., chap. 7, this volume; Foltz, Gilliam, & Kendall, 2000; Kintsch, 1998; Landauer & Dumais, 1997; Landauer, Foltz, & Laham, 1998). The size may vary from being a single word to a sentence, paragraph, or lengthier document. A cosine is calculated between the LSA vector associated with Expectation E (or Misconception M) and the vector associated with learner input I. Expectation E (or Misconception M) is scored as covered if the match between E or M and the learner's text input I meets some threshold, which has varied between .40 and .85 in previous instantiations of AutoTutor (Graesser et al., 2000; Olde, Franceschetti, Karnavat, Graesser, & Tutoring Research Group, 2002). As the threshold parameter increases, the learner needs to be more precise in articulating information and thereby cover the expectations.

Suppose that there are five key expectations in an ideal answer that the tutor wants to cover in an answer to a question. AutoTutor directs the dialogue in a fashion that finesses the students to articulate each of these expectations. AutoTutor directs the dialogue through prompts, hints, and embedded three-dimensional simulations that are targeted for particular expectations. AutoTutor stays on topic by completing the subdialogue that covers Expectation E before starting a subdialogue on another expectation. For example, suppose an answer requires this expectation: *The force of impact will cause the car to experience a large forward acceleration.* The following family of prompts is available to encourage the student to articulate particular content words in the expectation:

1. The impact will cause the car to experience a forward _____?
2. The impact will cause the car to experience a large acceleration in what direction? _____.
3. The impact will cause the car to experience a forward acceleration with a magnitude that is very _____?
4. The car will experience a large forward acceleration after the force of _____?
5. The car will experience a large forward acceleration from the impact's _____?
6. What experiences a large forward acceleration?

The particular prompts that are selected are those that fill in missing information if answered successfully. That is, the dialogue management component adaptively selects hints, prompts, and targeted three-dimensional simulations in an attempt to achieve pattern completion. The expectation is covered when enough of the ideas underlying the content words in the expectation are articulated by the student so that the LSA threshold is met or exceeded.

Once again we believe that these dialogue mechanisms of AutoTutor are both computationally manageable and similar to what human tutors do. Human tutors cannot deeply comprehend all of the contributions of students, most of which are imprecise, vague, fragmentary, incomplete, and ungrammatical (Graesser et al., 1995). The best that most human tutors can do is compare student input to anticipated good answers and misconceptions. The repertoire of anticipated content grows incrementally with tutoring experience. Comparisons between student input and anticipated content are approximate and scruffy, rather than precise and tidy. LSA provides a suitable algorithm for such comparison operations. Moreover, the Expectation and Misconception Tailored (EMT) dialogue moves of AutoTutor and most human tutors are not particularly sophisticated from the standpoint of ideal tutoring strategies that have been proposed in the fields of education and artificial intelligence (Graesser et al., 1995). Graesser and colleagues videotaped over 100 hours of naturalistic tutoring, transcribed the data, classified the speech act utterances into discourse categories, and analyzed the rate of particular discourse patterns. These analyses reveal that human tutors rarely implement intelligent pedagogical techniques such as bona fide Socratic tutoring strategies, modeling-scaffolding-fading, reciprocal teaching, frontier learning, building on prerequisites, or diagnosis/remediation of deep misconceptions (Collins, Brown, & Newman, 1989; Palincsar & Brown, 1984; Sleeman & Brown, 1982). These sophisticated techniques are summarized in Table 8.2. Instead of implementing these and many other sophisticated tutoring strategies, tutors tend to coach students in constructing explanations according to the EMT dialogue patterns (Strategy 1 in Table 8.2). The EMT dialogue strategy is substantially easier to implement computationally than are the sophisticated tutoring strategies. On this dimension, the computational and psychological solutions are perfectly compatible.

TABLE 8.2
Pedagogical Strategies of Human Tutors and Ideal Tutors

Strategies	Explanations
Expectation and misconception tailored dialogue	The tutor coaches the student to articulate expectations and corrects student misconceptions that are manifested in the dialogue. This is the most common strategy that most human tutors implement.
Socratic tutoring	The tutor asks the student illuminating questions that lead the student to discover and correct his or her own knowledge deficits in a self-regulated fashion.
Modeling-scaffolding-fading	The tutor first models a desired skill, then has the student perform the skill while the tutor provides feedback and explanation, and finally fades from the process until the student performs the skill all on his or her own.
Reciprocal teaching	This is a form of modeling-scaffolding-fading that encourages the student to implement strategies of asking questions, answering self-generated questions, articulating explanations, and summarizing content.
Frontier learning and zone of proximal development	The tutor selects problems and gives guidance that slightly extends the boundaries of what the student already knows or has mastered.
Building on prerequisites	Prerequisite concepts and skills are covered in the session before moving on to more complex problems and tasks that require mastery of the prerequisites.
Diagnosis and remediation of deep misconceptions	The tutor diagnoses deep misconceptions that can explain many of the errors and missing information manifested in the student's performance. These deep misconceptions are corrected after they are diagnosed.

Adapting to Learner Emotions

We are in the process of developing a version of AutoTutor that perceives and responds to learner emotions in addition to the learner's knowledge states. AutoTutor is augmented with sensing devices and signal processing algorithms that classify learners' affective states. Emotions are classified on the basis of dialogue patterns during tutoring, the content covered, facial expressions, body posture, mouse haptic pressure, and keyboard pressure. This recent project has two specific objectives. First, AutoTutor analyzes patterns of facial, body, and dialogue activity that arise while interacting with AutoTutor and classifies this input into basic affect states (such as confusion, frustration, boredom, interest, excitement, and insight). Second, we investigate whether learning gains and learners' impressions of AutoTutor are influenced by dialogue moves of AutoTutor that are sensitive to the learners' emotions. For example, if the student is extremely frustrated, AutoTutor presumably should give a good hint or prompt that directs the student in a more positive learning trajectory. If the student is bored, AutoTutor should give more engaging, challenging, and motivating problems. If the student is absorbed and happy, AutoTutor should be minimally invasive and stay out of the student's way.

There is already some evidence that emotions might be intimately interwoven with complex learning. We recently conducted an experiment in which we observed six different affect states (frustration, boredom, flow, confusion, eureka, and neutral) that potentially occur during the process of learning introductory computer literacy with AutoTutor (Craig, Graesser, Sullins, & Gholson, in press). The participants were 34 low-domain-knowledge college students. Expert judges recorded emotions that learners apparently were experiencing at random points during the interaction with AutoTutor. Observational analyses revealed significant relationships between learning gains (posttest–pretest scores on multiple-choice tests) and the affective states of boredom ($r = -.39$), flow ($r = .29$), and confusion ($r = .33$). Correlations with eureka ($r = .03$) and frustration ($r = -.06$) were near zero.

These results fit some available theoretical frameworks that interrelate emotions and cognition. The positive correlation between confusion and learning is somewhat provocative, but is actually consistent with a model that assumes that *cognitive disequilibrium* is one precursor to deep learning (Graesser & Olde, 2003; Otero & Graesser, 2001). Cognitive disequilibrium occurs when the learner experiences contradictions, discrepancies, novel input, obstacles to goals, decision deadlocks, and major knowledge gaps. Both cognitive activities and emotions are experienced until equilibrium is restored. The findings that learning correlates negatively with boredom and positively with flow are consistent with predictions from Csikszentmihalyi's (1990) analysis of flow experiences. Conscious flow occurs when the student is so absorbed in the material that time disappears, fatigue disappears, and extraneous interruptions get unnoticed. Experiences of eureka were much too rare in the experiment; there was only one recorded eureka experience in 17 total hours tutoring among the 34 students.

At this point in the project, we have assembled and installed most of the emotion-sensing technologies with AutoTutor. We have analyzed the components, features, and representations of each of the sensing technologies (i.e., dialogue patterns during tutoring, content covered, facial expressions, body posture, mouse haptic pressure, and keyboard pressure). Software is currently being developed to interpret the input. These channels include (a) the AutoTutor log file with speech acts of student and tutor turns, as well as knowledge states achieved from the tutorial dialogue; (b) the body posture pressure measurement system purchased from Tekscan; (c) the upper facial sensor device developed by Roz Picard's Affective Computing Lab at MIT (Kapoor & Picard, 2002; Picard, 1997); (d) a haptic pressure sensor for the mouse (supplied by MIT); and (e) a keyboard pressure sensor purchased from Tekscan. Affect states are interpreted and/or classified on the basis of these five input channels of information. Computational models are being explored to perform these emotion analyses. These models have quantitative foundations in Bayesian, hidden Markov, neural network, and/or dynamical systems, but are substantially more complex than the standard architectures.

EMPIRICAL EVALUATIONS OF AUTOTUTOR

AutoTutor should be declared a success to the extent that it meets various performance criteria. Four criteria have been considered in our previous evaluations of AutoTutor. One type is technical and is not addressed in this chapter. In essence, do particular computational modules of Auto-Tutor produce output that is valid and meets the intended technical specifications? We are satisfied, for example, that our LSA component performs conceptual pattern-matching operations almost as well as human judges (Graesser, Hu, & McNamara, in press; Graesser et al., 2000; Olde et al., 2002) and that our speech act and question classifier has a high degree of accuracy (Olney et al., 2003). A second type of evaluation assesses the quality of the dialogue moves produced by AutoTutor. That is, to what extent are AutoTutor's dialogue moves coherent, relevant, and smooth? A third criterion is whether AutoTutor produces learning gains. A fourth criterion is whether learners like interacting with AutoTutor. This section briefly presents what we know so far about the second and third types of evaluation.

Expert judges have evaluated AutoTutor with respect to conversational smoothness and the pedagogical quality of its dialogue moves (Person, Graesser, Kreuz, Pomeroy, & Tutoring Research Group, 2001). The experts' mean ratings lean to the positive end of the rating scales on conversational smoothness and pedagogical quality, but there is room to improve in the naturalness and pedagogical effectiveness of its dialogue. One intriguing evaluation has been a *bystander Turing test* on the naturalness of AutoTutor's dialogue moves (Person, Graesser, & Tutoring Research Group, 2002). In these studies, there was a random selection of tutor moves in the tutorial dialogues between students and AutoTutor. Six human tutors (from the tutor pool on computer literacy at the University of Memphis) were asked to fill in what they would say at these random points. At each of these random tutor turns, the corpus contained what the human tutors generated and what AutoTutor generated. A group of computer literacy students was asked to discriminate between dialogue moves generated by a human versus a computer; in fact half were by human and half were by computer. The results surprisingly reveal that the bystander students were unable to discriminate whether particular dialogue moves had been generated by a computer versus a human. The d' discrimination scores were near zero.

These results of the bystander Turing test support the claim that AutoTutor is a good simulation of human tutors. AutoTutor manages to have productive and reasonably smooth conversations, although it does not completely understand what the student expresses. There is an alternative interpretation, however, which is just as interesting. Perhaps tutorial dialogue is not highly constrained, so the tutor has a high degree of latitude on what can be said without disrupting the conversation. In essence, there might be a large landscape of options on what the tutor can say at most points in the dialogue. The conversations are flexible and resilient, not fragile.

Evaluations of tutoring systems on learning gains is perhaps the most important performance criterion. It is well established that one-to-one human tutoring is a powerful method of promoting learning (Cohen, Kulik, & Kulik, 1982; Corbett, 2001), although the vast majority of the human tutors have moderate domain knowledge and little or no training in pedagogy or tutoring. These unaccomplished human tutors enhanced learning with an effect size of .4 standard deviation units (called sigmas), which translates to approximately an improvement of half a letter grade. According to Bloom (1984), accomplished human tutors can produce effect sizes as high as 2 sigma in basic mathematics. However, the magnitude of this effect is suspect because only two studies have investigated the impact of accomplished tutors on learning gains. In the arena of computer tutors, intelligent tutoring systems with sophisticated pedagogical tactics, but no natural language dialogue, produce effect sizes of approximately 1 sigma in the topics of algebra, geometry, and quantitative physics (Corbett, 2001; VanLehn et al., 2002). Learning gains from tutors have been most pronounced on subject matters that are quantitative, with precise, clear-cut answers.

AutoTutor has been evaluated on learning gains in several experiments on the topics of computer literacy (Graesser et al., 2004; Graesser, Moreno et al., 2003; Person, Graesser, Bautista, Mathews, & Tutoring Research Group, 2001) and conceptual physics (Graesser, Jackson et al., 2003; VanLehn et al., 2004). The results of nine experiments have been quite positive. Previous versions of AutoTutor have produced gains of .2 to 1.5 sigma (a mean of .8) depending on the learning performance measure, the comparison condition (either pretest scores or a control condition, in which the learner reads the textbook for an equivalent amount of time as the tutoring session), the subject matter, and the version of AutoTutor. Approximately a dozen measures of learning have been collected in these assessments on the topics of computer literacy and physics, including: (a) multiple-choice questions on shallow knowledge that tap definitions, facts, and properties of concepts; (b) multiple-choice questions on deep knowledge that tap causal reasoning, justifications of claims, and functional underpinnings of procedures; (c) essay quality when students attempt to answer challenging problems; (d) a cloze task, which has subjects fill in missing words of texts that articulate explanatory reasoning on the subject matter; and (e) performance on problems that require problem solving. These results place previous versions of AutoTutor somewhere between an unaccomplished human tutor and an intelligent tutoring system. Moreover, one recent evaluation of physics tutoring remarkably reported that the learning gains produced by accomplished human tutors in computer-mediated communication were equivalent to the gains produced by AutoTutor (VanLehn et al., 2004). It is informative to note that the largest learning gains from AutoTutor have been on deep reasoning measures, rather than measures of shallow knowledge. AutoTutor's problems and dialogue facilities were designed to target deep reasoning, so this result was quite expected.

One persistent question is, what is it about AutoTutor that facilitates learning? For example, is it the dialogue content or animated agent that explains the learning gains? What roles do motivation and emotions play over and above the cognitive components? We suspect that the animated conversational agent will fascinate some students and possibly be more motivating. Learning environments have only recently had animated conversational agents with facial features synchronized with speech and, in some cases, appropriate gestures (Cassell & Thorisson, 1999; Johnson et al., 2000). Many students are fascinated with an agent that controls the eyes, eyebrows, mouth, lips, teeth, tongue, cheekbones, and other parts of the face in a fashion that is meshed appropriately with the language and emotions of the speaker (Picard, 1997). The agents provide an anthropomorphic human–computer interface that simulates having a conversation with a human. This is exciting to some, frightening to a few, annoying to others, and so on. There is some evidence that these agents tend to have a positive impact on learning or on the learner's perceptions of the learning experience, compared with speech alone or text controls (Atkinson, 2002; Moreno, Mayer, Spires, & Lester, 2001). However, additional research is needed to determine the precise conditions, agent features, and levels of representation that are associated with learning gains. According to Graesser, Moreno et al. (2003), it is the dialogue content, not the speech or animated facial display, that influences learning, whereas the animated agent can have an influential role on motivation (positive, neutral, or negative). As expressed in Graesser, Moreno et al. (2003), "the medium is not the message—the message is the message." Learning apparently is facilitated by a tutor that communicates the right content at the right time to the right student, whereas motivation is influenced by the aesthetics of the animated agent. One rather provocative result is that there is a near zero correlation between learning gains and how much the students like the conversational agents (Moreno, Klettke, Nibbaragandla, Graesser, & Tutoring Research Group, 2002). Therefore, it is important to distinguish liking from learning in this area of research. Although the jury is still out on what it is exactly about AutoTutor that leads to learning gains, the fact is that students learn from the intelligent tutoring system, and some enjoy having conversations with AutoTutor in natural language.

ARCHITECTURE OF AUTOTUTOR

In the introductory chapter to this volume, Forsythe and Xavier argue that a cognitive system uses "plausible computational models of human cognitive processes as a basis for human–machine interactions." This is a distinctive conception of what an intelligent system interacting with a human should be, a stance for which we have considerable sympathy. Forsythe and Xavier propose two requirements for such a system: The system should possess an accurate model of both the user's knowledge and cognitive processes. AutoTutor's user modeling does in fact attempt to recover some of the knowledge and cognitive processes of the student learner, but it does so only statistically and coarsely, not symbolically and precisely. For example, LSA provides a statistical approximation of what the student knows about each expectation, as well as the student's overall knowledge about the subject matter. AutoTutor's conversation logs also keep track of how verbose the student is (measured as words per student turn) and how much the student takes the initiative (measured as the number of student questions). However, that is the limit on what AutoTutor knows about the student. This learner modeling of AutoTutor is intentionally minimal because of the vagueness and indeterminacy of student contributions and because we know there are limits to how much human tutors know about the students' knowledge states (Graesser et al., 1995).

The computational model underlying AutoTutor is much more refined from the standpoint of its attempts to model what human tutors do. We indeed designed AutoTutor to incorporate the cognitive representations and processes of actual human tutors. For example, the Expectation and Misconception Tailored (EMT) dialogues are distinctly modeled to match the dialogue patterns and pedagogical strategies of human tutors.

This section describes the overall computational architecture of Auto-Tutor. Given that many versions of AutoTutor have been developed and described (Graesser et al., 1999, 2001), we describe our most recent version that accommodates interactive three-dimensional simulation. This version is called AutoTutor-3D, although there is the option of removing the interactive three-dimensional simulation module. We subsequently focus on one module that is particularly at the heart of AutoTutor—namely, dialogue management.

OVERALL ARCHITECTURE OF AUTOTUTOR-3D

AutoTutor-3D is a client-server application on the Internet that uses a thin client protocol with the asynchronous transmission of small data packets (< 20 K). In a dialogue turn, a *packet* is sent from the client (i.e., the computer or workstation that one learner interacts with) to the server (the central computer that handles many learners) and back again. These packets contain the global state of the tutoring session; all of the usable history and information of the tutoring session is stored in a packet. As a consequence, the server can forget about a client after a packet has been processed.

There are two major reasons for this asynchronous architecture. The first reason appeals to computational efficiency. In an asynchronous model, the server maintains no connection information or memory resources for a particular client. Consequently, memory resource demands do not increase with the number of clients. This process closely resembles the operating system's notion of a context switch, whereby a server gives each client the impression that he or she is the only user while serving thousands of clients in the background. The second reason appeals to ease of testing. Our asynchronous system can be tested more easily because all of the current state information is explicit in a packet. This greatly facilitates unit testing, debugging, and interoperability. It should be noted that these two reasons for the packet-based asynchronous architecture are entirely computational and practical, as opposed to being motivated by theoretical cognitive mechanisms. It is doubtful that this design decision makes any sense at all from the standpoint of psychological plausibility.

The packet is represented as a binary serialized class known as the *state object*. This class implements an interface for every component of the server. These interfaces have a dual purpose: to declare what data a component needs from other components, and to create storage for a component's state for the next turn. Therefore, all of the dependencies between modules are explicit in the state object. The state object further simplifies the system by being the input and output of every component. Therefore, to have a basic grasp of the system, one only needs to understand the dependencies and data in the state object. A packet is essentially a local data structure that permits the server to reconstruct the global history of all modules in the system for that one client.

The components of the system are divided into *modules, utilities*, and the *hub*. The AutoTutor-3D server is a distributed *hub and spokes* application that may reside on multiple servers or on a single server. In the standard hub and spokes configuration, only the hub knows about the existence of the modules. Therefore, any component that provides the data specified by the state object may be interchangeably used. As stated previously, the hub receives a state object from the client and then passes the state object to various modules in a scripted order. The basic architecture concept and hub are similar to the DARPA Communicator (Xu & Rudnicky, 2000). However, in AutoTutor-3D, modules are defined by the fact that they input and output state objects, which greatly simplifies communication and interoperability between modules. Modules may call various utilities, such as LSA facilities or databases that have their own distinctive interface. The AutoTutor-3D architecture is much like a production line, in that modules each do a small bit of the work and subsequent modules are dependent on preceding ones. Just as in a production line, the modules are only interested in the work in front of them and forget about previous work. The AutoTutor-3D architecture is somewhat like a blackboard model (Anderson, 1983; Laird, Newell, & Rosenbloom, 1987), in which items are written on a blackboard and modules are only interested in particular items. However, in the present model, the blackboard gets passed from one module to the next, and when the modules are finished with the blackboard they forget about it.

There are theoretical reasons for adopting a modular architecture with packets containing state objects. The architecture emulates a modular cognitive architecture that is also contextually rich. Fodor (1983) and many others in the cognitive sciences believe that the human mind can be segregated into a set of semi-autonomous modules that perform special-purpose functions, such as visual perception, syntactic language parsing, retrieval from episodic memory, executive decisions, and so forth. At the same time, however, the input and constraints operating on each module M should be sufficiently rich and informative about other modules that module M can perform its computations intelligently. Modules that can peak at a limited snapshot of outputs from other modules are inherently limited.

To gain a more concrete understanding of our architecture, consider Fig. 8.4. The Client computer sends a state object to the Hub after the student has entered an utterance. The state object is first passed to the Language Analyzer, which segments the utterance into main clauses, parses the clauses, and assigns a speech act to each main clause (Olney et al., 2003). The Language Analyzer uses the Conexor EngLite parser (Tapananinen & Järvinen, 1997) as a utility. The modified state object is sent to the Hub, which then sends it to the Assessor. The Assessor updates the student model and produces a set of predictions about the likely effects of alternative dialogue moves on the student model. The Assessor uses LSA and the Curriculum Script database (i.e., the major content repository of main questions and dialogue moves) to update the student model and make predictions. Next the Assessor passes the updated state object to the Hub, which forwards it to the Dialogue Manager. The Dialogue Manager consults the output of the previous modules as well as the dialogue information state of the previous turn (not shown). The Dialogue Manager subsequently updates the dialogue information state of the state object and provides it with dialogue for the tutor's turn. The updated state object is passed to the Hub, which forwards it back to the client. It should be noted that the state object presented in Fig. 8.4 is highly simplified, but the process of computation is accurately specified.

It is worthwhile to point out a few technical points for those who are interested in implementing similar systems. AutoTutor-3D is written in C# and Visual Basic .NET—both languages that run atop the managed .NET Framework and Common Language Runtime (CLR). The CLR offers language-level compatibility (*Microsoft .NET Technology Overview*, n.d.). In other words, any component of AutoTutor can easily communicate with any other component as long as the component is written in a CLR-compatible language. Over 30 programming languages have CLR-compatible compilers (Ritchie, 2004), so almost any programmer can use the language of their choice to add functionality to the system. The .NET

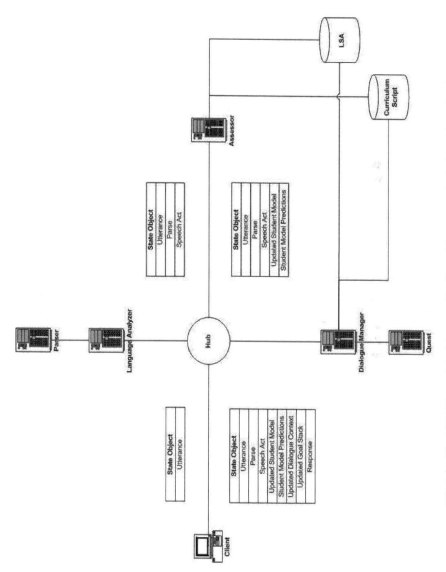

FIG. 8.4. The AT3D Network Architecture. The flow of data proceeds clockwise from the client, returning a response to the client.

Framework offers a variety of libraries, including the Remoting system that allows objects to be quickly and transparently accessed over the network and that forms the basis of the scalable infrastructure. Both the Framework and the CLR virtual machine run on Windows, Linux, Mac OS X, and other operating systems by using open source run-times such as Mono and Portable.NET.

The AutoTutor-3D server has a variety of protocol translators that convert the data stream from clients into state tables that the modules can understand. These multiprotocol personal translators are affectionately known as *muppets*. To make AutoTutor-3D compatible with a new piece of client software, regardless of the language it is written in or the way it transmits data, a programmer simply needs to write a new muppet to parse the data from the client and convert it into a state table. Each muppet can also have its own set of modules and utilities, and a muppet can be instantiated multiple times. This facility permits the construction of multiple virtual AutoTutor servers that work with the same client software, yet differ in functionality. Consequently, experimenters can quickly construct experimental conditions without altering the underlying server code and can save changes required to the modules to create the variant conditions. Currently, two muppets exist. One muppet reads raw text from a standard TCP/IP connection. The other reads partial state tables constructed by a .NET client that are transmitted through Remoting. An unlimited number of muppets can be constructed as distributed systems on the Internet become progressively more complex.

The standard AutoTutor-3D server we have developed uses four modules and two utilities. As shown in Fig. 8.4, the Hub first sends an incoming response, changed into a state table by one muppet, to the Language Analysis module. This module performs surface analyses on the input to determine what sort of speech act the student utterance is. It also performs some text segmentation to aid other modules. The next module in the sequence is the Assessor module. Using LSA and the Curriculum Script, the assessments module determines the quality of the student response with regards to the tutor's goals for the lesson. It also generates other metrics, such as the length of the response. With this information in hand, the Dialogue Manager module can draw a conversationally and pedagogically appropriate response from the curriculum script. Finally, the state table is passed to the Logger, which records the state of the system for the current turn, before being passed back to the muppet and from there to the client.

The utilities in the standard version of AutoTutor are the Curriculum script and an LSA utility. The curriculum script utility grants modules access to a script of topics and the concepts the tutor is to teach in those topics, tutor moves, correct and erroneous student responses, and common misconceptions on the topic. The LSA utility uses the LSA text similarity algorithm to determine how close a student response is to particular expectations and misconceptions about a topic. The LSA utility was trained on a large corpus of documents that are relevant to the subject matter. For the topic of physics, the corpus was a textbook and 10 articles on Newtonian physics. For the topic of computer literacy, the corpus was a textbook and 30 articles on hardware, the operating system, and the Internet.

Dialogue Manager

The Dialogue Manager is the architecture's major decision maker. Other modules provide the Dialogue Manager with information it uses to make decisions. One important input is the dialogue information state of the previous turn. This state information is not a history of all previous turns, but a summary snapshot of what information is required to successfully continue the conversation. The Dialogue Manager takes in the relevant information, updates the state object with a new dialogue information state, and produces a tutor turn for the client. However, there are multiple steps along the way.

The Dialogue Manager first receives a state object from the Hub. This state object is decompressed and translated into an internal format called a *context*. The context contains all dialogue information states and state object elements that are ever used in the Dialogue Manager's computations. In actuality, the Dialogue Manager is a confederation of submodules that work on a context. Thus, the context is the common currency for all parts of the Dialogue Manager in the same way that the state object is the common currency for AutoTutor-3D modules.

The planner chain is the first set of submodules that the context encounters. In this chain, each planner independently considers the context and suggests plans to move the dialogue forward and successfully tutor the student. Each planner considers a different kind of initiative, including a student initiative, an opportunistic alternative, and a tutor initiative. AutoTutor-3D is a mixed initiative system, which means that the student can ask questions and, to some degree, take control of the tutoring session. The student initiative planner looks for evidence of student initiative by interpreting student speech acts in the context of the dialogue. When a sufficient student initiative is detected (such as a student question), the student initiative planner pushes a plan tree on the context's plan stack. These plan trees range from question-answering subdialogues to motivational subdialogues to repetitions of previous turns. The opportunistic planner looks for opportunities to clarify or otherwise micro-adapt to the student's progress. For example, the opportunistic planner might push a plan tree to Pump (e.g., "Can you add to that?") when the student is doing well, but is not verbose. The opportunistic planner looks for instances of the student becoming confused or frustrated with the lack of progress, so the planner pushes a plan tree to let the student know how much more information the tutor is looking for. Finally, the tutor initiative planner has inbuilt knowledge of tutoring strategies and what elements a student should cover during the tutoring session. It is the tutoring initiative planner that advances the tutoring session's content in a structured way.

Once the planners have pushed their plan trees, the context is passed to a search module that performs a depth-first search against the plan trees on the plan stack. Each node in a plan tree is visited recursively. When a node in a plan tree is visited, its plan is instantiated. Plans must be instantiated because the plan trees on the plan stack are not specific recipes for action, but rather templates or intentions for action. When the plan is instantiated, a specific update rule is applied to the context, specific dialogue is generated, or both. For example, the Dialogue Manager chooses dialogue moves to maximize student learning. To do this, the Dialogue Manager uses the predictions provided by the Assessor and performs an agent-centered search (Koenig, 1996) akin to MiniMax (Winston, 1984), which is often used by artificial intelligence (AI) programs to play games such as chess. In this instance, however, the Dialogue Manager is not playing against the student, so it tries to maximize the student's score or potential for learning. A specific dialogue move is eventually chosen and added to the context, followed by a data structure in the context being updated to show that the added move has been used. Finally, the plan tree on the plan stack is advanced to the next node. Thus, the results of visitation include the dialogue to be spoken, the updated plans, and the updated context elements.

Plan trees consist of a core set of structural elements that control the flow of the visitation process, along with domain-specific plans. This core set includes sequence, iteration, alternation, terminal, and nonterminal elements. Any of these elements can be embedded in another, leading to arbitrarily complex objects. Each of these elements is both a container for plans and a plan itself. As plans, they have termination conditions that mark when the plan is complete. For example, a sequence is completed either when the plans contained within it are exhausted or some success condition is reached, which sets the plan complete. The success conditions of plans may be linked together systematically; when one plan is completed, all connected plans are simultaneously satisfied. Completed plans are popped from the plan stack. This process of plan tree traversal continues until a terminal node is visited. The terminal node is a plan to wait for student input. At this point, the context is translated back into a state object, and the state object is passed out of the Dialogue Manager.

Our Dialogue Manager has similarities to dialogue managers developed by other researchers, but there are some important differences. In systems that implement a general model of collaborative discourse, there is a great emphasis on the negotiation of plans between the agent and user (Allen et al., 1995). The goals are negotiated as well as the steps or plans to reach them. A collaboration requires that the user and system share the same goals and that they are capable of monitoring progress toward these goals. Nevertheless, we know from research on human tutoring that students rarely take the initiative, so it is the tutor that controls the lion's share of the tutoring agenda (Graesser et al., 1995). Students rarely ask information-seeking questions or introduce new topics, for example. Moreover, most students are poor judges of their own progress toward goals (Glenberg, Wilkinson, & Epstein, 1982; Weaver, 1990). For example, Person et al. (1995) reported a near zero correlation between students' answering positively to a tutor's comprehension gauging question (e.g., "Do you understand?") and the students' objective understanding of the material. Both Graesser and Person (1994) and Chi et al. (1989) reported a positive correlation between students' answering "no" to such comprehension-gauging questions and their objective understanding. The deeper students are better able to identify their knowledge deficits and say they do not understand. Tutoring is a complex activity in which speech participants have a low amount of shared knowledge and students do not judiciously control their agenda. As a consequence, tutoring is not a conversational context that is or should be collaborative and cooperative in the standard ways that are discussed in the fields of computational linguistics and discourse processing.

In the absence of student initiative, Graesser et al. (1995) found that conventional tutors rely heavily on curriculum scripts (McArthur, Stasz, & Zmuidzinas, 1990; Putnam, 1987) with topics, subtopics, example problems, and topic-specific questions. A pervasive pattern in conventional tutoring is the five-step dialogue frame (Graesser & Person, 1994; Person et al., 1995):

1. Tutor asks question
2. Student answers question
3. Tutor gives short feedback on quality of answer
4. Tutor and student collaboratively improve the quality of the answer
5. Tutor assesses student's understanding of the answer

As a reflection of conventional tutoring, AutoTutor-3D's learning goals and the plans to reach them are often set in advance. The Dialogue Manager dynamically constructs few plans; it dynamically sequences plans based on the current session, but most of those plans are prebuilt. In general models of dialogue, the purposes of utterances must be inferred and depend on the task structure. Generating such inferences is manageable in a narrow situational context, such as dialogues between callers and telephone operators or between customers and flight reservation systems. However, there is no successful general dialogue model that has successfully scaled up to handle a large class of contexts or all conversational contexts. In AutoTutor-3D, as with all conversation systems that have been successfully implemented, the purposes of nearly all types of utterances are known a priori. This greatly simplifies the process of discourse interpretation: The tutor has a loosely specified lesson plan, whereas student questions are seen as information-seeking interruptions to this plan.

Comparisons of AutoTutor-3D With Previous Dialogue Managers

AutoTutor-3D plans share similarities with previous work on dialogue modeling in computational linguistics, such as TRINDI (Larsson & Traum, 2000; Traum & Larsson, 2003; The TRINDI Consortium, 2001) and COLLAGEN (Rich & Sidner, 1998; Rich, Sidner, & Lesh, 2001). Historically, different authors have used the term *plan* in a variety of contexts, so it is worth exploring how the AutoTutor-3D notion of plan fits in this history. One distinction that has been made is the distinction between plans and recipes (Lochbaum, 1998). Recipes are merely sequences of actions, whereas plans have beliefs and desires that must be identified and that help drive the actions. The Dialogue Manager of AutoTutor-3D fits the recipe model more than the plan model, although there are vestiges of bona fide plans that are implicitly present (as opposed to being explicitly declared as goals and plans in the computer code).

The objective of the TRINDI project (The TRINDI Consortium, 2001) is to create an approach to dialogue modeling that is suitable for rapid prototyping, promoting domain portability, and accommodating varied theories of dialogue processing. To achieve these three goals, the TRINDI project focuses on information state; the information makes the dialogue distinct and supports the successful continuation of the dialogue. The information state approach is general enough to accommodate dialogue systems from the simplest finite-state script to the most complex Belief-Desire-Intention (BDI) model (Larsson & Traum, 2000; Traum & Larsson, 2003). AutoTutor-3D follows the information state theory of dialogue modeling, which requires:

1. Description of the informational components that constitute the information state.
2. Formal representations of these components.
3. External dialogue that triggers the update of the information state.
4. Internal update rules that select dialogue moves and update the information state.
5. Control strategy for selecting update rules to apply given a particular information state.

AutoTutor-3D uses a context as its model of dialogue information state. Based on a student's utterance, the resulting speech act classification of that utterance, and the current context (as defined in the previous section), the Dialogue Manager updates the context and generates dialogue for the tutor turn. The control strategy consists of both the recursive search over plan trees and the local rules that are applied when a plan is instantiated.

COLLAGEN (Rich & Sidner, 1998; Rich et al., 2001) is based on a theory of discourse structure (Grosz & Sidner, 1986; Lochbaum, 1998) that distinguishes among three kinds of structure: linguistic, intentional, and attentional. Linguistic structure is the sequence of utterances, whereas intentional structure is the structure of purposes, and attentional state is the focus of attention that records salient elements of the discourse at a particular point. The Dialogue Manager of AutoTutor-3D recognizes linguistic structure (how utterances aggregate into discourse segments) first by interpreting speech acts in the context of the dialogue. Given a speech act, there are three possible relations of that act to the current discourse segment purpose (DSP; Grosz & Sidner, 1986). Either the speech act continues the existing DSP, ends the existing DSP, or begins a new DSP. The Dialogue Manager determines this by looking at both the individual act and its role in the current plan. For example, an information-seeking speech act like a student question will start a new DSP, whose purpose is to deliver the sought after information to the student. Noninformation-seeking contributions will either continue the existing DSP or end the current DSP depending on whether a plan is satisfied. Shifts in DSP are communicated to the user via discourse markers and canned expressions.

Grosz and Sidner (1986) identified two relations in the intentional structure: dominance (satisfying X partly contributes to the satisfaction of Y) and satisfaction precedence (X must be satisfied before Y). The Auto-Tutor-3D plan stack models dominance and precedence relations. For example, in answering a problem, the student must demonstrate mastery of all elements of the problem. Each of these elements stands in a dominance relationship to the problem; coverage of each contributes to the partial coverage of the problem. Precedence likewise is evident in plan trees for question/answer/clarification dialogues in which the answer must be given before clarification.

Existing implementations of COLLAGEN are still only an approximation of the discourse theory of Grosz and Sidner (1986) because the attentional state is modeled by a stack of plans rather than a stack of focus spaces (Rich et al., 2001). The Dialogue Manager of AutoTutor-3D is similar in this respect: Although the Dialogue Manager does use the context as a cache approach to attentional state (Grosz & Gordon, 1999; Walker, 1996), it also uses a stack of plan trees. The major difference between Collagen plan trees and our Dialogue Manager plan trees is that the former include information about who speaks, the particular conversational participant who is performing what act. This information is wired in more directly in the separate roles and machinery of the tutor versus learner in AutoTutor.

FINAL COMMENTS

The vision of having a computer communicate with humans in natural language was entertained shortly after the computer was invented. Weizenbaum's (1966) Eliza program was the first conversation system that was reasonably successful, popular, and widely used. Eliza simulated a Rogerian client-centered psychotherapist. Like a typical Rogerian therapist, Eliza tried to get the patient to do the talking by asking the patient questions about the patient's verbal contributions. Eliza detected keywords and word combinations that triggered rules, which in turn generated Eliza's responses. The only intelligence in Eliza was the stimulus–response knowledge captured in production rules that operated on keywords and performed syntactic transformations. What was so remarkable about Eliza is that 100 or 200 simple production rules could often create an illusion of comprehension, although Eliza had no depth. It is conceivable that an Eliza with 20,000 well-selected rules might exhibit a responsive, intelligent, compassionate therapist, but no one ever tried.

Unfortunately, by the mid-1980s, most researchers in cognitive science and AI were convinced that the prospect of building a good conversation system was well beyond the horizon. The chief challenges were (a) the inherent complexities of natural language processing; (b) the unconstrained, open-ended nature of world knowledge; and (c) the lack of research on lengthy threads of connected discourse. In retrospect, this extreme pessimism about discourse and natural language technologies was premature. There have been a sufficient number of technical advances in the last decade for researchers to revisit the vision of building dialogue systems. The primary technical breakthroughs came from the fields of computational linguistics, information retrieval, cognitive science, AI, and discourse processes. The representation and processing of connected discourse is much less mysterious after two decades of interdisciplinary research in discourse processing (Graesser, Gernsbacher, & Goldman, 2003). The field of computational linguistics has produced an impressive array of lexicons, syntactic parsers, semantic interpretation modules, and dialogue analyzers that are capable of rapidly extracting information from naturalistic text for information retrieval, machine translation, and speech recognition (Allen, 1995; Harabagiu, Maiorano, & Pasca, 2002; Jurafsky & Martin, 2000; Voorhees, 2001). These advancements in computational linguistics represent world knowledge either symbolically, statistically, or a hybrid of these two foundations. For instance, Lenat's CYC system represents a large volume of mundane world knowledge in symbolic forms that can be integrated with a diverse set of processing architectures (Lenat, 1995). The world knowledge contained in an encyclopedia can be represented statistically in high-dimensional spaces such as LSA. An LSA space provides the backbone for statistical metrics that score essays as reliably as experts in English composition (Foltz et al., 2000; Bauer et al., chap. 7, this volume).

Natural language dialogue facilities are not expected to do a reasonable job in all conversational contexts. It depends on the subject matter, knowledge of the learner, expected depth of comprehension, and expected sophistication of the dialogue strategies. We doubt that natural language dialogue facilities will be impressive when the subject matter requires mathematical or analytical precision, when the knowledge level of the user is high, and when the user would like to converse with a humorous, witty, or illuminating partner. A natural language dialogue facility would not be well suited to an eCommerce application that manages precise budgets that a user carefully tracks. Nor would a computerized dialogue system be a good spouse, parent, comedian, or confidant. However, a natural language dialogue facility is feasible in applications that have the following characteristics: (a) imprecise verbal content, (b) low to medium user knowledge about a topic, (c) low to medium common ground (shared knowledge) between the user and the system, and (d) earnest literal replies.

AutoTutor fits the bill for tutoring students on qualitative domains when the common ground between the tutor and learner is low or moderate rather than high. If the common ground is high, then both dialogue participants (i.e., the computer tutor and the learner) can expect a higher level of precision of mutual understanding and therefore a higher risk of failing to meet each other's expectations. We believe that automated tutoring systems with natural language dialogue will be disappointing to the extent that they fail to have one or more of these four characteristics.

ACKNOWLEDGMENTS

The Tutoring Research Group (TRG) is an interdisciplinary research team comprised of approximately 35 researchers from psychology, computer science, physics, and education (visit http://www.autotutor.org). The research on AutoTutor was supported by the National Science Foundation (SBR 9720314, REC 0106965, REC 0126265, ITR 0325428) and the DoD Multidisciplinary University Research Initiative (MURI) administered by ONR under grant N00014-00-1-0600. Any opinions, findings, conclusions, or recommendations expressed in this chapter are those of the authors and do not necessarily reflect the views of DoD, ONR, or NSF. Kurt VanLehn, Carolyn Rose, Pam Jordan, and others at the University of Pittsburgh collaborated with us in preparing AutoTutor materials on conceptual physics.

REFERENCES

Aleven, V., & Koedinger, K. R. (2002). An effective metacognitive strategy: Learning by doing and explaining with a computer-based Cognitive Tutor. *Cognitive Science, 26*, 147–179.

Allen, J. F. (1995). *Natural language understanding*. Redwood City, CA: Benjamin/Cummings.

Allen, J. F., Schubert, L. K., Ferguson, G., Heeman, P., Hwang, C. H., Kato, T., Light, M., Martin, N. G., Miller, B. W., Poesio, M., & Traum, D. R. (1995). The TRAINS project: A case study in defining a conversational planning agent. *Journal of Experimental and Theoretical AI, 7*, 7–48.

Anderson, J. R. (1983). *The architecture of cognition*. Cambridge, MA: Cambridge University Press.

Anderson, J. R., Corbett, A. T., Koedinger, K. R., & Pelletier, R. (1995). Cognitive tutors: Lessons learned. *Journal of the Learning Sciences, 4*, 167–207.

Atkinson, R. K. (2002). Optimizing learning from examples using animated pedagogical agents. *Journal of Educational Psychology, 94*, 416–427.

Bloom, B. S. (1984). The 2 sigma problem: The search for methods of group instruction as effective as one-to-one tutoring. *Educational Researcher, 13*, 4–16.

Bransford, J. D., Brown, A. L., & Cocking, R. R. (Eds.). (2000). *How people learn: Brain, mind, experience, and school*. Washington, DC: National Academy Press.

Cassell, J., & Thorisson, K. (1999). The power of a nod and a glance: Envelope vs. emotional feedback in animated conversational agents. *Applied Artificial Intelligence, 13*, 519–538.

Chi, M. T., Bassock, M., Lewis, M. W., Reimann, P., & Glaser, R. (1989). Self-explanations: How students study and use examples in learning to solve problems. *Cognitive Science, 13*, 145–182.

Chi, M. T. H., de Leeuw, N., Chiu, M., & LaVancher, C. (1994). Eliciting self-explanations improves understanding. *Cognitive Science, 18*, 439–477.

Chi, M. T. H., Siler, S. A., Jeong, H., Yamauchi, T., & Hausmann, R. G. (2001). Learning from human tutoring. *Cognitive Science, 25*, 471–533.

Cohen, P. A., Kulik, J. A., & Kulik, C. C. (1982). Educational outcomes of tutoring: A meta-analysis of findings. *American Educational Research Journal, 19*, 237–248.

Collins, A., Brown, J. S., & Newman, S. E. (1989). Cognitive apprenticeship: Teaching the craft of reading, writing, and mathematics. In L. B. Resnick (Ed.), *Knowing, learning, and instruction: Essays in honor of Robert Glaser* (pp. 453–494). Hillsdale, NJ: Lawrence Erlbaum Associates.

Corbett, A. T. (2001). Cognitive computer tutors: Solving the two-sigma problem. *Proceedings of the 8th International Conference on User Modeling 2001* (pp. 137–147). New York: Springer-Verlag.

Craig, S. D., Graesser, A. C., Sullins, J., & Gholson, B. (in press). Affect and learning: An exploratory look into the role of affect in learning. *Journal of Educational Media.*

Csikszentmihalyi, M. (1990). *Flow: The psychology of optimal experience.* New York: HarperRow.

Fodor, J. A. (1983). *The modularity of mind.* Cambridge, MA: MIT Press.

Foltz, P. W., Gilliam, S., & Kendall, S. (2000). Supporting content-based feedback in on-line writing evaluation with LSA. *Interactive Learning Environments, 8,* 111–128.

Fox, B. (1993). *The human tutorial dialogue project.* Hillsdale, NJ: Lawrence Erlbaum Associates.

Glenberg, A. M., Wilkinson, A. C., & Epstein, W. (1982). The illusion of knowing: Failure in the self-assessment of comprehension. *Memory & Cognition, 10,* 597–602.

Graesser, A. C., Gernsbacher, M. A., & Goldman, S. (Eds.). (2003). *Handbook of discourse processes.* Mahwah, NJ: Lawrence Erlbaum Associates.

Graesser, A. C., Hu, X., & McNamara, D. S. (in press). Computerized learning environments that incorporate research in discourse psychology, cognitive science, and computational linguistics. In A. F. Healy (Ed.), *Experimental cognitive psychology and its applications: Festschrift in honor of Lyle Bourne, Walter Kintsch, and Thomas Landauer.* Washington, DC: American Psychological Association.

Graesser, A. C., Jackson, G. T., Mathews, E. C., Mitchell, H. H., Olney, A., Ventura, M., et al. (2003). Why/AutoTutor: A test of learning gains from a physics tutor with natural language dialogue. In R. Alterman & D. Hirsh (Eds.), *Proceedings of the 25th Annual Conference of the Cognitive Science Society* (pp. 1–6). Mahwah, NJ: Lawrence Erlbaum Associates.

Graesser, A. C., Lu, S., Jackson, G. T., Mitchell, H., Ventura, M., Olney, A., & Louwerse, M. M. (2004). AutoTutor: A tutor with dialogue in natural language. *Behavioral Research Methods, Instruments, and Computers, 36,* 180–193.

Graesser, A. C., Moreno, K., Marineau, J., Adcock, A., Olney, A., Person, N., & Tutoring Research Group. (2003). AutoTutor improves deep learning of computer literacy: Is it the dialogue or the talking head? In U. Hoppe, F. Verdejo, & J. Kay (Eds.), *Proceedings of Artificial Intelligence in Education* (pp. 47–54). Amsterdam: IOS Press.

Graesser, A. C., & Olde, B. A. (2003). How does one know whether a person understands a device? The quality of the questions the person asks when the device breaks down. *Journal of Educational Psychology, 95,* 524–536.

Graesser, A. C., & Person, N. K. (1994). Question asking during tutoring. *American Educational Research Journal, 31,* 104–137.

Graesser, A. C., Person, N. K., Harter, D., & Tutoring Research Group. (2001). Teaching tactics and dialogue in AutoTutor. *International Journal of Artificial Intelligence in Education, 12,* 257–279.

Graesser, A. C., Person, N. K., & Magliano, J. P. (1995). Collaborative dialogue patterns in naturalistic one-on-one tutoring. *Applied Cognitive Psychology, 9,* 359–387.

Graesser, A. C., VanLehn, K., Rose, C., Jordan, P., & Harter, D. (2001). Intelligent tutoring systems with conversational dialogue. *AI Magazine, 22,* 39–51.

Graesser, A. C., Wiemer-Hastings, K., Wiemer-Hastings, P., Kreuz, R., & Tutoring Research Group. (1999). AutoTutor: A simulation of a human tutor. *Journal of Cognitive Systems Research, 1,* 35–51.

Graesser, A. C., Wiemer-Hastings, P., Wiemer-Hastings, K., Harter, D., Person, N. K., & Tutoring Research Group. (2000). Using latent semantic analysis to evaluate the contributions of students in AutoTutor. *Interactive Learning Environments, 8,* 129–148.

Gratch, J., Rickel, J., Andre, E., Cassell, J., Petajan, E., & Badler, N. (2002). Creating interactive virtual humans: Some assembly required. *IEEE Intelligent Systems, 17,* 54–63.

Grosz, B. J., & Gordon, P. C. (1999). Conceptions of limited attention and discourse focus. *Computational Linguistics, 25*(4), 617–624.

Grosz, B. J., & Sidner, C. L. (1986). Attention, intentions, and the structure of discourse. *Computational Linguistics, 12*(3), 175–204.

Harabagiu, S. M., Maiorano, S. J., & Pasca, M. A. (2002). Open-domain question answering techniques. *Natural Language Engineering, 1,* 1–38.

Johnson, W. L., Rickel, J. W., & Lester, J. C. (2000). Animated pedagogical agents: Face-to-face interaction in interactive learning environments. *International Journal of Artificial Intelligence in Education, 11,* 47–78.

Jurafsky, D., & Martin, J. H. (2000). *Speech and language processing: An introduction to natural language processing, computational linguistics, and speech recognition.* Upper Saddle River, NJ: Prentice-Hall.

Kapoor, A., & Picard, R. (2002). Real-time, fully automated upper facial feature tracking. *Proceedings of the 5th International Conference on Automated Face and Gesture Recognition,* Washington, DC.

Kintsch, W. (1998). *Comprehension: A paradigm for cognition.* New York: Cambridge University Press.

Koenig, S. (1996). Agent-centered search: Situated search with small look-ahead. In *Proceedings of the Thirteenth National Conference on Artificial Intelligence* (p. 1365). Menlo Park, CA: American Association for Artificial Intelligence.

Laird, J. E., Newell, A., & Rosenbloom, P. (1987). SOAR: An architecture for general intelligence. *Artificial Intelligence, 33,* 1–64.

Landauer, T., & Dumais, S. (1997). An answer to Plato's problem: The latent semantic analysis theory of acquisition, induction, and representation of knowledge. *Psychological Review, 104,* 2111–2240.

Landauer, T., Foltz, P. W., & Laham, D. (1998). An introduction to latent semantic analysis. *Discourse Processes, 25,* 259–284.

Larsson, S., & Traum, D. (2000). Information state and dialogue management in the TRINDI dialogue move engine toolkit. *Natural Language Engineering, 6*(3–4), 323–340.

Lenat, D. B. (1995). CYC: A large-scale investment in knowledge infrastructure. *Communications of the ACM, 38,* 33–38.

Lochbaum, K. E. (1998). A collaborative planning model of intentional structure. *Computational Linguistics, 24*(4), 525–572.

Massaro, D. W., & Cohen, M. M. (1995). Perceiving talking faces. *Current Directions in Psychological Science, 4,* 104–109.

McArthur, D., Stasz, C., & Zmuidzinas, M. (1990). Tutoring techniques in algebra. *Cognition and Instruction, 7,* 197–244.

Microsoft .NET Technology Overview. (n.d.). Accessed April 15, 2004, at http://msdn. microsoft.com/netframework/technologyinfo/overview/default.aspx

Moore, J. D. (1995). *Participating in explanatory dialogues.* Cambridge: MIT Press.

Moreno, K. N., Klettke, B., Nibbaragandla, K., Graesser, A. C., & Tutoring Research Group. (2002). Perceived characteristics and pedagogical efficacy of animated conversational agents. In S. A. Cerri, G. Gouarderes, & F. Paraguacu (Eds.), *Proceedings of the Sixth International Conference on Intelligent Tutoring Systems* (pp. 963–971). Berlin: Springer-Verlag.

Moreno, R., Mayer, R. E., Spires, H. A., & Lester, J. C. (2001). The case for social agency in computer-based teaching: Do students learn more deeply when they interact with animated pedagogical agents? *Cognition & Instruction, 19,* 177–213.

Olde, B. A., Franceschetti, D. R., Karnavat, A., Graesser, A. C., & Tutoring Research Group. (2002). The right stuff: Do you need to sanitize your corpus when using Latent Semantic Analysis? In W. D. Gray & C. D. Schunn (Eds.), *Proceedings of the 24th Annual Meeting of the Cognitive Science Society* (pp. 708–713). Mahwah, NJ: Lawrence Erlbaum Associates.

Olney, A., Louwerse, M. M., Mathews, E. C., Marineau, J., Mitchell, H. H., & Graesser, A. C. (2003). Utterance classification in AutoTutor. In J. Burstein & C. Leacock (Eds.), *Building educational applications using natural language processing: Proceedings of the Human Language Technology—North American Chapter of the Association for Computational Linguistics Conference 2003 Workshop* (pp. 1–8). Philadelphia: Association for Computational Linguistics.

Otero, J., & Graesser, A. C. (2001). PREG: Elements of a model of question asking. *Cognition & Instruction, 19*, 143–175.

Palincsar, A. S., & Brown, A. (1984). Reciprocal teaching of comprehension-fostering and comprehension-monitoring activities. *Cognition & Instruction, 1*, 117–175.

Person, N. K., Graesser, A. C., Bautista, L., Mathews, E., & TRG. (2001). Evaluating student learning gains in two versions of AutoTutor. In J. D. Moore, C. L. Redfield, & W. L. Johnson (Eds.), *Artificial intelligence in education: AI-ED in the wired and wireless future* (pp. 286–293). Amsterdam: OIS Press.

Person, N. K., Graesser, A. C., Kreuz, R. J., Pomeroy, V., & Tutoring Research Group. (2001). Simulating human tutor dialogue moves in AutoTutor. *International Journal of Artificial Intelligence in Education, 12*, 23–39.

Person, N. K., Graesser, A. C., & Tutoring Research Group. (2002). Human or computer? AutoTutor in a bystander Turing test. In S. A. Cerri, G. Gouarderes, & F. Paraguacu (Eds.), *Proceedings of the Sixth International Conference on Intelligent Tutoring Systems* (pp. 821–830). Berlin: Springer-Verlag.

Person, N. K., Kreuz, R. J., Zwaan, R., & Graesser, A. C. (1995). Pragmatics and pedagogy: Conversational rules and politeness strategies may inhibit effective tutoring. *Cognition and Instruction, 13*(2), 161–188.

Picard, R. W. (1997). *Affective computing.* Cambridge: MIT Press.

Putnam, R. T. (1987). Structuring and adjusting content for students: A live and simulated tutoring of addition. *American Educational Research Journal, 24*, 12–48.

Rich, C., & Sidner, C. L. (1998). COLLAGEN: A collaborative manager for software interface agents. *User Modeling and User-Adapted Interaction, 8*, 315–350.

Rich, C., Sidner, C. L., & Lesh, N. (2001). COLLAGEN: Applying collaborative discourse theory to human-computer interaction. *AI Magazine, 22*(4), 15–25.

Rickel, J., & Johnson, W. L. (1999). Animated agents for procedural training in virtual reality: Perception, cognition, and motor control. *Applied Artificial Intelligence, 13*, 343–382.

Ritchie, B. (2004). *.NET languages.* Accessed April 15, 2004, at http://www12.brinkster.com/brianr/languages.aspx

Sleeman, D., & Brown, J. (Eds.). (1982). *Intelligent tutoring systems.* New York: Academic Press.

Traum, D., & Larsson, S. (2003). The information state approach to dialogue management. In J. van Kuppevelt & R. Smith (Eds.), *Current and new directions in discourse and dialogue* (pp. 325–353). Dordrecht: Kluwer.

The TRINDI Consortium. (2001). *The TRINDI book.* Gothenburg: Gothenburg University, Department of Linguistics.

VanLehn, K., Jones, R. M., & Chi, M. T. H. (1992). A model of the self-explanation effect. *Journal of the Learning Sciences, 2*, 1–60.

VanLehn, K., Lynch, C., Taylor, L., Weinstein, A., Shelby, R., Schulze, K., et al. (2002). Minimally invasive tutoring of complex physics problem solving. In S. A. Cerri, G. Gouarderes, & F. Paraguacu (Eds.), *Proceedings of the Sixth International Conference on Intelligent Tutoring Systems 2002* (pp. 367–376). Berlin: Springer-Verlag.

Voorhees, E. (2001). The TREC question answering track. *Natural Language Engineering, 7,* 361–378.

Walker, M. A. (1996). Limited attention and discourse structure. *Computational Linguistics, 22*(2), 225–264.

Weaver, C. A., III. (1990). *Calibration and assessment of comprehension.* Unpublished doctoral dissertation, University of Colorado, Boulder, CO.

Weizenbaum, J. (1966). ELIZA—A computer program for the study of natural language communication between man and machine. *Communications of the ACM, 9,* 36–45.

Winston, P. H. (1984). *Artificial intelligence.* Reading, MA: Addison-Wesley.

Xu, W., & Rudnicky, A. (2000, May). *Task-based dialog management using an agenda.* Presented at the ANLP/NAACL Workshop on Conversational Systems, Somerset, NJ.

CHAPTER NINE

Cognitive and Computational Models in Interactive Narrative

R. Michael Young
North Carolina State University

The number and type of computer system using interactive three-dimensional interfaces continue to grow as the processing power of commercial graphics cards increases. Although a significant portion of the most popular virtual world applications are in the $9 billion per year interactive entertainment market, it is now common for users to interact with virtual worlds in applications ranging across simulation, training, education, and social interaction. Many of these environments, especially those focused on entertainment, exploit informal adaptations of narrative techniques drawn from conventional narrative media in their design. Much of that work, however, conflates two central aspects of narrative structure that limit (a) the range of techniques that can be brought to bear on the narrative's generation, and (b) the range of narrative structures that can be generated for a given environment. These two aspects of narrative are the structure of story and the structure of narrative discourse.

In this chapter, I describe an approach to the generation of narrative-oriented interaction within virtual worlds that treats story and discourse as its two foundational elements. In this approach, I adapt models of narrative from narrative theory, computational linguistics and cognitive psychology, integrating these approaches with techniques from artificial intelligence to create interactive intelligent narrative virtual worlds systems. The following section describes related work from both computer science and narrative theory. Next, I give a brief introduction to Mimesis, the system used to create interactive virtual world applications, and describe the processes Mimesis uses for generating story-world and discourse-level narrative structure. Then I describe several examples of Mimesis plan fragments and show the means used to generate effective narrative structure from them. Finally, I characterize the role of story and discourse plans in several virtual world applications built using Mimesis, give a short description of the benefits of this approach to managing interactivity with our system, and describe work in progress that builds on story and discourse structure.

RELATED WORK

Story and Discourse in Narrative Theory

The work described here adapts and extends existing work in artificial intelligence (AI) to account for specific story-oriented applications within three-dimensional virtual environments. This approach is based on concepts and methods first developed in narrative theory. Narratologists have provided an extensive characterization of narrative and its elements, describing the fundamental building blocks used by an author to create a compelling story (Bal, 1998; Chatman, 1990; Rimmon-Keenan, 2002). Narrative-theoretic approaches, however, are analytic in nature and do not directly lend themselves to a computational model capable of being used in a generative capacity. A central challenge of any computational approach that seeks to operationalize concepts from narrative theory is to determine appropriate methods to translate concepts derived from analysis into concrete, formal models capable of being put to use in the creation of an interactive virtual environment.

Although a broad range of approaches to the analysis of narrative exists, our work makes use of a structure that divides a narrative into two fundamental parts—the *story* and the *discourse* (Chatman, 1990; Emmot, 1999)—and we construct distinct representations and tools to manage each. From a narratological perspective, a *story* consists of a complete conceptualization of the world in which the narrative is set. This includes all the characters, locations, conditions, and actions or events that take place during the story's temporal extent. Two fundamental components of a narrative—its plot and characters—are defined within the story.

Distinct from the story, but closely tied to it, is the narrative *discourse*. Our discourse model represents those elements responsible for the *telling* of the story, rather than containing the story elements. This notion of discourse differs from its conventional meaning. Specifically, the discourse we are generating is not communication between the user and the characters within the story. Rather, it is concerned with that communication between the system and user that conveys the storyline (which may include character dialogue as individual elements).

In my approach, the construction of a narrative discourse can be divided into two conceptual aspects. One aspect is the determination of both the content of the discourse and its organization. To compose a narrative discourse, an author makes choices about those elements from the story to include in the story's telling and those elements to leave out. Further, the author determines additional information about the story world to convey to the reader (e.g., properties of relevant objects, internal properties of the story's characters). Finally, the author must organize the discourse, determining what is to be told first, what second, and so on, and how the subparts of the discourse should be arranged so as to achieve the intended communicative effects on a reader.

A second aspect to the generation of narrative discourse is the selection of the specific communicative resources to be used to convey the story's elements to the reader. In a three-dimensional virtual environment, these resources include a range of media—from voice-over narration to three-dimensional camera control to background music. The work that we describe here focuses on the generation of coherent, cinematic camera control, although our results are applicable to aspects of communicative actions across media.

Computational Approaches to the Generation of Narrative

There are many examples of narrative-oriented interactive computer games, but the majority of this work involves interaction with storylines that are carefully crafted by game designers at design time rather than generated automatically at run time. In contrast, several AI researchers have addressed the problem of narrative generation using techniques related to the approach we define here. Szilas (2001), for instance, used a bipartite system composed of (a) a narrative logic component used to generate story elements, and (b) a virtual narrator used essentially to filter the story elements to determine which actions are to be communicated to the user. Beyond this filtering process, however, no reasoning is performed to determine appropriate discourse structure.

Similarly, Cavazza and his collaborators (Cavazza, Charles, & Mead, 2002) focused primarily on story structure, rather than the discourse structure, using a hierarchical plan-based model similar to the one we describe next to control the characters within their narrative systems. In their recent work (Charles et al., 2003), they used a novel heuristic search algorithm for creating plans; the structures that they create, however, are roughly equivalent in representational expressiveness to those used in their previous work.

Unlike plan-based approaches, Sgouros' (1999) work used an iterative approach to generate story actions. In his system, the action that occurs at a given moment is selected by a three-step process. First, aspects of the story-world context are considered by a rule set that generates a set of potential actions that could occur next. Second, these actions are filtered based on contextual weighting factors, and a single action is selected. Finally, the action is carried out or resolved within the system. This approach has two limitations. First, the creation of story elements is essentially opportunistic; actions are selected one at a time at the moment of their execution. Because there is no means for considering the relationships between current action choices and the execution of potential future actions, the degree of coherence of story actions may be quite limited.

Second, like much of the work related to narrative generation, Sgouros' work focuses on the generation of story-world actions to the exclusion of a sophisticated model of narrative discourse. Explicit description of the unfolding storyline is handled through prescripted text presented via pop-up dialogue boxes, prescripted audio clips, and character animations viewed via a user-controlled camera.

GENERATING STORY AND DISCOURSE

Action and change are central to the nature of narrative. In most narratives, story-world action is initiated by the narrative's characters as they attempt to achieve their individual and collective goals. Goals play a role at the discourse level as well. In film narratives, for example, a cinematographer acts in a goal-directed manner to build the cinematic discourse, intentionally composing shots and shot sequences to effectively communicate unfolding story action. The goal-oriented focus in operation at both the story and discourse levels in conventional narrative media motivates us to use a plan-based model of the control of activity within virtual worlds. We have constructed an architecture called Mimesis that uses this model to generate plans for controlling characters operating within a narrative as well as controlling media resources used for telling the narrative. We briefly describe the Mimesis architecture here. More details can be found in Young et al. (2004), Young and Riedl (2003), and Riedl, Saretto, and Young (2003).

The Mimesis system integrates a suite of intelligent control tools with a number of existing virtual world environments and conventional programming environments (Young et al., 2004). In this chapter, we restrict our discussion to applications built using Unreal Tournament (UT)—a commercially available three-dimensional graphical game engine. Although UT is well suited as an engine for building conventional three-dimensional interactive game titles, the representation of the environments that it models does not match well with those typically used by AI researchers. Like most virtual world engines, UT's internal representation is *procedural*—it does not utilize any formal or declarative model of the characters, setting, or actions of the stories that take place within it. Consequently, direct integration of intelligent software components is not straightforward.

To facilitate this integration, Mimesis overrides UT's default mechanisms for controlling its virtual environment, using instead a client/server architecture in which low-level control of the game environment is performed by a customized version of the game engine (called the *MWorld*), and high-level reasoning about narrative structure and user interaction is performed remotely by a suite of intelligent agents (called *Mimesis Components [MCs]*). The architecture is presented in Fig. 9.1 and described briefly here. In later sections, we characterize several example virtual world applications built for and controlled by the Mimesis architecture.

Within Mimesis, the MCs act collectively as a narrative server, determining the narrative elements of the user's experience within the virtual world. The MCs are responsible for

- the generation of a story (in the form of a *story-world plan* characterizing all character actions to be performed within the environment).
- the generation of a *discourse plan* characterizing the media-specific communicative actions used to convey the story to the user, and the maintenance of a coherent narrative experience in the face of unanticipated user activity.

At startup, the MWorld sends a message to the MCs requesting a story. This request identifies a goal state for the story, the MWorld's current world state, and the library of actions that are available for characters in the MWorld's world. The MCs then generate a story-world plan (Young, 1999) that describes all the actions that the characters will execute in the story world. It sends this plan as input to the discourse planner, which generates a specification of the communicative action (in our case, three-dimensional camera shot specifications) that will convey the elements of the story plan to the user. These two plans are integrated and passed to the *Execution Manager*, the Mimesis component responsible for driving the story's action. From the combined story and discourse plan, the Execution Manager builds a directed acyclic graph whose nodes represent individual actions in the plans and whose arcs define temporal constraints between actions' orderings. The Execution Manager encodes nodes from

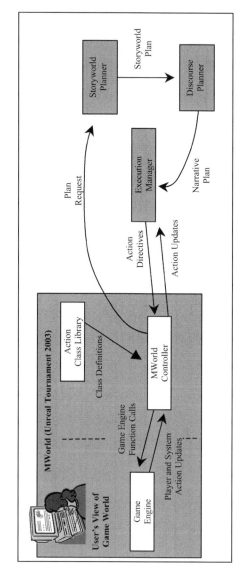

FIG. 9.1. The Mimesis system architecture shown with an MWorld built using Unreal Tournament 2003 as a sample game engine. Individual gray boxes indicate components described later. Within the MWorld component, the vertical dashed line represents the boundary between code created by the Mimesis developer (to the right of the line) and that created by the game engine developer (to the left of the line).

the graph into XML messages and transmits these messages to the MWorld for execution as the action corresponding to each node becomes ready for execution. The MWorld translates the XML messages by using a one-to-one mapping from the action types of the nodes in the Execution Manager's graph to game engine functions and from the parameters of each action to instances of game engine objects to construct function calls that will drive the appropriate animations and state changes within the virtual world. The structures created and used by these elements are described in more detail in the following sections.

Creating the Story-World Plan

The plan structures that we employ are produced by the Decompositional Partial Order Causal Link (DPOCL) planner (Young, Pollack, & Moore, 1994). DPOCL plans are composed of steps corresponding to the actions that characters carry out within a story; in DPOCL, each step is defined by a set of preconditions, the conditions in the world that must hold immediately prior to the step's execution for the step to succeed, and a set of effects, the conditions in the world that are altered by the successful execution of the action. In addition to a set of steps, a DPOCL plan contains a set of temporal constraints defining a partial temporal ordering on the execution of the plan's steps and a set of causal links connecting pairs of steps. Two steps—s_1 and s_2—are connected by a causal link with associated condition c (written $s_1 \rightarrow^c s_2$) just when c is an effect of s_1 and a precondition of s_2, and the establishment of c by s_1 is used in the plan to ensure that c holds at s_2.

Further, DPOCL plans contain information about the hierarchical structure of a plan, similar to the representation used by hierarchical task network (HTN) planners (Sacerdotti, 1977). Because action sequences within narratives are often episodic—that is, because they follow common patterns of action—these hierarchical structures are particularly amenable to representing story fragments. A DPOCL plan fragment is shown in Fig. 9.2.

Adopting a plan-based model of story structure allows the system to compose new stories in response to novel starting states or goal specifications, or to customize a story based on a user's interests and knowledge. The use of DPOCL plans has two additional advantages. First, the formal properties of the planning algorithm guarantee that the plans contain adequate structure to effectively control the story world's virtual environment. Specifically, DPOCL plans are provably sound—that is, when executed, each action in them is guaranteed to execute correctly, and the plans are guaranteed to achieve their top-level goals. These properties of DPOCL make the plans it produces well-suited for use in controlling the

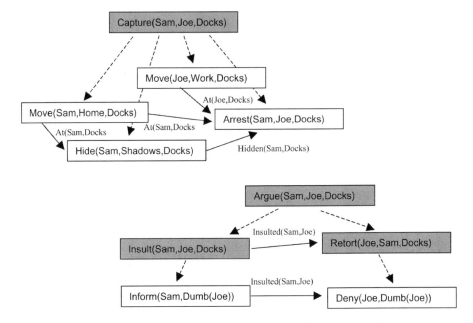

FIG. 9.2.   A DPOCL plan fragment meant to be part of a larger story-plan structure. White boxes indicate primitive actions, gray boxes indicate abstract actions,
dashed arcs indicate subplan relationships, and solid arcs indicate causal links
from effects of one action to the preconditions of another. Temporal ordering is
indicated in rough left to right order.

execution of a virtual environment (Cavazza, Charles, & Mead, 2002;
Young, 1999b).[1]

A second benefit to the use of plans to drive a narrative is in the plan's
structural correspondence to a user's mental model of the story it defines.
Recent research (Ratterman et al., 2002; Young, 1999a) suggests that hierarchical causal link plans like DPOCLs, as well as the techniques used by
the DPOCL algorithm to create them, make for effective models of human
plan reasoning. Our empirical studies indicate that the core elements of
DPOCL plans match up with the models of narrative structure defined and
validated by psychologists (Christian & Young, 2004). By using a formal
representation for story structure that corresponds to users' models of
stories, we can make more direct predictions about the users' understanding of the stories we create. We rely on this correspondence when designing techniques to create specific narrative effects, such as the models of
suspense discussed in the following sections.

---

[1]Not all narrative plans require sound structure, however. For instance, stories in which a
hero's plan fails contain story elements that are unsound.

Creating the Narrative's Discourse

A narrative system must not only create engaging story-world plans, it must use its resources to tell the story effectively. In this chapter, we discuss one particular strategy used in the effective creation of a narrative: Building narrative discourse involves the central task of determining the content and organization of a sequence of camera shots that film the action unfolding within a story world.

In the work described here, we build on our previous research on the generation of natural language discourse to generate discourse plans for controlling an automated camera that is filming the unfolding action within a three-dimensional story world. To create these discourse plans, we use a discourse planning system named Longbow (Young, Moore, & Pollack, 1994). The Longbow planner is built on the core DPOCL algorithm, and so the two planners' representations are quite similar. In our approach, three-dimensional camera shots and shot sequences are viewed as planned, intentional action whose effects obtain in the cognitive state of the user. Individual camera shots are treated as primitive communicative actions, multishot sequences and cinematographic idioms are characterized using hierarchical plan operators, and, as in conventional discourse planning, plan structure that specifies the communicative content of a discourse is created to achieve particular effects on the mental state of the user.

Conventional discourse planners take as input a set of propositions intended to be conveyed to the user of a system, along with a model of the user's existing knowledge of the domain of discourse and a library of plan operators describing both the primitive communication actions available to the planner (e.g., typically speech acts such as INFORM or REQUEST) and definitions for a set of abstract actions and their subplan schemas, sometimes referred to as *recipes*. Abstract operators often specify rhetorical structure (Mann & Thompson, 1988; Moore & Paris, 1993) in a discourse (e.g., when one part of a discourse stands as evidence for the claim set forth in a second part of a discourse), and their subplan schemas specify how more primitive collections of communicative actions can be combined to achieve the abstract act's communicative effects.

There are several important ways that the task of narrative discourse generation—and our approach to it—differ from the task of discourse generation in conventional contexts. In our approach, the propositional content that the narrative discourse planner receives as input refers not just to relations that hold in the domain of discourse, but also to propositions describing the structure of the story-world plan. For instance, in addition to generating discourse which conveys that a character has a gun, the narrative discourse must also convey the action of the character using the gun to rob a bank. The task of the discourse planner is, in part, to generate camera action sequences that convey the execution of story-world plan actions to the user.

Beyond the requirement to communicate a different type of content in narrative discourse, our approach to the generation of plans for three-dimensional narrative discourse addresses two key problems. First, the narrative discourse that we generate must contain structure beyond that which simply mirrors the structure of the actions executed in the story world. Cinematic discourse contains both rhetorical structure, aimed at conveying propositions about the story world to a user, and idiomatic structure, mirroring the use of patterns for shot composition used in film (Arijon, 1976; Monaco, 1981). Our plan operators capture these aspects of discourse structure and combine them effectively to tell the story.

Consider the schematic of a hierarchical discourse plan operator shown here:

```
establish_scene_change(current_action)
constraints:
    previous_action(current_action,previous_action)
    location(previous_action,previous_location)
    current_action_being_filmed(current_action)
    location(current_action,current_location)
    not(equal(current_location,previous_location))
    participants(current_action, agent1, agent2)
    location(agent1,current_location)
    location(agent2,current_location)
    surrounding_location(exterior,current_location)
    not(equal(exterior, previous_location))
substeps:
    establish_exterior_location(exterior)
    establish_character_location(agent1,agent1)
ordering:
    establish_exterior_location < establish_character_location
```

This operator provides an abstract description of the communicative actions involved in conveying a scene change that also involves a change of location. The constraints of the operator, represented as a set of logical clauses, bind variables (indicated in italics) to entities within the story world and its plan. The operator is applicable only when all its constraints can be satisfied. These constraints serve to (a) pick out the previously filmed action, and the location for both this past action and the next action to be filmed; (b) ensure that the locations of the two actions are distinct; (c) pick out the two characters involved in the new action to be filmed and ensure that they are both located in the same place; and, (d) finally, pick out a larger location that surrounds the characters' location, checking to ensure that this surrounding location is not the same as the location of the previous action.

The substeps created in the discourse plan involve filming the surrounding location and filming the location of the two characters. A temporal ordering imposed by the operator requires the shot filming the surrounding location to occur before the shot that shows the location of the characters. These two substeps are abstract, and a plan that contains them will make context-specific choices about the ways in which they can be further refined, eventually creating specific constraints for camera actions. For instance, an `establish_character_location` action might be refined into one long shot in which both characters and their setting can be seen. Alternatively, it might be refined into a sequence of two shots—one medium shot where the first character can be seen, with her location visible in the background, and a shot of the second character, with the first character visible in the background. By placing the appropriate constraints on the operators that create the hierarchical structure of the discourse plan, we can effectively embed the rhetorical structure of a film into the plan for filming the story world's actions.

A second key problem addressed by our approach to discourse planning is the temporal integration of the story-world and discourse-level plans. The actions in discourse plans for narrative in virtual worlds, unlike actions in plans for textual narrative, must execute. Camera actions for panning, tracking, fading, and so on all require time to play out, a physical location from which the camera films, physical objects that must be included or excluded from the field of view, and so on (Bares & Lester, 1998). A particularly complicating aspect of this is that these camera actions must execute in the same temporal and spatial environment as the objects of the story that they must convey to the user. A knowledge representation for narrative discourse must take this shared environment into account or risk creating suboptimal (or even inconsistent) plans.

For instance, consider the case where camera action C_1 is responsible for filming action s_1 and camera action C_2 is responsible for filming action s_2. If s_1 completes its execution prior to s_2 beginning, then C_1 must complete its execution prior to C_2. In plans where the successful execution of C_1 depends on the user knowing some property of the domain first established in C_2, the inconsistency must be detected and remedied. If s_1 and s_2 happen concurrently in the same spatial location, then C_1 and C_2 could be replaced by a single appropriately positioned shot C_3. Without considering their co-location/co-occurrence, a planner would not be able to generate this option.

To allow the operator writer to specify the temporal relationships between the execution of camera actions and the story-world actions that they must film, primitive camera actions in the discourse planner can be annotated with temporal constraints between the two plans.

These constraints relate the start and end times of the camera actions to the start and end times of the actions they film. The constraints are listed in Table 9.1. Constraints can be composed using logical operators (e.g., *and*, *not*, *or*) to create complex temporal relationships between filming and acting.

By relating a precise computational model of action to a mental model of narrative, we are able to make predictions about the cognitive and affective consequences to a user that is experiencing the execution of specific kinds of plan structures. For instance, we have been exploring the role of plans and planning on suspense, an essential property of conventional narrative forms such as the film or novel. Although suspense can be of many forms and arise in many kinds of situations, we have focused on sus-

TABLE 9.1

Temporal Constraints Relating Primitive Camera Actions
to the Execution of the Story-World Actions That They Film

Constraint	*Explanation*
begin_before_start(*swa*)	Begin current action any time before start of story-world action *swa*.
begin_at_start(*swa*)	Begin current action at the same time as the start of story-world action *swa*.
begin_after_start(*swa*)	Begin current action any time after the start of story-world action *swa*.
begin_before_end(*swa*)	Begin current action any time before the end of story-world action *swa*.
begin_at_end(*swa*)	Begin current action at the same time that story-world action *swa* ends.
begin_after_end(*swa*)	Begin current action any time after the end of story-world action *swa*.
end_before_start(*swa*)	End current action any time before the start of story-world action *swa*.
end_at_start(*swa*)	End current action at the same time as the start of story-world action *swa*.
end_after_start(*swa*)	End current action any time after the start of story-world action *swa*.
end_before_end(*swa*)	End current action any time before the end of story-world action *swa*.
end_at_end(*swa*)	End current action at the same time that story-world action *swa* ends.
end_after_end(*swa*)	End current action any time after story-world action *swa* ends.

Note.   In these actions, *swa* is a variable bound to the story-world action being filmed.

pense deriving from a user's knowledge of the unfolding plans of a narrative's characters. In particular, we focus on suspense arising from the anticipation of future events and their consequences on the goals of the narrative's protagonist (whether that protagonist is the user or another character within the narrative).

Suspense and Narrative Plans

Recent work in cognitive psychology (Comisky & Bryant, 1982; Gerrig & Bernardo, 1994; Ohler & Neidling, 1996; Trabasso & Sperry, 1985) has considered the role of narrative structure in the creation and maintenance of this type of suspense in film and literature. Gerrig and Bernardo (1994) suggested that people who read fiction act as problem solvers, continuously looking for solutions to the plot-based dilemmas faced by the characters in a story world. Their work indicates that a reader's suspense is dependent on the number of solutions he or she can find to the protagonist's problem: Suspense is greater when there are fewer solutions accessible.

Our approach approximates the problem-solving activity that a user performs when seeking solutions to plot-related problems as planning in a space of story-world plans. Our cognitive model employs the model of planning as refinement search defined by Khambamphati, Knoblock, and Yang (1995). A refinement planning algorithm represents the space of plans that it searches using a directed graph; each node in the graph is a (possibly partial) plan. An arc from one node to the next indicates that the second node is a refinement of the first (i.e., the plan associated with the second node is constructed by repairing some flaw present in the plan associated with the first node). In typical refinement search algorithms, the root node of the plan space graph is the empty plan containing just the initial state description and the list of goals that together specify the planning problem. Nodes in the interior of the graph correspond to partial plans, and terminal nodes in the graph are identified with completed plans (solutions to the planning problem) or plans that cannot be further refined due, for instance, to inconsistencies within the plans that the algorithm cannot resolve.

We have successfully used this model to approximate the plan-based reasoning performed by readers when understanding instructional texts (Young, 1999a). By characterizing the space of plans that a user might consider when solving problems faced by a protagonist at a given point in a plot, the model can be used to make predictions about the amount of suspense a user will experience at that point. To do this, we model the set of beliefs held by a user as she experiences an unfolding narrative. At any point in the narrative, a user will have a set of beliefs about that state of the story world, a set of beliefs about the goals of the story's protagonist, and a set of beliefs about the action operators available to the characters acting within the story. These three elements are used to create a DPOCL planning problem, the specification used as input to DPOCL to create a plan (in this case, a plan that solves the protagonist's goals given the story world's current state as known by the user). DPOCL's refinement search algorithm creates not just a single plan that solves the protagonist's goals, but the space of possible plans given the problem specification. To the extent that DPOCL's configuration mirrors the user's planning process, this plan space approximates the space of solutions considered by the user when searching for solutions to the protagonist's current problems (see Fig. 9.3).

To determine the level of suspense a user may experience at a particular point in a story, we have developed and empirically evaluated a model

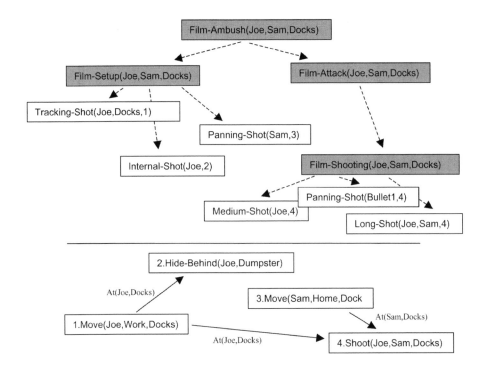

FIG. 9.3. A narrative plan fragment showing both DPOCL and Longbow plan structures. The DPOCL plan fragment, shown below the dividing line, represents a simple plan for an ambush between two characters, Joe and Sam. The Longbow plan fragment is shown above the horizontal divider and represents the plan for controlling the camera. For clarity, DPOCL plan steps have been given unique numeric labels. Arguments to camera actions specify both the story-world objects to be filmed as well as the story-world action during which the filming must occur (indicated by corresponding numeric labels).

(Christian & Young, 2004) that relates characteristics of this space to the psychological results described earlier. For instance, when there are a large number of successful solution plans at the leaves of the plan space graph, our model correctly predicts that a user's experience of suspense would be lower than when there were few successful solutions to the current planning problem.

Additional features of this space (e.g., the ratio of failed plans to total plans) also prove to be an element of an effective prediction of suspense. As a result of initial experimental results, we are considering extending the representation of plans to include additional features, such as the perceived probabilities of success for each of the plans, and are evaluating those new features for their role in the problem-solving process of users.

Results from this work also suggest means by which suspense can be increased or decreased. The features of a plan space that a user considers differ depending on the planning problem she is attempting to solve. By controlling what facts the user believes about the story world at a given time (e.g., by generating camera sequences that explicitly convey some facts while explicitly eliding others), the system can, in effect, define a planning problem with the suspense properties appropriate for each point in the narrative.

In general, the use of plan-based models of task reasoning serve to predict inferences about future world states, future event occurrence, and/or potential conflicts between the actions of multiple agents and their collective goals. Although the models of suspense provided by cognitive psychologists match well with techniques for creating plans and plan spaces, it may be that other cognitive phenomena (e.g., reasoning about action choice, task-based decision making, human–machine collaboration) can be approximated by the computational tools we use here. As such these phenomena might be candidates for modeling in a similar manner.

THE CHALLENGES OF INTERACTIVITY
IN STORY AND DISCOURSE

Control and Coherence

Our work described earlier takes an idealized stance in which the user is not accounted for except as a passive observer. Although this assumption is entirely valid for conventional narrative media such as film or literature, the assumption is almost always invalid for narrative-oriented virtual worlds. A key feature of these worlds is the level of interactivity that they offer the user. The ability to step into the narrative world and play a character in the story, to take substantive action within the unfolding story, is a key distinguishing feature of virtual worlds and stories.

A central issue in the development of effective and engaging interactive narrative environments is the balance between coherence and control. The understandability of any narrative is determined, in part, by its coherence—that is, by the user's ability to comprehend the relationships between the events in the story, both within the story world (e.g., the causal or temporal relations between actions) and in the story's telling (e.g., the selection of camera sequences used to convey the action to the user). Dramatists often refer to narrative as having a premise or point; stories are told for a reason, and much of our comprehension of a story involves the construction of cognitive models that predict or explain these relationships. Systems that construct actions for telling a story should respect the story's coherence by clearly linking each action in the narrative to its overall structure.

The degree of engagement by a user within an interactive narrative lies, to a great extent, with the user's perceived degree of control over her character as she operates within the environment. The greater the user's sense of control over her character, the greater will be her sense of presence (Lombard & Ditton, 1997)—that is, the sense that she is part of the story world and free to pursue her own goals and desires. Unfortunately, control and coherence are often in direct conflict in an interactive narrative system. To present a coherent narrative, the actions within an interactive narrative are carefully structured (either at design time by human designers, in the case of conventional computer games, or at run time by intelligent systems, like the one described here) so that actions at one point in the story lead clearly to state changes necessitated by actions occurring at subsequent points in the story. When users exercise a high degree of control within the environment, it is likely that their actions will change the state of the world in ways that may interfere with the causal dependencies between actions as intended within a storyline.

Conventional forms of narrative (e.g., film and novel) resolve the issue of coherence versus control by completely eliminating control; the audience is a passive observer. Computer game developers, in contrast to film makers, introduce interactivity in their systems, but carefully limit the control exercised by the user by designing the environment so that the user's choices for action at any point reduce to a small set of options moving the user through a predefined branching structure. In the remainder of this chapter, we discuss a technique used in the Mimesis architecture called *narrative mediation*, which allows a degree of control and coherence that lies between that of computer games and conventional narrative media.

Managing Interactivity

As described before, Mimesis drives the action within its story world based on the structure of a plan produced by a narrative planner. As users issue commands for their characters to perform actions within the story world, these actions have the potential to undo conditions in the world that are critical to the success of actions in the narrative plan that have not yet been executed. Consequently, before carrying out directives from the user, the corresponding actions must be checked against the narrative plan to determine how they fit with the plan's structure. This is accomplished by relating each input command from the user's keyboard or mouse activity to some predefined action α specified by a plan operator.

Each action α performed by the user is automatically characterized in one of three ways with respect to the unexecuted portion of the plan. One possibility is that α is *constituent* to the plan—α matches an action prescribed by the narrative plan for execution by the user, in which case the user is doing exactly the action that the system desires her to do to perform that portion of the storyline. The second possibility is that α is *consistent* with the plan—α is not constituent, and none of the effects of α interact with any of the plan's remaining structure. For example, it may be consistent if the user rotates her character in a circle to orient herself spatially before walking out of a room, as long as her act of walking out of the room is part of the narrative and is successfully performed during the appropriate time frame. The third possibility is that α is *exceptional*—α is not constituent, and one or more of α's effects threaten the conditions in the world required by future agent actions. Specifically, an exception occurs whenever a user attempts to perform some action α, where some effect $\neg e$ of α threatens to undo some causal link $s_1 \to^e s_2$ between two steps, s_1 and s_2, with condition e, where s_1 has occurred prior to α and s_2 has yet to occur.

If a user performs an exceptional action, the effects of the exception on the virtual world undoes the condition of at least one causal link in the plan, invalidating some or all of the plan's subsequent structure. It is the responsibility of the system to detect exceptions when they arise and to respond accordingly in a manner that balances the need to preserve the coherence of the narrative with the need to preserve the user's sense of control. Within the Mimesis system, response to exceptions occurs in one of two ways. Either the system allows the exception to occur and restructures the narrative plan midstory, or it prevents the exception from actually executing, in effect coercing the user into compliance with the existing plan structure. We refer to this process of exception detection and response as *narrative mediation*.

The most straightforward response to an exception is via intervention. Typically, the success or failure of an action within a virtual environment is determined by function calls that approximate the physical rules of the underlying story world (e.g., setting a nuclear reactor's control dial to a particular setting may cause the reactor to overload). However, when a user's action would violate one of the story plan's constraints, Mimesis can intervene, causing the action to fail to execute. In the reactor example, this might be achieved by surreptitiously substituting an alternate set of action effects for execution, one in which the natural outcome is consistent with the existing plan's constraints. A control dial momentarily jamming, for instance, will preserve the apparent consistency of the user's interaction while also maintaining safe energy levels in the story world's reactor system.

The second response to an exception is to adjust the narrative structure of the plan to accommodate the new activity of the user. The resolution of the conflict caused by the exception may involve only minor restructuring of the narrative—for instance, selecting a different, but compatible location for an event when the user takes an unexpected turn down a new path. Accommodation may involve more substantive changes to the story plan, however, and these types of modifications can be computationally expensive. For instance, should a user instigate a fight with a character that is intended to be a key ally later in the story or unintentionally destroy a device required to rescue a narrative's central character, considerable replanning is required on the part of the MCs' narrative planner.

To handle exceptions in an interactive narrative system, the narrative planner analyzes its plans prior to execution. Analysis begins at the start of the plan and proceeds forward in time in discrete steps corresponding to the execution of each action in the plan. Because the plan structure contains explicit representations of all causal and temporal dependencies between the plan's steps, it is possible to examine each world state between actions, looking for points where enabled user actions (i.e., actions whose preconditions for execution are satisfied at that point in the plan) can threaten the plan structure. When potential exceptions are identified, the planner weighs the computational cost of replanning required by accommodation against the potential cost incurred when intervention breaks the user's sense of agency in the virtual world. The reader is encouraged to see Riedl, Saretto, and Young (2003) for a discussion of the approach used for narrative mediation within Mimesis, including techniques for precomputing responses to exceptions to increase system response time.

Narrative mediation has already proved useful with story-world actions; the efficacy of the technique comes, in part, because of the nature of user actions that might raise exceptions. Exceptions can typically be identified with discrete and instantaneous user activity (e.g., firing a laser blaster, starting a car engine), rather than with continuous, substantial duration (e.g., capturing a space station, driving to Pittsburgh). Further, most story-world actions that a user will perform are going to be consistent rather than exceptional. Because of these two features, exceptions are straightforward to identify and rarely place high computational demands on the system. In contrast, detecting and responding to exceptions at the level of narrative discourse is more difficult. Camera actions are inherently continuous, making it difficult to determine what the current effects of a camera movement will be. Further, camera actions happen almost all the time inside most game-related virtual worlds.

To date, we have avoided this issue by using mediation techniques to contexts where a user's camera control is explicitly limited (e.g., in cut scenes where the user has a menu for controlling camera views). To address the problem, however, we are building a component that monitors features of a user's field of view (e.g., what is the level of lighting, what entities are in or out of view) and the motion of the camera to anticipate changes in camera position that may violate the structure of the discourse plan. This extension will take into account the changes in knowledge state caused by a user's choice of shot composition; by integrating this model into a discourse-level mediation scheme, we expect that techniques similar to the accommodation approach described in the previous section will be applicable. However, a discourse level equivalent to intervention seems more problematic. Because camera control is tightly coupled with a user's input actions (e.g., mouse manipulation), an approach that substitutes alternate camera control actions without disrupting a user's sense of agency in the virtual world is a challenge to define.

This issue has ramifications to broader aspects of human interaction with cognitive systems as well. Cognitive systems typically reason about activities performed both by system and user, and they may make recommendations for actions to be taken by humans. Unlike systems that operate autonomously in the absence of human users, cognitive systems often rely on the actions of their users to implement needed change in their operating environment. As such the preservation of the human's sense of agency is central; mediation techniques applied to contexts in which a more collaborative and explicit relationship exists between user and cognitive system may contribute to the sense of engagement experienced by human users.

System Performance Summary

To date we have constructed several test-bed environments for use with Mimesis; performance results from these experiments are encouraging. The number of characters in these worlds ranges from 2 to 20, including a single user. Because characters are treated by the planners like any other resource available within the story world, the number of characters or users in the story is not a limiting factor for the planner's performance. Rather, the number and complexity of the actions in the operator library are more often the determining factor in the speed of the planners' execution. We currently generate plans for several test problem domains described briefly next. These planning problems include 40 to 60 action operators in their operator libraries and goal expressions containing 5 to 15 predicates. The planning process considers roughly 3,000 alternate plans during plan generation, running in under a half second on a Pentium 4 1GHz. Typical plans that are produced contain about 60 steps. Although this length is not sufficient to capture an entire story, future tests will expand the complexity of the planning task to generate longer action sequences.

Performance for DPOCL and Longbow planning is roughly identical given comparably complex planning problems. Integration between discourse and story plans serves to improve overall performance because the addition of temporal constraints between the two plan structures can serve to filter out plans that are temporally inconsistent earlier in the planning process, cutting down on the extra planning work that would have been performed on the unexecutable plans.

Performance of the narrative mediation component has also been encouraging, although precomputing and caching techniques are required for this technique to be feasible. In our approach, a recursive algorithm is run on the initially created narrative plan to determine all potential responses to exceptions that might arise. For those exceptions that require accommodation, replanning is done at that point in the plan, determining appropriate new plans to put in place should the exception arise. These new plans are then analyzed for exceptions, and so on until a time limit is reached. This approach requires a greater startup time, but improves overall system response time as exceptions arise. Results of these computations are cached in the MWorld, facilitating quick lookup. When the MCs' processor load is low during execution—for instance, when the user is idle—additional precomputing can be done, anticipating responses to exceptions at a greater look-ahead depth.

SUMMARY AND CONCLUSIONS

In this chapter, we set out a basic approach to the modeling of narrative in interactive virtual worlds. This approach adopts a bipartite model of narrative as story and discourse in which story elements—plot and character—are defined in terms of plans that drive the dynamics of a virtual environment. Narrative discourse elements—the narrative's communicative actions—are defined in terms of discourse plans whose communicative goals include conveying the story-world plan's structure. To ground the model in computational terms, we have provided examples from the Mi-

(a)   (b)   (c)

FIG. 9.4. The images show example worlds controlled by Mimesis, including (a) a virtual tour of the Monterey Bay Aquarium, (b) a futuristic bank robbery story, and (c) the great hall of a medieval castle.

mesis system (Fig. 9.4), including features of the system that have already been implemented, and features that are under development, targeted at the theoretical division we set out previously. Although there are many possible means to approach a story-and-discourse model of interactive narrative, our goal is to demonstrate the effectiveness of this model using the Mimesis system as a test bed; our initial results, mentioned here and in the work we cite, are encouraging.

ACKNOWLEDGMENTS

We are grateful to the many students who have contributed to the Liquid Narrative Group and the development of the Mimesis system. Significant contributors to the work described in this chapter include Dan Amerson, Mark Branly, D'Arcey Carol, Arnav Jhala, Shaun Kime, Milind Kulkarni, R. J. Martin, Mark Riedl, C. J. Saretto, and Sirish Somanchi. This work was supported by National Science Foundation CAREER award #0092586.

REFERENCES

Arijon, D. (1976). *Grammar of the film language. Communication arts books.* New York: Hastings House.

Bal, M. (1998). *Narratology: An introduction to the theory of narrative.* Toronto: University of Toronto Press.

Bares, W., & Lester, J. (1998). Intelligent multi-shot visualization interfaces for dynamic 3D worlds. *Proceedings of the Fourth International Conference on Intelligent User Interfaces* (pp. 119–126), Los Angeles, CA.

Cavazza, M., Charles, F., & Mead, S. (2002). Planning characters' behaviour in interactive storytelling. *Journal of Visualization and Computer Animation, 13*(2), 121–131.

Charles, F., Lozano, M., Mead, S., Bisquerra, A., & Cavazza, M. (2003). Planning formalisms and authoring in interactive storytelling. *Proceedings of the First International Conference on Technologies for Interactive Digital Storytelling and Entertainment*, Darmstadt, Germany.

Chatman, S. (1990). *Story and discourse: Narrative structure in fiction and film*. Ithaca, NY: Cornell University Press.

Christian, D., & Young, R. M. (2004). Comparing cognitive and computational models of narrative structure. *Proceedings of the National Conference on Artificial Intelligence*, San Jose, CA.

Comisky, P., & Bryant, J. (1982). Factors involved in generating suspense. *Human Communication Research, 9*(1), 49–58.

Emmot, K. (1999). *Narrative comprehension: A discourse perspective*. New York: Oxford University Press.

Gerrig, R., & Bernardo, D. (1994). Readers as problem-solvers in the experience of suspense. *Poetics, 22*, 459–472.

Khambamphati, S., Knoblock, C., & Yang, Q. (1995). Planning as refinement search: A unified framework for evaluating design tradeoffs in partial-order planning in artificial intelligence. *Artificial Intelligence, 76*(1–2), 167–238.

Lombard, M., & Ditton, T. (1997). At the heart of it all: The concept of presence. *Journal of Computer-Mediated Communication, 3*(2).

Mann, W., & Thompson, S. (1988). Rhetorical structure theory: Toward a functional theory of text organization. *Text 8*(3), 243–281.

Monaco, J. (1981). *How to read a film: The art, technology, language, history and theory of film and media*. New York: Oxford University Press.

Moore, J., & Paris, C. (1993). Planning text for advisory dialogues: Capturing intentional and rhetorical structure. *Computational Linguistics, 19*(4), 651–695.

Ohler, P., & Niedling, G. (1996). Cognitive modeling of suspense-inducing structures in narrative films. In P. Vorderer et al. (Eds.), *Suspense: Conceptualizations, theoretical analyses and empirical explorations*. Mahwah, NJ: Lawrence Erlbaum Associates.

Rattermann, M. J., Spector, L., Grafman, J., Levin, H., & Harward, H. (2002). Partial and total-order planning: Evidence from normal and prefrontally damaged populations. *Cognitive Science, 25*(6), 941–975.

Riedl, M., Saretto, C. J., & Young, R. M. (2003). Managing interaction between users and agents in a multiagent storytelling environment. *Proceedings of the Second International Conference on Autonomous Agents and Multi-Agent Systems*, New York, NY.

Rimmon-Keenan, S. (2002). *Narrative fiction: Contemporary poetics*. New York: Routledge.

Sacerdotti, E. (1977). *A structure for plans and behavior*. New York: Elsevier.

Sgouros, N. M. (1999). Dynamic generation, management and resolution of interactive plots. *Artificial Intelligence, 107*(1), 29–62.

Szilas, N. (2001). A new approach to interactive drama: From intelligent characters to an intelligent virtual narrator. *The Working Notes of the AAAI Spring Syposium on AI and Interactive Entertainment*. Stanford, CA: AAAI Press.

Trabasso, T., & Sperry, L. (1985). Causal relatedness and importance of story events. *Journal of Memory and Language, 24*, 595–611.

Young, R. M. (1999a). Cooperative plan identification: Constructing concise and effective plan descriptions. *Proceedings of the National Conference of the American Association for Artificial Intelligence* (pp. 597–604), Orlando, FL.

Young, R. M. (1999b). Notes on the use of plan structures in the creation of interactive plot. *The Working Notes of the AAAI Fall Symposium on Narrative Intelligence*. Cape Cod, MA: AAAI Press.

Young, R. M., Pollack, M. E., & Moore, J. D. (1994, July). Decomposition and causality in partial order planning. *Proceedings of the Second International Conference on AI and Planning Systems* (pp. 188–193), Chicago, IL.

Young, R. M., Riedl, M., Branly, M., Jhala, A., Martin, R. J., & Saretto, C. J. (2004). An architecture for integrating plan-based behavior generation with interactive game environments. *The Journal of Game Development, 1*(1), 51–70.

CHAPTER TEN

Building Augmented Cognition Systems for Automotive Applications

Wilhelm E. Kincses
DaimlerChrysler

The role of the driver has changed tremendously over time. In the beginning of the automobile era, the driver's most important skill was that of a mechanical engineer ensuring the operational reliability of the vehicle. These skills have been successfully replaced by technological advancements that provide us with highly reliable and safe systems. Today, we are facing a paradigm switch, moving from the traditional picture, in which the driver is engaged in solely driving-related tasks, toward a situation where the driver is involved in nondriving actions. We are both witnesses and facilitators of this change by transforming our automobiles from a simple means of transportation to a place of work and leisure. The most dramatic changes are taking place in the military domain. Here the operator of a vehicle has to fulfill requirements that are primarily mission related, such as surveillance and gun fire, at least for short periods of time.

The driving force behind this development is the information and communication technology (ICT). This technology bears risks as well as chances. On the one hand, ITC systems represent a source of distraction. On the other hand, they offer the operator significant and sometimes even vital support. Therefore, it is of particular importance to promote the utilization of ITC systems with focus on the chances offered by these technologies—namely, as a means to increase driver safety as well as improve the performance of the nondriving-related tasks.

Within the automotive sector, DaimlerChrysler has always been a driving force behind technological advancement, especially regarding issues related to vehicle safety. With a focus on the vehicle, systems have been developed such as Active Body Control (ABC), Electronic Stability Program (ESP), Antilock Braking System (ABS), and so on, which all support the driver in demanding driving situations and which even compensate driving failures.

The future of vehicle safety will move beyond a focus purely on vehicle systems (i.e., the physical or mechanical aspect) and move into the neurophysiological realm by including the driver and thereby taking on a holistic approach to vehicle safety. The necessity of a holistic approach results primarily from the increased employment of driving-related as well as nondriving-related systems.

Due to the rapid pace of technological developments, an evolutionary adaptation of the human capabilities to deal with these new challenges is only partly possible. To guarantee an optimal if not symbiotic cooperation between the human and digital worlds, with the ultimate goal of expanding the limits of human performance, consciousness, and quality of life, two prerequisites must be fulfilled:

- Technical systems of the future will have to have cognitive abilities, meaning that the system "knows what it does"; and
- the optimization of safety and reliability of the interaction between humans and machines will have to take into account intrinsic neural human abilities and deficits.

By fulfilling these criteria, it will be possible to compensate for the lagging evolutionary adaptation to the challenges of the digital environment. The reliability and effectiveness of the human–machine interface (HMI) will play a decisive role. The requirements are easily defined: The interaction must be designed such that the driver is neither distracted, disturbed, nor cognitively overloaded by the information provided. The fundamental knowledge necessary for the design of a safe and reliable HMI, however, is far from being sufficiently developed. The interaction of driver, vehicle, and environment is extremely complex, and the traditional analytical methods of behavioral psychology are often insufficient and, furthermore, difficult to assess. With the newly developed brain imaging methodology in the neurosciences, for the first time it is possible to establish an effective and objective measurement procedure for this issue. Since the last decade of the past century, known as the "Decade of the Brain," this approach has been refined to such a degree that HMI-relevant cognitive processes such as attention, learning, cognitive overload, and so on can be directly correlated with brain activity. The focus of this discipline up to now, however, has been primarily on relatively simple recognition patterns or actions.

With our current research efforts, we have resolved to address this exact issue, with the ultimate goal of making a significant contribution to the improvement of vehicle and traffic safety as well as an improvement in mission-related task resolution. Our current activities are embedded into our broad research activities focusing on the interaction among the cognitive, perceptual, neurological, and digital domains, with the goal of developing new and forward-looking concepts of performance-relevant applications.

The most natural way to tackle this challenge is to understand the vehicle–driver system as one entity that solves problems together as a team. This rationale consequently leads to the premise that both members of this entity (a) take advantage of each other's strengths, (b) take into account each other's weaknesses, and (c) share a common basis of knowledge.

PERCEIVING AND UNDERSTANDING
THE ENVIRONMENT

Significant advancements in the field of sensor technology and microelectronics; gains in computational power, information capacity, speed and memory growth in digital machinery; and success in the miniaturization, powering, and ruggedization of hardware—all these factors have contributed to the development of a large number of vehicle systems designed to inform, warn, and support the driver in various situations. As part of its contribution to the vision of "Accident-Free Driving," DaimlerChrysler is continuously developing driver assistance systems and active safety systems designed to assist drivers in perceiving, interpreting, and more safely handling traffic situations. With regard to the nature of the performed processes—be it to warn the driver, support him or her, and/or even to take corrective actions—these systems fall into three main categories: (a) *reactive processes*, where system responses are provided with low latency in direct response to inputs; (b) *deliberative processes*, where planning and other reasoning processes are carried out; and (c) *reflective processes* which operate based on observations made about the system (intrinsic system states).

An example of such systems is the GHz radar-based advanced cruise control (Distronic), which was launched in 1999 by DaimlerChrysler in premium class vehicles. Distronic is more *intelligent* than an ordinary cruise control (Tempomat) in that it ensures the vehicle maintains the cruising speed the driver has selected while keeping a safe distance from the vehicle ahead. The main supplier of data to Distronic is a 77-GHz radar sensor with three transmitters and receivers that constantly emit signals and register traffic scenarios of a distance up to 150 meters (ca. 500 feet) ahead. The relative speed to nonstationary vehicles in front is calculated by the Distronic using the Doppler Effect, whereas their distance is derived from the transit time of the reflected radar signals. The computing power required for these calculations is provided by digital signal processors, which evaluate the data streams much faster than conventional microchips. In addition to sensing the traffic scene ahead, the system takes corrective longitudinal control actions within set limits. When the vehicle in front slows down, thereby reducing the safety distance, the electronic system automatically applies the brakes. As soon as traffic conditions allow, the system accelerates to the preset speed. If the situation is too hazardous to leave the braking maneuver to the system alone, the system warns the driver and calls on him or her to brake accordingly.

Primarily due to technical characteristics of the sensor used, however, the Distronic does have technical limitations. For example, the narrow angle of the radar does not allow for satisfactory object recognition in the immediate front and proximity of the vehicle. Because the radar system is rigidly pointing toward the front, the radar beam is prone to lose sight of the tracked vehicle in sharp curves. In these conditions, the electronic system might also erroneously interpret oncoming vehicles as rapidly approaching threats.

Both detriments can be overcome if the scope of environment recognition is expanded. A second sensor with a wider beam angle can be used to detect objects within the immediate vicinity of the vehicle, including vehicles on parallel lanes that are only 5 to 10 meters away from the vehicle. An additional video-based sensor equipped with an according image processing unit can maintain a view of even the sharpest curves.

Already the analysis of this example makes it clear that a prerequisite for a perfect interaction of the vehicle with the driver and the environment (i.e., traffic) is a comprehensive digital representation of the situation of which the vehicle is a part. This is possible by combining and integrating information from several different sensors, with computer vision-based systems playing a fundamental role to this end.

Computer Vision for Advanced Driver Assistance Systems

Driving on public roads is characterized by a strict and comprehensive set of traffic rules marked by traffic signs and supportive information (e.g., demarcation lines of traffic lanes, etc.). Humans are good at perceiving and integrating these signs into a conclusive environmental model, which allows them to safely maneuver through traffic. To appropriately support the driver, driver assistance systems have to be able to obtain a correct model of the external world, which has to match the human one (i.e., comprehending the same set of rules). Consequently, the system must reliably identify objects of particular interest, such as traffic participants, traffic signs, traffic lanes, and so on, and subsequently build a realistic model of the traffic scenery.

We envision the car of the future being equipped with several video cameras because no other sensor can provide comparably detailed information about the vehicle's surroundings. The information supplied by video cameras is also the closest approximation to human perception and, accordingly, is the prerequisite for comprehensive recognition. Rapidly falling costs of sensors and processors, in combination with increasing image resolution, are further accelerating the dissemination of this technology.

Just like the human brain, computerized visual perception systems have to handle an immense volume of data. Within each second, they have to extract relevant information from tens of millions of pixels, which is subsequently routed to further processes generating reactive, deliberative, or reflective actions. The first part of this processing chain is fast object recognition (i.e., the concentration on decision-relevant areas of the image). Two methods of optical image recognition play a particular importance: (a) optical flow, and (b) stereo image technology (see Fig. 10.1). A combination of both approaches allows fast reduction to the essential matter at hand: the threat of a collision.

In 1983, for the first time camera systems were able to detect motion. Unfortunately, the evaluation of images recorded within a second took almost an entire weekend! Currently, computers can compute the motion patterns from an entire scene several times a second. This achievement is only in part the result of huge gains in raw computational power. Equally

FIG. 10.1.   Stereo cameras are used to measure a vehicle's distance to objects. Close objects are marked red, distant objects are colored green (left). A stereo camera is used to calculate movement from frame to frame. The movement vectors are shown as colored lines (right).

significant progress has been made with new and more effective computing algorithms developed by researchers at DaimlerChrysler.

In terms of object recognition, current approaches are similar to what
we, as humans, do when we interact with our surrounding world as novices: We learn by example. Supervised learning techniques use samples
that are labeled by a human supervisor to train machines to identify these
objects when encountered. Images of a particular traffic situation containing the significant objects marked by hand are used as input for machine
learning algorithms. For example, a specific traffic sign is presented in up
to 100,000 different images and in the widest variety of traffic situations.
In the subsequent learning process, computerized learning procedures filter the typical features and contexts of the sign without human intervention. As a result, the computer can recognize this sign during all common
weather and ambient light conditions (Fig. 10.2).

Within the last years, several vision-based systems such as pedestrian
detection (Gavrila, Giebel, & Munder, 2004; Giebel, Gavrila, & Schnörr,
2004), lane detection (Lindner, Kressel, & Kaelberer, 2004), and blind

FIG. 10.2.   The traffic sign recognition unit repeatedly analyzes an approaching sign in fractions of a second. In the first step, it determines whether the
sign is round, square, or triangular. After it has determined that the sign is
round, a polynomial classifier ascertains whether the sign is prohibitive or informative in nature. Finally, after the sign has been identified as informative,
it is compared with stored pictograms of all traffic signs and subsequently
identified as a sign indicating an approaching traffic circle.

spot detectors have been developed. A detailed overview of these systems and the underlying techniques can be found in Franke et al. (2001).

Sensor Fusion for Enhanced Situation Interpretation

All driver assistance systems are based on sensors that deliver information about the vehicle's immediate environment: Video cameras recognize traffic signs and traffic lanes, infrared scanners monitor lateral movements of the vehicle, and radar sensors perform long- and short-range object detection. However, each type of sensor has its strengths and weaknesses. Video-based sensors, for example, experience detection problems under low-visibility conditions, whereas radar sensors have the disadvantage of lacking object classification properties.

By using the approach of sensor fusion and, consequently, combining and integrating the data of all available sensors as well as the output of the according subsequent analysis, it is possible to overcome the detriments of each separate sensor and obtain a more comprehensive and conclusive digital representation of the vehicle's relevant traffic environment (Fig. 10.3).

A further significant advantage of fusing the information from different sensors is a higher reliability of the computed representation. Because some parameters are measured by several sensors simultaneously, the system has a better statistical basis for the computed model. Furthermore, the system uses probabilistic models to take into account the uncertainties associated with each measurement to obtain a more accurate and reliable representation of the computed models (Dagli, Brost, & Breuel, 2003). Finally, advanced mathematical models take into consideration the reliability of the sensors as well.

FIG. 10.3. Interplay between two sensors: A radar sensor recognizes the vehicle in front and marks it with a red cross. A video camera serves as the lane-recognition system, with the detected side and center lines marked in green.

Such probabilistic approaches also have the advantage of enabling the system to have predictive capabilities, being able to predict certain events a few moments ahead. In this way, the system can predict the probability of, for example, a vehicle within the range of observation changing lanes at a specific moment. Such a situation analysis allows detecting lane changes of a vehicle about 1.5 seconds earlier than the Distronic would based solely on its radar sensor.

The importance of sensor fusion becomes even more obvious when we take a comparative look at the human physiology, which is an example of a system perfectly tuned by evolution to maximize the knowledge output from sensory information input.

Multisensory stimuli are known to improve perceptual performance (e.g., bimodal stimuli may speed up reactions; Schröger & Widmann, 1998). Recent studies suggest the existence of a distributed, hierarchical cortical network that contributes to the binding of auditory, tactile, and visual objects. Studies in primates report multisensory neurons (i.e., spiking activity in response to stimulation in different modalities) in parietal (e.g., Hyvarinen & Shelepin, 1979), temporal (e.g., Benevento, Fallon, Davis, & Rezak, 1977), and frontal regions of the neocortex (e.g., Rizzolatti et al., 1981). Feed forward patterns in the transcortical profile suggest that direct excitatory connections exist (e.g., from somatosensory cortex to secondary auditory areas; Schroeder et al., 2001). Tactile-visual integration has been found in the fusiform gyrus (Macaluso, Frith, & Driver, 2000). Moreover, sensory-evoked potentials to bimodal stimuli exhibited reduced amplitudes, compared with summed unimodal responses reflecting early interactions in the human (Foxe et al., 2000; Giard & Peronnet, 1999). A recent study by Menning et al. (2005) indicated that multisensory systems do not require attentional shifts to enhance object processing across different modalities. Instead spatial integration at early processing levels might in turn be considered an automatic process that provides a basis for selective attention and orienting reactions.

COGNITIVE STATE DETECTION

As discussed earlier, driver assistance as well as active safety systems are able to compute an accurate representation of the environment and reliably identify possible threats. Taking into account additional information about its internal state—part of it being driver's responses (i.e., steering wheel activity, braking, etc.)—the system takes appropriate supportive actions. In this context, the term *appropriate supportive actions* refers to the system's ability to initiate actions that take into account context information (traffic rules, behavior of other traffic participants, road conditions, etc.) as well as information about the driver's ability to cope with that specific situation (driver's intentions and limitations). The electronic stability program (ESP), a standard feature in modern cars, is a good example of how current driver assistance systems compensate for the driver's erroneous or insufficient behavior in certain driving maneuvers. The Brake Assistance System (BAS), developed by DaimlerChrysler and introduced in 1996 for the first time in the Mercedes-Benz vehicles, represents a system that interprets the driver's braking behavior and initializes a complete stop of the vehicle, thus compensating for the driver's often insufficient braking action.

However, in most cases, drivers' behavioral data alone do not allow for an accurate estimation of their capability to cope with a specific situation. Unfortunately, in some cases, a definite relationship can be asserted only after the effects of an accident are inevitable. The driver's ability to cope with a specific situation highly depends on his or her cognitive state at that specific moment. Statistical data based on the evaluation of accidents suggest that the main cause of accidents is a deteriorated cognitive state of the driver (i.e., fatigue, inattention, drowsiness, cognitive overload, etc.; Treat, 1979; Wang, Knipling, & Goodman, 1996).

Consequently, future driver assistance systems will have to take into account information regarding the driver's intrinsic capabilities—not just as part of the system's design process, but rather permanently during the entire operation of the vehicle. Information about the operator's cognitive state, his or her level of alertness and stress—will be indispensable in facilitating a perfect match between humans and machines. This rationale inevitably leads to a closed-loop system in which operator and system (e.g., driver and vehicle) form a cognitive entity, taking into account each other's capabilities and limitations.

Cognitive State Detection Under Real Operational Conditions

Driving is a complex, everyday task that requires multiple cognitive mechanisms such as attention, perception, memory, learning, decision making, motor control, and so on. Consequently, this complex task involves the engagement and interaction of a variety of brain networks. Within the past 4 years, functional brain imaging studies have tackled the identification of the neural correlates of driving (Calhoun et al., 2002; Walter et al., 2001). These studies, in conjunction with paradigms studying more specific aspects of cognition, enhance our overall understanding of the neural correlates of complex behaviors and the interaction between humans and the systems under consideration.

However, the complexity of the involved processes makes it extremely difficult to understand and study in detail all neural processes involved in driving. Studies are further complicated by the restrictions of a real operational setting, making it difficult to control experimental conditions. For this reason, in our current research efforts, we adopt a top–down strategy to tackle this challenge (i.e., a task-specific approach). This means that we are focusing on just specific driving situations and tasks. We designed our system such that it detects the cognitive state changes of the driver as well as the according context information relevant to the tasks under consideration.

Mental Workload

Despite its extensive use, there is neither a common understanding of the term *workload* nor a shared methodology for measuring it, especially in the context of driving. Historically, the concept of *mental workload* was first introduced in the 1940s in the context of optimizing human–machine systems (e.g., Gopher & Donchin, 1986). In our approach, we follow O'Donnell and Eggemeier (1986), who defined *driver workload* as that portion of a person's limited capacity required to perform a particular task (i.e., driving). From the neural-processing perspective, the general term *workload* summarizes the parallel and serial processing of several neural units that are part of different hierarchical processing levels, ranging from sensory perception over multisensory integration to cognitive processes such as working memory, decision making, and motor-response execution. With respect to neurophysiological function, perceptual and cognitive processing relies on limited neural resources. Any increase of information being transmitted from the system (e.g., vehicle) or the environment to the driver increases the driver's workload due to engaging additional neural units of the respective sensory and cognitive processing pathways.

States of different types and levels of cognitive workload are measurable using neurophysiological parameters (e.g., obtained from EEG signals). There is ample evidence that a large variety of EEG signal parameters allow discrimination among different cognitive states, such as the P300 amplitude as an indicator of cognitive resources (e.g., Donchin, 1987; Fowler, 1994), spectral band-power dissociating between different forms and levels of attention (e.g., Gevins, Smith, McEvoy, & Lu, 1997; Wrobel, 2000), or certain types of signal coupling within limited frequency ranges indicating working-memory processes (e.g., Burgess & Gruzelier, 1997; Gevins & Smith, 2000; Sarnthein, Petsche, Rappelsberger, Shaw, & von Stein, 1998; Tallon-Baudry, Bertrand, & Fischer, 2001).

Different types as well as levels of cognitive workload can also, to some degree, be predicted by online evaluation of environmental factors, as long as these factors have a well-defined influence on the driver's cognitive resources. In the operational environment of our current investigation, we assume that critical traffic situations and highly dynamic states of the vehicle absorb some of the driver's attention and sensory input capacity.

Additionally, classification of workload conditions may also be performed on the basis of the driver's behavioral data. Head tracking or monitoring of the driver's seat posture, for example, allows detection of preparatory movements that are likely to be followed by certain driving maneuvers. Combining this approach with context recognition, it is possible to recognize situations indicative of certain (upcoming) cognitive states, providing anticipatory capabilities.

FIRST CLOSED-LOOP AUGMENTED COGNITION SYSTEM FOR AUTOMOTIVE APPLICATIONS

DaimlerChrysler broke new ground with the integration and development of an augmented cognition system for automotive applications, concluded by a concept validation experiment demonstrating the feasibility, applicability, and potential of such a closed-loop system. Specifically, by using a Mercedes-Benz S-Class vehicle-based platform, we demonstrated improvement of driver's information-processing performance during a number of different cognitive tasks executed while driving.

Our first objective was the technical integration and practical application of a sensor suite in the vehicle platform. The sensor suite comprises devices for EEG recording, seat posture recognition, audio monitoring of vehicle interior, and logging of driver-behavioral variables. Together with vehicle data relating to assessment of driving, traffic situations, and context, the output of this sensor suite feeds into the developed cognitive state classifiers. These in turn interpret the current driver condition in terms of sensory and cognitive processing on the basis of previously developed cognitive models.

Our second objective consisted of the implementation of a trigger logic—the mitigation strategy—that uses the classifiers' interpretations for flexible cognitive-task manipulation in response to the driver's estimated workload. This step closes the measurement–interpretation–manipulation loop, thereby completing the framework of our Closed-Loop Integrated Prototype (CLIP). To maintain control over changes of cognitive states at the best possible rate from an experimental point of view, we defined secondary tasks, deliberately inducing the cognitive states under investigation. Based on these states, dedicated mitigation strategies were chosen and implemented. A key aspect of our approach is the fact that we did not use any simulated environment. Instead all experiments were performed under real traffic conditions. We are convinced that, under the current considerations, the advantage of running a field experiment under real driving conditions outclasses the disadvantages of a not fully controllable experimental setup by offering high validity and practical relevance of the collected data.

Experimental Design

Five male subjects participated in the study as drivers. The following experimental protocol was carried out twice for each subject—once with the augmented cognition (AugCog) system disabled (*Reference Session*) and once with the system enabled (*AugCog Session*). Each of these two sessions had an approximate duration of 2 hours. Subjects drove on a predefined route on a German highway, which represented the *primary* task.

While driving, *secondary* tasks were performed in a block design, with each block being followed by a baseline period (without secondary task), which served as the control condition. The different secondary tasks deliberately induced different types of cognitive and sensory load. The tasks used were an auditory workload task (AWT), a mental arithmetic task (MAT), and a driving maneuver task (DMT).

In addition to the secondary tasks, a *tertiary* task was continuously performed. On the one hand, this task served to impose additional workload onto the drivers, and therefore was subject to our mitigation strategies (i.e., its form of presentation [continuous vs. scheduled, visual vs. auditory] was flexibly adapted to the driver's current cognitive state). On the other hand, tertiary task performance (comprising accuracy and reaction time) provided a measure for quantifying the closed-loop augmented system's success.

Sensor Suite

In this first study, we focused on recognizing the driver's information processing related mainly to two cognitive bottlenecks: sensory input and working memory. For this purpose, we used three groups of sensors for estimating the driver's cognitive state. The first group collected (neuro-) physiological signals from the driver consisting of a 29-channel electroencephalography (EEG) (10–20) system, supported by EOG and EMG recordings to facilitate artifact recognition. EEG represents the most robust and best-documented brain imaging method that, in addition, directly registers electrophysiological activity (as opposed to secondary phenomena like blood-vessel dynamics), features high temporal and sufficient spatial resolution, and, most important, is easily realizable with portable equipment. In our opinion, other brain imaging methods such as (functional) magnetic resonance imaging (fMRI), positron emission tomography (PET), single-photon emission tomography (SPET), or magnetoencephalography are inadequate for our purposes due to technical limitations.

A main challenge of our approach pertains to the EEG-based classifiers, in that EEG signals show high interindividual differences due to anatomical and functional variety among subjects (e.g., Haan, Streb, Bien, & Rösler, 2000). There are two ways to address this challenge: Either the classifiers are trained with EEG data from a large number of subjects, or the classifiers are individually tuned to each subject. The first alternative would deliver reliable estimators of the *mean* signal patterns characterizing certain cognitive states, but would still present the problem that individual patterns may show large deviations from these prototypes. Therefore, and because of the complexity and novel character of the present research endeavor, the second approach was followed. Although more time-consuming, it was expected to yield better and more reliable results. In addition to these physiological signals, the driver's seat posture and head movements were captured by a second group of sensors consisting of a seat mat and a head tracker device.

The third group of sensors comprised all vehicle devices that are suitable for recognizing the current context situation and estimating its influence on the driver's cognitive state. Sensor values from each of the three groups are fed into classification algorithms (EEG signals directly, vehicle-sensor values via CAN data bus), the output of which represents interpretations of the driver's current workload or the context's impact on it.

Two types of classification algorithms were employed. One of them, developed in collaboration with the Fraunhofer Institut für Rechnerarchitektur und Softwaretechnik (FIRST, Berlin, Germany), utilizes neurophysiological (EEG) data. In the studied environment, it was trained to distinguish between a baseline condition and high-workload conditions. Two different configurations of the classifier were used, with the first one trained on the AWT and the second one trained on the MAT. The second classifier used was developed in collaboration with Sandia National Laboratories (Albuquerque, NM) and the University of Pittsburgh (Pittsburgh, PA). It incorporates the driver's body movements and information regarding the driving situation as context information. The system recognizes several different traffic and driving situations (DMT), which are assumed to increase the driver's workload (e.g., entering highway, changing lanes, dynamic state of the vehicle, approaching a slower vehicle).

Mitigation Strategy

Outputs of all classifiers are updated at a regular time interval of 200 ms and transformed into binary values that represent the cognitive-state values. Subsequently, the gauge outputs are multiplied by weighting factors and summed. At this level, there are still separate meta-gauges for the EEG- and context-based elementary gauges. The meta-gauges in turn have to exceed certain thresholds to trigger mitigation measures. Further refinements of this model take into account special requirements associated with the respective operational environment.

The augmentation manager decides whether to trigger the mitigation measures, which consists of either scheduling (in the case of AWT and MAT) or changing the modality (DMT) of the tertiary task presentation. These mitigation measures are intended to reduce the amount of task load imposed on the driver, thereby leading to shorter reaction times and higher accuracy in the tertiary task.

Results and Discussion

Both the EEG- and the context-based classifiers yielded outputs accurately corresponding to the deliberately induced cognitive states and/or driving situations (i.e., 77% classification accuracies for the EEG classifiers and 95% for the context classifiers).

Figure 10.4 exemplarily shows the temporal pattern of tertiary task stimuli during the AWT and MAT blocks for one subject. There are only a few episodes in which tertiary stimuli were presented in combination with the secondary task or in which tertiary stimuli were absent, with there being no secondary task. When considering these episodes, however, one has to bear in mind that what appears as an imperfection with regard to the experimental design is always a correct decision from the augmented cognition system's point of view. It may well be that the driver's workload was sometimes low during the secondary-task blocks or high during the baseline periods. In the current experimental setup, it is not possible to identify periods of high or low workload by means of an additional gauge that works independently of the cognitive-state classifiers.

Because the real cognitive state is always unknown, it is not possible to exactly determine the time it takes for mitigation measures to be activated. Figure 10.4 shows that the augmentation manager usually responded with some delay to cognitive-state changes. Speeding up the reaction time of the system would have decreased its reliability and vice versa. The configuration used in the present study seems to be a reasonable compromise between response speed and classification reliability. Delay times after task onsets showed that the system was capable of reacting as fast as within a few seconds. In cases where delays were longer, it has to be assumed that the driver actually did not experience an instantaneous cognitive state change, and that the output changes of the gauges were correspondingly slow. It is also important to bear in mind that the time which elapsed until

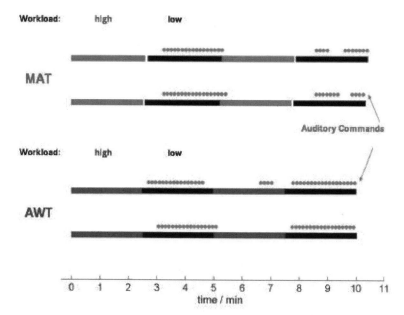

FIG. 10.4. Mitigation by scheduling results from one subject. Some slight imperfections (i.e., inconsistencies with the putatively induced cognitive states) can be seen during the second and fourth baseline period of the MAT task and during the second AWT task block. In most cases, there were delays of some seconds after cognitive-state transitions before the corresponding classifiers responded. There is a trade-off between these delays and the classifiers' reliability.

the reaction of the mitigation system became obvious (in the form of disappearing or reappearing of tertiary stimuli) can be as large as the interstimulus interval of the tertiary task. All in all, it can be considered a conservative estimation to say that the augmentation manager responded to cognitive state changes within 10 seconds.

Results obtained from the driving maneuver conditions show much faster system reaction times. Exact quantification of classification accuracy is not possible without exact documentation of every single driving maneuver. During test sessions, however, the accuracy of the context-based classifier was observed to be around 95%, and it reliably reacted to critical driving situations in real time (i.e., within less than 1 second).

Mean operator performances on the tertiary task were significantly higher during the *AugCog Sessions* than during the *Reference Sessions*. For the final assessment of the experiment and the success of the augmented cognition system, it is most important to know how the driver performance depended on the state of the system (i.e., being disabled or enabled). We were especially interested in the tertiary-task performance increase as a consequence of the AugCog system being enabled. This increase was defined as

$$improvement = 100 \times \frac{performance_{AugCog} - performance_{reference}}{performance_{reference}} \%.$$

There was an increase in mean subjects' tertiary-task performances due to activating the augmented cognition system during all three conditions—AWT, MAT, and DMT (93% averaged over all three conditions). Because the number of performance values ($N = 15$; 3 tasks $\times$ 5 subjects) is too small to estimate their distribution, and because values cannot be assumed to be normally distributed, performance was tested for a significant increase using a one-tailed Wilcoxon (rank-sum) test. The performance increase was significant at $p < 05$.

OUTLOOK

We envision vehicles of the future being equipped with advanced perception technologies that process streaming sensor data from multiple sources and physical sensors with low latency to detect important objects, events, and situations in the environment.

Advanced computational models supporting reflective processes and reasoning will facilitate an accurate digital representation of the vehicle's environment. Current studies already show that large improvements in the system's digital representation can be obtained by integrating information from digital maps as well as other telematics applications, enabling the system to have predictive analytic behavior.

By taking into account information about the operator's cognitive state, two further advantages are expected. First, by understanding the impact of specific situations on the driver's cognitive state and combining this knowledge with the system's analytical predictive behavior, it is possible to avoid critical situations. Second, by adapting to the operator's dynamically changing intrinsic capabilities, it is possible to have universally applicable systems that do not require intensive training prior to operation.

The prior presentation is a brief illustration of our current efforts to develop a technology that provides the best fit between driver and vehicle. The mitigation strategy presented earlier applies to the warning and information management of the vehicle. In the future, with a better understanding of the driver's intrinsic capabilities, it will be possible to dynamically reallocate driving tasks and other duties between the driver and the autonomous capabilities of the vehicle. For example, the level of autonomy and the warning characteristics of future driver assistance systems can be a function of the driver's cognitive state.

The closed-loop augmented system presented before is the first of its kind within the automotive application domain, representing a successful first step toward an optimal interaction among driver, vehicle, and environment. However, the challenges associated with the final goal are manifold. Further improvements of the neurophysiological sensor technology for noninvasive cognitive state assessment are necessary to allow for remote measurements, which are currently not possible. Further research efforts also have to be dedicated to better understanding the neural correlates of complex operational tasks in real environments and the associated cognitive states, as well as the neurophysiological basis of driver vehicle interaction with respect to different levels of cognitive load.

This approach will enable us to use the human's cognitive abilities more effectively and efficiently and will create natural, cooperative human–machine collaborations. The success of our approach will change the human–machine design paradigm from "human learns to operate the system" to "human and machine cooperate to solve problems, arrive at decisions and master challenges as a team."

ACKNOWLEDGMENTS

The author thanks Dr. Andreas Bruns for his excellent technical assistance and helpful discussions and Melinda Ewert-Kincses for her editorial assistance. Parts of the research presented herein were supported by grant NBCH3030001 awarded to Dr. Wilhelm E. Kincses (DaimlerChrysler AG).

REFERENCES

Benevento, L. A., Fallon, J., Davis, B. J., & Rezak, M. (1977). Auditoryvisual interaction in single cells of the superior temporal sulcus and the orbito frontal cortex of the macaque monkey. *Experimental Neurology, 57*, 849–872.

Burgess, A., & Gruzelier, J. H. (1997). Short duration synchronization of human theta rhythm during recognition memory. *Neuroreport, 8*, 1039–1042.

Calhoun, V. D., Pekar, J. J., McGinty, V. B., Adali, T., Watson, T. D., & Pearlson, G. D. (2002). Different activation dynamics in multiple neural systems during simulated driving. *Human Brain Mapping, 16*, 158–167.

Dagli, I., Brost, M., & Breuel, G. (2003). Action recognition and prediction for driver assistance systems using dynamic belief networks. In R. Kowalczyk, J. P. Müller, H. Tianfield, & R. Unland (Eds.), *Agent technologies, infrastructures, tools, and applications for E-services: NODe 2002 agent-related workshops, Erfurt, Germany, October 7–10, 2002. Revised Papers. Lecture Notes in Computer Science 2592* (pp. 179–194). Heidelberg, Germany: Springer-Verlag.

Donchin, E. (1987). The P300 as a metric for mental workload. *Electroencephalography and Clinical Neurophysiology Supplement, 39,* 338–343.

Fowler, B. (1994). P300 as a measure of workload during a simulated aircraft landing task. Human Factors, 36, 670–683.

Foxe, J. J., Morocz, I. A., Murray, M. M., Higgins, B. A., Javitt, D. C., & Schroeder, C. E. (2000). Multisensory auditory-somatosensory interactions in early cortical processing revealed by high-density electrical mapping. *Cognitive Brain Research, 10,* 77–83.

Franke, U., Gavrila, D. M., Gern, A., Görzig, S., Janssen, R., Paetzold, F., & Wöhler, C. (2001). From door to door—Principles and applications of computer vision for driver assistant systems. In L. Vlacic, F. Harashima, & M. Parent (Eds.), *Intelligent vehicle technologies* (chap. 6). Oxford: Butterworth Heinemann.

Gavrila, D. M., Giebel J., & Munder, S. (2004). Vision-based pedestrian detection: The PRO-TECTOR+ system. *Proceedings of the European Conference on Computer Vision,* Prague, Czech Republic.

Gevins, A., & Smith, M. E. (2000). Neurophysiological measures of working memory and individual differences in cognitive ability and cognitive style. *Cerebral Cortex, 10,* 829–839.

Gevins, A., Smith, M. E., McEvoy, L., & Yu, D. (1997). High resolution EEG mapping of cortical activation related to working memory: Effects of task difficulty, type of processing, and practice. *Cerebral Cortex, 7,* 374–385.

Giard, M. H., & Peronnet, F. (1999). Auditory-visual integration during multimodal object recognition in humans: A behavioral and electrophysiological study. Journal of Cognitive Neuroscience, 11, 473-490.

Giebel, J., Gavrila, D. M., & Schnörr, C. (2004). A Bayesian framework for multi-cue 3D object tracking. In T. Pajdla & J. Matas (Eds.), *Computer Vision—ECCV 2004, 8th European Conference on Computer Vision, Prague, Czech Republic. Proceedings, Part IV. Lecture Notes in Computer Science 3024* (pp. 241–252). Heidelberg, Germany: Springer-Verlag.

Gopher, D., & Donchin, E. (1986). Workload—An examination of the concept. In K. R. Boff, L. Kaufmann, & J. P. Thomas (Eds.), *Handbook of perception and human performance* (pp. 41-1–41-49). New York: Wiley.

Haan, H., Streb, J., Bien, S., & Rösler, F. (2000). Individual cortical current density reconstructions of the semantic N400 effect: Using a generalized minimum norm model with different constraints (L1 and L2 norm). *Human Brain Mapping, 11,* 178–192.

Hyvarinen, J., & Shelepin, Y. (1979). Distribution of visual and somatic functions in the parietal associative area 7 of the monkey. *Brain Research, 169,* 561-564.

Lindner, F., Kressel, U., & Kaelberer, S. (2004). Robust recognition of traffic signals. *Proceedings of the European Conference on Computer Vision,* Prague, Czech Republic.

Macaluso, E., Frith, C. D., & Driver, J. (2000). Modulation of human visual cortex by crossmodal spatial attention. *Science, 18,* 1206–1208.

Menning, H., Ackermann, H., Hertrich, I., & Mathiak, K. (2005). Spatial auditory attention is modulated by tactile priming. *Experimental Brain Research.* Epub ahead of print.

O'Donnell, C. R. D., & Eggemeier, F. T. (1986). Workload assessment methodology. In K. R. Boff, L. Kaufmann, & J. P. Thomas (Eds.), *Handbook of perception and human performance* (pp. 42–43). New York: Wiley.

Rizzolatti, G., Scandolara, C., Matelli, M., & Gentilucci, M. (1981). Afferent properties of periarcuate neurons in macaque monkeys: II. Visual responses. *Behavioural Brain Research, 2*(2), 147–163.

Sarnthein, J., Petsche, H., Rappelsberger, P., Shaw, G. L., & von Stein, A. (1998). Synchronization between prefrontal and posterior association cortex during human working memory. *Proceedings of the National Academy of Sciences of the United States of America, 95,* 7092–7096.

Schroeder, C. E., Lindsley, R. W., Specht, C., Marcovici, A., Smiley, J. F., & Javitt, D. C. (2001). Somatosensory input to auditory association cortex in the macaque monkey. *Journal of Neurophysiology, 85,* 1322–1327.

Schröger, E., & Widmann, A. (1998). Speeded responses to audiovisual signal changes result from bimodal integration. *Psychophysiology, 35,* 755–759.

Tallon-Baudry, C., Bertrand, O., & Fischer, C. (2001). Oscillatory synchrony between human extrastriate areas during visual short-term memory maintenance. *Journal of Neuroscience, 21,* RC177 (1–5).

Treat, J. (1979). *Tri-level study of the causes of traffic accidents* (Tech. Rep. Federal Highway Administration). Washington, DC: U.S. Department of Transportation.

Walter, H., Vetter, S. C., Grothe, J., Wunderlich, A. P., Hahn, S., & Spitzer, M. (2001). The neural correlates of driving. *NeuroReport, 12*(8), 1763–1767.

Wang, J. S., Knipling, R. R., & Goodman, M. J. (1996). The role of driver inattention in crashes: New statistics from the 1995 Crashworthiness Data System. *Proceedings of the 40th Annual Meeting of the Association of Automotive Medicine,* Vancouver, Canada.

Wrobel, A. (2000). Beta activity: A carrier for visual attention. *Acta Neurobiologiae Experimentalis, 60,* 247–260.

PART FOUR

TOPICS IN COGNITIVE SYSTEMS

CHAPTER ELEVEN

Automated Knowledge Capture and User Modeling

Terran Lane
University of New Mexico

A critical issue in computational modeling of human cognition is acquisition and encoding of the models and model parameters. Early work in Artificial Intelligence (AI) took the position that such models could be directly manually encoded (Luger, 2002; Russell & Norvig, 2002), whereas more recent exemplars of that tradition assume that cognitively plausible behavior will emerge from sufficiently thorough sets of hand-coded axiomatic world knowledge or heuristics (Lenat, 1995; Rosenbloom, Laird, & Newell, 1993). Although it is clear that manually encoded knowledge will continue to be a significant part of cognitive models for the indefinite future, it currently appears that complete manual development is not scalable, either to developing a single model of general cognition or individualizing models to a variety of different human subjects. Thus, a key facet of current cognitive modeling efforts is an automated knowledge capture component. This component employs techniques drawn from the fields of User Modeling (UM), Machine Learning (ML), Human–Computer Interaction (HCI), and preference elicitation to derive knowledge representations and model parameters for individualized cognitive models. In this chapter, we give an overview of such techniques, focusing on their application to cognitive modeling.

In this context, it is worth clarifying precisely what kind of knowledge acquisition/learning we are discussing. We are specifically interested in the semi-automated development of models of individual humans by monitoring their behavior and/or querying them about their internal states, beliefs, or preferences. We call this the process of *user modeling*. This is distinct from learning that the model might perform (e.g., through exploration, monitoring the environment, etc.). Both types of learning are rooted in some form of experience and act to modify the cognitive model, both may be used for/by a single cognitive model, and both may even use the same state monitoring or parameter updating techniques, but there are two key differences. The first is the agent performing the learning: In the former case, the agent is some software system *external* to the cognitive model that takes observations about the human user and acts to update the model. In some sense, the learning agent is simply replacing the human system designers as architect of the cognitive model. In the latter case, the model is the learning agent, taking observations about the *environment* and updating itself. This is a function much closer to what animals do as they interact with their environments, and is close to what we typically think of as learning.

The second key distinction between the two types of learning derives from the first: By virtue of being separate from the cognitive model, a user modeling system need not be constrained to employ mechanisms that are cognitively plausible, although it must produce a model that *is* cognitively plausible. The cognitive agent, however, is constrained to use learning methods and state monitoring techniques that are cognitively plausible.

BACKGROUND

We begin with a high-level overview of the mathematical formulation of a user modeling system (UMS) as a state monitoring and parameter estimation system. UMSs vary widely in specific technique, but it is convenient to have a uniform language for describing them.

State Variables, System Parameters, and Probabilities

User modeling systems typically take a state monitoring point of view, illustrated in Fig. 11.1. The UMS perceives the user, U, through a set of *sensors* or *observables*, which are viewed as variables, denoted $o^1, \ldots, o^n$. These variables could be effectively static (e.g., the user's gender, job title, etc.), but are more usually dynamic and observed over time: $o^i_1, o^i_2, \ldots,$ $o^i_t, \ldots, o^i_T$ (e.g., the software application or keystroke rate that the user is currently employing). For convenience, we denote the set of all variables observed at time t as $\mathbf{o}_t$, the time series of a single variable, o^i, from time 1 to T as $o^i_{1:T}$, and the time series of all observables as $\mathbf{o}_{1:T}$.

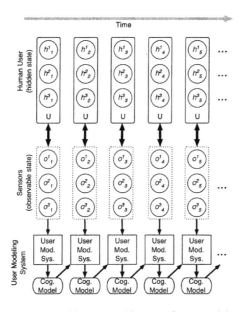

FIG. 11.1. Sensor and latent variable view of user modeling. The circles indicate random variables that evolve over time, divided into the observable (sensor) variables, o_t^i, and the unobservable (latent or hidden) variables, h_t^j, which represent facets of the user's cognitive state, U. Arrows indicate the flow of information: The user generates observable state and, in turn, responds to the environment; the user modeling system tracks the observable variables and uses them to continually update the user model.

Although modeling only the observable sensor variables may be sufficient to describe or predict the user's *behavior*, when we are interested in *cognitive* models, it is also necessary to model the user's *hidden* or *latent* cognitive state. Again we denote this state with a set of variables, $h^1, \ldots, h^m$, and the cognitive state of the user as $\mathbf{h}$. Similarly, over time we can think of $h_{1:T}^i$ and $\mathbf{h}_{1:T}$.

It is important to note that we do not intend $\mathbf{h}$ to capture the *entire* cognitive state of the user, but only the *salient* variables—that is, the variables that are likely to be correlated with observable behaviors. For example, salient hidden variables may include the user's current goal, the set of all tasks on the user's to-do list, the user's current cognitive load or emotional state, and so on. Such variables are not directly observable, but we can hope to infer their state through their correlation to observables.

Over time the user model tracks observables and infers the states of hidden variables, using both to update all parameters of the user model, denoted Θ. A primary axis of variation among different UMSs is the method by which they carry out this update.

Often many of the variables in the system are noisy or difficult to fully capture, so they are thought of as random variables, and we work with joint, marginal, or conditional probabilities over them. For example,

$$\Pr[\mathbf{o}_{1:T}, \mathbf{h}_{1:T} | \Theta] \qquad (1)$$

represents the complete joint probability of all observable and hidden states over all time, whereas

$$\Pr[\mathbf{h}_t | \mathbf{o}_{1:t-1}; \Theta] \qquad (2)$$

represents the conditional probability of the user's cognitive state at time t given knowledge of the complete history of sensor data up to time $t - 1$. We write the system parameters, Θ, as a set of random variables in this context simply because they are free variables that need to be selected; the actual probability assessed for a specific time series of observables is a function of the parameters we select. In a Bayesian statistical framework, we can regard Θ precisely as random variables; in other frameworks, it is simply convenient to view them as tunable free parameters.

Model Performance and Objective Functions

To validate a user model, it is necessary to establish a function that measures the quality of the model with respect to a known target such as the user. Ideally, this would be a measure of the similarity between the model and the user's cognitive structure. Of course if the user's true cognitive structure were known, we would have little need for a UMS. Therefore, we are typically most interested in behavioral measures—similarities between the user's observed behaviors and the model's predictions. Our notion of similarity is encoded by an *objective function* or *loss function*, $L(\ )$. In addition to validation, the objective function is critical for model learning/acquisition—the learning algorithm attempts to locate the model that minimizes the loss function relative to user behaviors. The specific model that is obtained depends strongly on the loss function employed so we can, to some extent, control the resulting model and its behaviors through proper choice of the loss function.

Let the sequence of observed data generated by the user be $\mathbf{o}_{1:T}$ and the sequence of predicted observations generated by the model be $\hat{\mathbf{o}}_{1:T}$. The objective function then takes these two sequences and returns a real value that assesses their similarity: $L : \mathbf{o}_{1:T} \times \hat{\mathbf{o}}_{1:T} \rightarrow \mathbb{R}$. For example, the standard *average accuracy* for discrete-valued observables (a.k.a., *zero-one loss*) can be obtained by assuming temporal independence and uniform cost for mismatches:

$$L_{acc}(\mathbf{o}_{1:T}, \hat{\mathbf{o}}_{1:T}) = \frac{1}{T}\sum_{t=1}^{T}[\![\mathbf{o}_t = \hat{\mathbf{o}}_t]\!] \tag{3}$$

where the operation $[\![\cdot]\!]$ denotes the indicator function that is 1 when its argument is true and is otherwise 0. A similar function for real-valued observables is the *mean squared error* loss,

$$L_{mse}(\mathbf{o}_{1:T}, \hat{\mathbf{o}}_{1:T}) = \sqrt{\frac{1}{T}\sum_{t=1}^{T}\mathbf{o}_t^{T}\hat{\mathbf{o}}_t} \ . \tag{4}$$

Both of these loss functions are appropriate when the temporal distribution of behavioral errors is considered unimportant, but can fail to reveal some critical performance differences. For example, Fig. 11.2 shows three different time traces of errors made by a hypothetical user model. In (a), the user model makes uniformly distributed mistakes, indicating uniformly mediocre performance. In (b), the model performs strongly in the early time segment, but quite poorly in the later section, indicating that the user has changed significantly and outdated the model. Finally, in (c), the model displays a periodic burst of errors, indicating that there is some periodically occurring user behavior that the model is not capturing. Because of the commutativity of addition, L_{acc} and L_{mse} are incapable of distinguishing these three cases. In the next section, we discuss loss functions for temporal models that are capable of distinguishing some of these cases.

Decision Theory and Utility Functions

The background material in this section is based heavily on standard works in decision-theoretic control, planning, and learning in the Markov decision process (MDP) formulation. For more in-depth discussion of these issues, we refer the reader to standard texts on MDPs and reinforce-

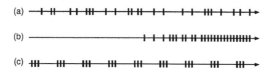

FIG. 11.2. Hypothetical examples of the need for sophisticated cost functions. In each timeline, the vertical ticks indicate times when the user model made an incorrect prediction. In (a) the model makes uniformly distributed errors, in (b) most errors occur at the end of time, while in (c) errors occur in periodic clusters. The three cases are indistinguishable with respect to the loss functions of Eqs. (3) and (4).

ment learning by Puterman (1994) and Sutton and Barto (1998), respectively.

Some classes of user modeling systems view the user as a decision-making agent with preferences and attempt to infer user behavior by first modeling those preferences (or *utilities*). This branch of work is based on decision (utility) theory and typically makes an assumption of rationality or bounded rationality.[1] A *rational agent* is defined to be one who always takes actions so as to maximize some long-term aggregate notion of expected utility. A boundedly rational agent also maximizes aggregate expected utility, but is not expected to be capable of exploring all possible consequences of actions and so may reach only an approximately optimal action choice.

In many ways, such a utility function is similar to the loss functions described in the previous section, but rather than describing the fit of the model to behavioral data, it describes the fit between the current true state of the world and the agent's desired state. For example, a utility function might describe the value of a user's stock portfolio, whether a security system has been compromised, or a student's progress through a university curriculum. States that the user prefers (valuable portfolio, secure system, graduation) are assigned higher utility than unpreferred states (bankruptcy, data theft, failure). Given such a utility function, the UMS can predict the user's actions by assessing the consequences of those actions on expected utility—actions that lead to higher expected utility are preferred by the agent and predicted by the UMS. Thus, the UMS's ability to model a user's behaviors is reduced to its ability to model the user's preferences. Again the UMS's performance is assessed with a loss function, as described under "Model Performance and Objective Functions."

Formally, a utility function is a function, $R(\ )$, that assigns a real valued utility to every world state: $R : \mathbf{o} \times \mathbf{h} \to \mathbb{R}$. That is, for every assignment of observable and hidden state, the utility of that assignment is a reflection of how much the agent values being in that world state. The agent's desire is to choose its actions so as to maximize some measure of its lifetime utility. The goal of the UMS in this framework is to induce $R(\ )$ by watching the agent's behaviors or, possibly, through direct queries to the agent (e.g., "If given the choice, would you prefer outcome A or B?").

Because agents are almost always temporal, it is necessary to consider the evolution of utility over time and introduce a notion of time aggregation of utility. Agents typically need to trade off immediate gain against

---

[1]In this context, the term *rational* is used in the technical sense from the decision theory literature. The choice of terminology is somewhat unfortunate because it does not precisely align with the commonsense notion of rationality, but we do not have the freedom to choose a better term now.

long-term needs, expressed via a function that assesses the long-term consequences on utility of the choice of actions. If the agent experiences states $\langle \mathbf{h}_{1:T}, \mathbf{o}_{1:T} \rangle$ over the bounded time interval $1, \ldots, T$ then a common utility aggregation function is the *finite horizon average value*:

$$V = \frac{1}{T} \sum_{t=1}^{T} R(\mathbf{h}_t, \mathbf{o}_t) . \tag{5}$$

Often, however, the agent acts for an indefinite amount of time, so the *infinite horizon discounted value* is more appropriate:

$$V = \sum_{t=1}^{\infty} \gamma R(\mathbf{h}_t, \mathbf{o}_t) . \tag{6}$$

In this expression, γ is a discount factor, $0 \leq \gamma < 1$, that prevents divergence of the infinite sum and reflects the decreasing utility of states that occur further in the future.

If the agent takes no actions to influence the world and the system state evolves deterministically, then Eqs. (5) and (6) fully describe the agent's aggregate utility. In our case, however, the agent is a human user who actively participates in the world, and the evolution of the world state is effectively stochastic—unpredictable factors such as interruptions by phone calls, power outages, unexpected project delays, and so on all prevent perfect prediction of the future. Our value functions must, therefore, account for both the user's actions and stochasticity of the world.

To model an agent's actions, we introduce a *policy function*, $\pi(\ )$, that describes the action that the agent takes in any world state: $\pi : \mathbf{h} \times \mathbf{o} \rightarrow A$, where A is the set of actions available to the agent at any point (e.g., A might contain actions like "close the current application," "send e-mail," "get up and stretch," etc.). In general, $\pi(\ )$ could be a stochastic function or a function of the complete history of states, but it suffices for our purposes to describe $\pi(\ )$ as a deterministic function of state. With respect to the user modeling system, actions can be regarded as a subset of observables—the actions are chosen by the user, but are merely monitored by the UMS.

To account for the stochasticity of the world, we write value functions as expectations over world states:

$$V_{avg}^{\pi}(\mathbf{h}_1, \mathbf{o}_1) = E_{\pi}[\frac{1}{T} \sum_{t=1}^{T} R(\mathbf{h}_t, \mathbf{o}_t)]$$

$$= \frac{1}{T} \sum_{t=1}^{T} \sum_{\mathbf{h}_t, \mathbf{o}_t} \Pr[\mathbf{h}_t, \mathbf{o}_t | \mathbf{h}_1, \mathbf{o}_1, \pi] R(\mathbf{h}_t, \mathbf{o}_t) \tag{7}$$

$$V_{\text{disc}}^{\pi}(\mathbf{h}_1,\mathbf{o}_1) = E_{\pi}[\sum_{t=1}^{\infty}\gamma^t R(\mathbf{h}_t,\mathbf{o}_t)]$$

$$= \sum_{t=1}^{\infty}\gamma^t \sum_{\mathbf{h}_t,\mathbf{o}_t}\Pr[\mathbf{h}_t,\mathbf{o}_t\,|\,\mathbf{h}_1,\mathbf{o}_1,\pi]R(\mathbf{h}_t,\mathbf{o}_t) \qquad (8)$$

The agent's goal, now, is to select $\pi(\ )$ so as to maximize one of these functions, whereas the UMS's goal is to induce $R(\ )$ from observation of the user's actions and then to use knowledge of $R(\ )$ to induce $\pi(\ )$ and, therefore, be able to model or predict the user's actions. Unfortunately, exact maximization of Eqs. (7) or (8) are typically intractable for systems that we care about (e.g., humans acting in real-world environments). Further, it is clear that humans do not precisely optimize V_{avg} or V_{disc}, nor do they even necessarily maintain consistent preference functions. We discuss such issues, their consequences, and approaches to handling them further under "Preference Elicitation Approaches."

A TAXONOMY OF USER MODELING METHODOLOGIES

The user modeling problem has been conceptualized in a number of different ways by a myriad of authors, drawing techniques from a wide spectrum of fields. In this section, we attempt to lay out the most widespread ways to conceptualize the problem and describe the results of each method and the relationships among them.

Atemporal Models

One branch of user modeling assumes that behaviors can be predicted instantaneously from current observations, with no knowledge of the past. Essentially, these models assume statistical independence among behaviors:

$$\Pr[\mathbf{o}_{1:T},\mathbf{h}_{1:T}\,|\,\Theta] = \prod_{t=1}^{T}\Pr[\mathbf{o}_t,\mathbf{h}_t\,|\,\Theta]. \qquad (9)$$

This assumption is appropriate in many situations, when we are interested in a user's response to widely separated events or when the temporal coupling between events is low. Note that in this case the lack of temporal coupling allows us to rewrite the inner term of the product:

$$\Pr[\mathbf{o}_t,\mathbf{h}_t\,|\,\Theta] = \Pr[\mathbf{h}_t\,|\,\Theta]\,\Pr[\mathbf{o}_t\,|\,\mathbf{h}_t;\,\Theta]$$

which is essentially a mixture model. For such models, direct maximum likelihood estimation of the system parameters, Θ, is not closed form, but an effective local optimum can be obtained via the Expectation Maximization (EM) algorithm (Dempster, Laird, & Rubin, 1977; Moon, 1996) or gradient ascent methods. In practice, some authors do not attempt to model the hidden state of the user at all, focusing instead on modeling only observable behaviors, in which case Eq. (9) takes the especially simple form:

$$\Pr[\mathbf{o}_{1:T} | \Theta] = \prod_{t=1}^{T} \Pr[\mathbf{o}_t | \Theta] . \tag{10}$$

Lacking any hidden state, such a model is simpler to parameterize, and often a closed form maximum likelihood estimator is available. Although this model is generally more tractable than Eq. (9), it models *only* behavior and neglects the hidden state component that is precisely of interest to us in this context. Furthermore, for complex domains, even Eq. (10) may be difficult to model exactly. In such cases, it is often reasonable to approximate Eq. (10), for example, with a naive Bayes model (Duda, Hart, & Stork, 2001; Hastie, Tibshirani, & Friedman, 2001) or a Bayesian network (Pearl, 1988).

The atemporal model of Eq. (9) is often adopted for applications such as collaborative filtering, recommender systems, or text classification methods, in which user observations are typically sparsely sampled (e.g., a buyer may purchase books at Amazon.com only once a month or so). In such conditions, the temporal coupling between events is fairly low, and most of the information is carried in the aggregate of past interactions. Although these systems often do not attempt to explicitly model a user's internal state, they often model a user's behaviors as a mixture of behaviors drawn from different populations. Thus, a user's cognitive parameters are implicitly modeled as a mixture of the cognitive parameters of their population pool.

Breese, Heckerman, and Kadie (1998) reviewed a number of collaborative filtering techniques including *memory-based* and *model-based* methods. In the memory-based approach, each user's model is taken to be an average over all other users, weighted by the mutual similarity between the target user and the background users. The primary difference among the various collaborative filtering techniques is in the assessment of similarity between pairs of user profiles. Common methods include correlation and vector (or cosine) similarity, possibly including adjustments for default voting, inverse user frequency, or weight amplification. All of these methods essentially represent the user model implicitly as a function of other users' models. Model-based methods, in contrast, attempt to construct an explicit user model that is either exactly or approximately of the form of Eq. (9) or Eq. (10). The authors test the performance of these various methods on a number of collaborative filtering tasks and conclude that, when the data are rich enough to support it, strong model-based methods have better performance. That is, the more closely one can approximate Eq. (9) or Eq. (10), the better. However, the authors also show that, in many cases, one can do quite well with the simple correlation measure.

Although collaborative filtering and recommender systems can be thought of as a type of preference modeling, other similar approaches can be viewed more directly as models of human knowledge states. Latent semantic analysis (LSA), for example, represents texts produced by users as clusters in a high-dimensional *semantic space* (Foltz, Kintsch, & Landauer, 1998; Landauer, Laham, Rehder, & Schreiner, 1997). This technique is similar to the memory-based vector (cosine) analysis examined by Breese et al. (1998), but is intended for use in document similarity and content analyses. After constructing an atemporal, "bag of words" representation of a set of documents, the document matrix is reduced via singular value decomposition (SVD) into a (relatively) low-dimensional semantic space. The knowledge content of any new document can then be assessed by projecting it into this semantic space and comparing it to other known documents in that projected space. Although LSA does make the "bag of words" assumption (essentially Eq. [10]), it turns out to do surprisingly well at assessing user expertise and knowledge. In multiple tests, LSA has been shown to perform competitively with human graders in assessing essay content and expertise (Foltz et al., 1998; Landauer et al., 1997).

Although atemporal methods have achieved great success in some domains, methods that explicitly account for temporal coupling are probably more popular, especially for modeling relatively densely sampled, rapid processes such as user interface behaviors.

Temporal Behavior Modeling and Prediction

A more widespread form of user modeling attempts to take into account the temporal structure of user data, in which case the full independence decomposition of Eq. (9) is inappropriate. In the worst case, it is, in principle, necessary to model the complete joint distribution of Expression (1). This model explodes exponentially with time, however, and is both computationally intractable and utterly infeasible to measure sufficiently to parameterize (e.g., for even modest size systems, this model may possess more parameters than there are particles in the universe). However, it is almost always feasible to make some sort of limiting assumption, such as a *first-order Markov* assumption (Papoulis, 1991; Rabiner, 1989; Smyth,

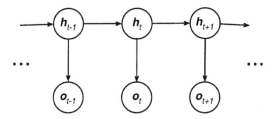

FIG. 11.3. Hidden Markov model of user behaviors. The hidden state vector $\mathbf{h}_t$ encompasses the user's cognitive state at time t, while the observable vector, $\mathbf{o}_t$, captures the user's observed behaviors. The arrows indicate statistical dependencies so, for example, $\mathbf{o}_t$ is statistically dependent on $\mathbf{h}_t$, but is (conditionally) independent of $\mathbf{o}_{t+1}$ or $\mathbf{o}_{t-1}$ given the user's cognitive state at time t. The cognitive model and modeling system are omitted from this diagram.

Heckerman, & Jordan, 1997). Such a model is displayed in Fig. 11.3, where for simplicity we have represented hidden and observables only as vectors.

Under such an assumption, Expression (1) can be rewritten:

$$
\Pr[\mathbf{o}_{1:T}, \mathbf{h}_{1:T} | \Theta] =
$$
$$
\Pr[\mathbf{h}_1 | \Theta] \Pr[\mathbf{o}_1 | \mathbf{h}_1; \Theta] \prod_{t=2}^{T} \Pr[\mathbf{h}_t | \mathbf{h}_{t-1}; \Theta] \Pr[\mathbf{o}_t | \mathbf{h}_t; \Theta]. \qquad (11)
$$

Further decomposition (e.g., factoring out the components of $\mathbf{h}_t$ or $\mathbf{o}_t$) may also be possible depending on the structure of the system. Furthermore, it is also usual to assume *parameter stationarity*—that is,

$$
\Pr[\mathbf{h}_i | \mathbf{h}_{i-1}; \Theta] = \Pr[\mathbf{h}_j | \mathbf{h}_{j-1}; \Theta] \ \forall i, j \qquad (12)
$$

$$
\Pr[\mathbf{o}_i | \mathbf{h}_i; \Theta] = \Pr[\mathbf{o}_j | \mathbf{h}_j; \Theta] \ \forall i, j \qquad (13)
$$

This representation is vastly more tractable than that of Expression (1). Equation (11) means that we need condition any time slice only on one other time slice, rather than all previous history (a bounded, rather than unbounded, conditional probability distribution), whereas Eqs. (12) and (13) allow us to build only a single conditional probability distribution that is stable for all time. Essentially, Eqs. (12) and (13) are a form of parameter tying and allow us to build estimates by averaging over time, rather than having to restart the system to sample every time point multiple times.

One approach to temporal behavior modeling is to adapt atemporal classification methods to the temporal domain. For example, Lane and

Brodley (1997, 1998) and Lane (2000) adapted an instance-based learning technique by considering sliding windows over streams of command-line tokens. That is, instances are of the form $\langle o_{1:k} \rangle$, $\langle o_{2:k+1} \rangle$, $\langle o_{3:k+2} \rangle$, and so on. (Observations in this work were scalar.) Each fixed-length window captures local temporal information; considering overlapping windows ensures that all such local information is represented in at least one window. They introduced a string similarity measure (related to, but cheaper to compute than, edit distance) for describing the similarity between instances. Given a database of sequences and such a similarity measure, it is possible to cluster windows into groups of related behaviors. They found that the user data naturally clustered into a few dominant behavioral groups that reflected common activities, such as email or code development, along with a "heavy tail" of uncommon behaviors that constituted roughly half of the total user activity. While revealing little internal cognitive state, this work did identify discernable activity clusers and was successful in discriminating users by behavior.

A similar approach was taken by Fagan and Cunningham (2003) in their work on recognizing player plans in a video game environment. In their work, they monitored users playing the "Space Invaders" game and tracked sequences of $k = 3$ player actions to predict the fourth action in sequence. They used a case-based reasoning approach similar to the instance-based approach of Lane (2000), albeit employing a more descriptive representation. They also examined the individuality of players in this environment by attempting to predict Player i's behaviors using Player j's model and found that, although there are measurable individual differences, strong accuracy can be achieved with nonindividualized models.

A more direct approach to temporal modeling is to employ methods that are explicitly designed to capture temporal structure. For example, Markov chains (Brémaud, 1999; Kemeny & Snell, 1976), hidden Markov models (HMMs; Rabiner, 1989), dynamic Bayesian networks (Murphy, 2002), or finite state automata (Angluin, 1987; Dean, Angluin, Basye, Engelson, Kaelbling, Kokkevis, & Maron, 1995). Most of these models attempt to capture or approximate the probability distribution of Eq. (11) directly.

Davison and Hirsh (1998) employed Markov chain models to predict the command-line and Web-browsing behaviors of users. A Markov chain is a simplification of the model of Eqs. (11) to (13) by assuming that there is no hidden state and that observable variables are directly coupled together over time:

$$\Pr[\mathbf{o}_{1:T} | \Theta] = \Pr[\mathbf{o}_1 | \Theta] \prod_{t=2}^{T} \Pr[\mathbf{o}_t | \mathbf{o}_{t-1}; \Theta]. \tag{14}$$

Again parameter stationarity (the equivalent of Eqs. [12] and [13], with corresponding simplification to observable state only) is typically assumed. These models record temporal structure—the probability of seeing a specific future behavior given the current observed behavior, $\Pr[\mathbf{o}_{t+1}|o_t]$—but do not posit any additional cognitive variables (hidden state) beyond the transition probabilities. Nonetheless, these authors were able to demonstrate reasonable levels of behavior recognition and prediction.

In follow-up work to the instance-based user modeling work, Lane (1999, 2000) examined the same data sets with an HMM. He found that HMMs had similar classification accuracy to the instance-based method (Lane & Brodley, 1997, 1998), but were able to reveal important cognitive information about the user. The HMMs in this work assume a single, discrete hidden state. Yet even with this simple assumption, Lane found that HMM states captured clusters of user behaviors corresponding to activities such as directory navigation, editing, program development, email use, and so on.

A serious drawback to simple Markov chain and HMM models, however, is that they model time only at one granularity, and it is difficult to represent "metabehaviors" that exist at multiple time scales and span many atomic observations. For example, the observations corresponding to *editing text* may also be contributing to the higher level behavior *reporting results*, which in turn contributes to *forwarding research program*. To attempt to capture such higher level behaviors, a number of researchers have proposed various extensions to the standard HMM formulation.

For example, Oliver, Horvitz, and Garg (2002) applied a layered hidden Markov model to assess user activities in an office computer application environment. Their system integrates multimodal information from video, acoustic, and computer interface data into a series of probability estimates at multiple levels of temporal granularity. The layered model allows the state assessment of a low-level (short-time span) HMM to form the input (observable variable) to a higher level HMM. They examined both an exact, global probability model in which the joint likelihood of low-level models forms an input vector to the higher level model, as well as an approximate model in which the most likely low-level model is determined and then that single ID is provided as a scalar input to the higher level model. Although the former approach is, in principle, capable of using higher level information to mediate among ambiguous lower level assessments, the authors found the more complex general model not to perform any better than the approximate model in their application.

Albrecht, Zukerman, and Nicholson (1998) and Zukerman, Nicholson, and Albrecht (1999) examined the problem of detecting the goals of players in an online multiplayer text adventure game (a multi-user dungeon

[MUD]). In their formulation, there is a single, discrete hidden variable, h_g, which represents a user's current goal. In the MUD context, goals are defined to be quests with recognizable achievement criteria such as recovering specific items, reaching particular locations, and so on. The observable variables are discrete quantities such as player name, time stamp, location, and current command. The objective of the Albrecht et al. system, then, is to estimate the maximum likelihood current goal given a history of observations. They assume that h_g is stationary over a session and dependent only on the goal of the previous session, whereas other variables evolve over a session under various Markov dynamics. These assumptions lead naturally to various dynamic Bayesian network (DBN) models. Such models can be parameterized from the observed data and used to infer a maximum likelihood estimate of h_g. Note that because of the actions of other players and the nonobservability of the complete state of the game, this system is actually non-Markovian. Despite this, their system achieved reasonable success in identifying user goals. A larger difficulty with their model seems to be the assumption of stationarity—often users would suspend working on a particular goal temporarily to address a side quest or to socialize with other players, for example. In these cases, the models' estimates of goals were highly unstable because the model had no way to describe having multiple simultaneous goals, changing goals, or suspending a goal temporarily. They do achieve some improvements by introducing a type of state abstraction over game locations to overcome some of the model assumption violations.

In an approach that verges somewhere between a pure temporal modeling approach and a pure preference modeling approach, Nguyen, Bui, Venkatesh, and West (2003) proposed an "Abstract Hidden Markov mEmory Model" (AHMEM) for a video surveillance task. Their model extends the classical notion of hidden Markov models to include abstract states, which average over many low-level states to represent regimes of behavior as well as context-free behaviors. This model is similar to the Oliver et al. (2002) layered HMM approach, although the AHMEM includes additional state variables to provide a stochastic system memory—essentially a discrete variable that evolves according to finite automaton dynamics that allows the system to track its progress through a long series of tasks. The authors regard the high-level abstractions in this model as being policies, much in the same way that decision processes employ control policies, but there is no notion of utility in this model. It is a purely state monitoring model, and there is no assessment that one policy is preferable to another except insofar as it agrees with observational data. Models that incorporate a full notion of utility require preference elicitation techniques, as we discuss in the next section.

Preference Elicitation Approaches

A number of authors have attempted user modeling via the indirect route of preference elicitation—attempting to infer the user's utility function $R(\ )$ and deduce behaviors from that. This approach has the advantage of giving a more direct and plausible model of the user's internal state than the behavior monitoring methods of the previous sections, but it comes at the price of often drastically more intractable learning and prediction problems. One significant problem is that utility functions can, in principle, be almost entirely unconstrained—every system state could have a radically different utility—and each user can have drastically different preferences. Because the space of states is exponentially large in the number of hidden and observed variables, it is infeasible to simply tabulate preferences for all possible states—a more compact representation must be found.

To address this scaling issue, Chajewska and Koller (2000) developed a series of preference-elicitation methods based on treating utility functions as random variables and subject to Bayesian inference. They proposed a class of utility functions that represent the full utility as a product of compact, basis utility functions, each of which is defined only over a subset of the state variables. That is,

$$R(\mathbf{o}) = \prod_i R_i(s_i),$$

where s_i denotes the ith set of basis variables, $s_i \subseteq \{o^1, \ldots, o^n\}$, and $R_i(\ )$ is the basis function over the set s_i. Further, they assumed that the complete population of users is partitioned into types or classes of users, where all members of a type share a common utility factorization. A specific user's individual utility is developed from his or her base-factored utility, derived from the utility function of his or her class. Both a user's type and individual parameters can, in principle, be identified from data via Bayesian likelihood maximization. A more challenging problem is identifying the appropriate factorization or structure for a particular type. Chajewska and Koller also showed how to apply variants of Bayesian structure search (Heckerman, 1999) to identify these factorizations. By situating the utility elicitation problem in this Bayesian statistical framework, it is possible to obtain confidence bounds over individual utility functions, identify individuals with extremely unusual utilities, or smooth individual utility estimates with respect to the complete population. These authors were concerned primarily with single-step decision problems (e.g., "Would you prefer outcome A or outcome B?"), so they did not address the use of utility functions for modeling or predicting long-term behaviors.

Ng and colleagues developed a class of "inverse reinforcement learning" techniques that attempt to reconstruct a human's *behavioral policy* through observations of that person's activities in an environment (such as a driving simulation; Abbeel & Ng, 2004; Ng & Russell, 2000). In this viewpoint, the goal is to replicate the user's behaviors, and the user's utility function emerges as a consequence of doing so. Specifically, these methods accumulate behavioral traces and measure mean state occupancies (i.e., the average number of timesteps that the human spent in each state of the environment). The assumption is that these traces reflect an "expert policy," π_E, which is a (possibly approximate) solution to a Markov decision process formed by the dynamics of the environment and the user's preference structure. The authors observed that, to closely approximate π_E, it is sufficient to find a $\tilde{\pi}$ that yields the same mean state occupancies as observed from the user. To accomplish this, they employed an algorithm that searches for a utility function, R_w, which, when coupled to the environment, can be solved to produce a $\tilde{\pi}$ whose behavior closely approximates π_E. To render this search feasible, they introduced a set of feature functions, $\phi_i : S \rightarrow [0, 1]$, and then assumed that the utility function is a linear function of the feature vector:

$$R_w(s) = \sum_i w_i \phi_i(s) = \mathbf{w} \cdot \mathbf{\Phi}(s) .$$

Features, in this work, were functions that aggregate atomic states into cogent higher level concepts. In their driving domain, for example, features might be "driving in the right lane" or "just collided with another car." The linearity assumption means that their search algorithm only had to consider the set of possible hyperplanes $\mathbf{w}$, rather than any possible reward function. In practice, they found that they were able to replicate a wide variety of human behaviors in small simulation domains.

Rather than attempting to infer utilities from observations, Royalty, Holland, Goldsmith, and Dekhtyar (2002) employed a direct query approach to preference elicitation. As part of a larger project to develop an automated academic advisement system, they developed a tool to allow users to directly specify their preferences for different outcomes. They represented utility functions via decision trees—essentially nested sets of "if–then" rules. For example, a user might be able to specify preferences of the form: "If class A is offered by professor G in the morning, it is has utility 3, but if it is only offered in the afternoon, it has utility 1." Users are also allowed to specify "don't care" preferences. Such a structure allows representation of an extremely wide variety of outcomes (states of the environment). It is overly burdensome to require the user to explicitly enumerate and specify values for all of these possibilities. Therefore, it is critical to minimize the number of questions that the system requires of the human.

The preference-elicitation tool allows the user to initialize the process by selecting one of a small set of prototypical preference structures such as "graduate early," "graduate with a high GPA," or "party like a rock star." Thereafter, a simple customization interface allows the user to edit this default preference structure without having to specify utilities for every possible outcome or interact directly with the preference trees. Furthermore, humans typically find it difficult to assign quantitative, numeric values to individual outcomes. The authors, therefore, employed a qualitative user interface, presenting the user with slider bars with which to indicate the rough importance of different outcomes.

Boutilier and colleagues also developed a similar system for eliciting and manipulating human preference structures using a qualitative interface (Boutilier, Brafman, Hoos, & Poole, 1999a; Boutilier, Brafman, Domshlak, Hoos, & Poole, 2004). Their work is based on conditional *ceteris paribus* ("all other things being equal") preference assertions. For example, a user could state a preference that "outcome 'high salary' is preferred to 'low salary,' conditional on 'hours per week' being medium and 'medical benefits' being high and all other factors being equal between the two outcomes (independent of what actual values those other factors take on)." Rather than the tree representation employed by Royalty et al., these authors used a graph representation in which each outcome variable, o_i, can have a set of "parent" variables, $Pa(o_i)$, on which the user's preferences about o_i are conditioned. That is, the user's utility function can be written $R(o_i|Pa(o_i))$. The *ceteris paribus* assumption renders this utility function independent of all other variables once an assignment to the set $Pa(o_i)$ is specified. This representation is named "CP-nets" and the authors provided a formal syntax and semantics for it. In addition, they gave inference algorithms allowing assessment of the relative preferences of different outcomes or action selection so as to maximize utility.

One difficulty with allowing users to specify preferences directly, as do Royalty et al. (2002) or Boutilier et al. (1999a, 2004), is that it is conceivable that it may be possible for the user to specify contradictory preferences such as "I prefer A to B, B to C, and C to A." That is, preferences should represent a partial order over states of the world, and cycles should be disallowed. This difficulty does not arise for preference inference methods such as those of Chajewska and Koller (2000) or Abbeel and Ng (2004) and Ng and Russell (2000) because these methods employ an underlying representation that is incapable of representing such cycles. If the user exhibits contradictory behaviors, the update algorithms that build and maintain the underlying representation will resolve the contradictions either by dropping subsets of the evidence or averaging over it. For preference-specification methods, however, the language with which users can describe their preferences (e.g., preference trees or CP-nets) may allow such cycles. Although Royalty et al. did not examine this issue directly, it may not actually be possible to specify contradictory preferences in their system. CP-nets, however, allow the user to specify contradictory preferences. Boutilier et al. addressed this by giving formal conditions for CP-net consistency as well as algorithms to detect inconsistent networks.

SUMMARY AND RECOMMENDATIONS

In this chapter, we reviewed the mathematical foundations of modeling human cognitive states from data and examined a number of deployed examples of these techniques. In this section, we attempt to assemble the *big picture* of the current state of user modeling by focusing on a number of key issues that need to be addressed in any UMS implementation. This framework is intended to help the designer of an adaptive cognitive modeling system quickly narrow down the space of techniques to those relevant to a specific situation. Before undertaking construction of a user modeling system, a designer should assess the following aspects of the target domain.

Cognitive Variables

Probably the most important single question to answer is: What are the relevant cognitive variables that are important to model? Cognitive variables are those variables presumed to occur "within the user's head"— they are the object of principal interest here, but are not subject to direct observation and are, therefore, treated as hidden variables. Possible significant cognitive variables to model range from none, through small sets of individual variables (such as cognitive load, current goal, etc.), to complete models of full utility functions for individual humans.

In the first category, fall approaches like recommender systems (Breese et al., 1998), LSA models (Foltz et al., 1998; Landauer et al., 1997), or instance-based methods (Fagan & Cunningham, 2003; Lane & Brodley, 1997, 1998). Although we refer to these approaches as maintaining "no" cognitive variables, that is not, strictly speaking, correct. Although these models do not explicitly store any variables corresponding to human internal mental state, they do construct implicit representations of mental states and/or behaviors. Specifically, all of these approaches model an individual user as an average across a population of users or as a cluster of behaviors. These averages capture the aggregate influence of the hidden cognitive variables even if they do not represent those variables directly.

The second category comprises the bulk of the work on temporal user modeling, including Markov chains, hidden Markov models, various flavors of hierarchical or layered HMMs, and dynamic Bayesian networks. These systems do posit varying amounts of hidden, cognitive user state. They frame the user modeling problem as reconstructing this hidden state from observable information. The main difference among these systems is the amount of information they attempt to maintain about the user. Simple models, such as Markov chains (Davison & Hirsh, 1998), essentially only model transition probabilities—the chance of generating one behavior given the previous behavior. This captures only the user's structure of linkages between behaviors and says little about the goals of those behaviors. Slightly more sophisticated models, such as HMMs (Lane, 2000), additionally track a single hidden variable that can be interpreted as denoting clusters of behaviors. Yet more powerful models, such as layered or hierarchical HMMs (Nguyen et al., 2003; Oliver et al., 2002) or DBNs (Albrecht et al., 1998; Zukerman et al., 1999), effectively maintain multiple hidden variables that track behavioral groupings at different granularities or time scales. That is, rather than describing a single partition of behaviors into clusters, such as "editing activities" versus "emailing activities," they can maintain higher level views such as "activities related to project A" or "activities related to research in general." These higher level behaviors can then subsume lower level behaviors as subroutines. Such an approach fits nicely with well-established multiresolution models of human–computer interaction such as the Goals, Operators, Methods, and Selection (GOMS) model (Card, Moran, & Newell, 1983).

The final category includes methods that attempt to build a complete model of the user's utility or reward function (i.e., a mapping from world states to utility values). The premise here is that the utility function is the most complete possible representation of a person's goals and intentions. Knowledge of the complete utility function should, in principle, allow us to interpret and predict a user's actions. Unfortunately, for all practical problems, it is completely intractable to measure a complete reward function. Therefore, all of the approaches in this area require some assumptions that allow compact representation of general utility functions. Typically, these take the form of some sort of factored representation (Chajewska & Koller, 2000), a set of default assumptions (Boutilier et al., 2004; Royalty et al., 2002), or a dimensionality-reduction projection function (Abbeel & Ng, 2004; Ng & Russell, 2000). Only with that representation specified can practical learning of utilities be achieved.

Observable Data Sources

Once a designer of a cognitive modeling system has isolated the cogent cognitive variables, the next critical factor to determine is what data are available as inputs to the system. Possibilities vary from individual commands typed into a computer command-line prompt (Davison & Hirsh, 1998; Lane, 2000), to complete behavioral traces while driving a vehicle or simulator (Abbeel & Ng, 2004), to entire textual documents (Foltz et al., 1998; Landauer et al., 1997), to direct interactive queries of the user (Royalty et al., 2002). The richness and quality of data significantly constrain the design of the entire user modeling system and may force reconsideration of the relevant cognitive variables. Although the designer may wish to model the entire utility function of a user, if the only available data are historical textual documents from that user (with no surrounding context), it is probably not feasible to do any sort of preference elicitation. In such cases, the designer may have to scale back to more achievable goals and take a less data-intensive approach such as LSA.

In general, the atemporal models make the fewest assumptions about the user and require the sparsest data. More sophisticated temporal modeling strategies typically require more data, observed over longer periods of time. The presence of hidden variables in a model complicates things considerably because it can be difficult to determine the cardinality of these variables and, without some observations of the hidden state, state identifications are nonunique. (That is, the inference algorithms are incapable of associating a particular label with an underlying state. A system may be able to distinguish different regimes of behaviors, but be incapable of labeling each with an appropriate cognitive descriptor.) Finally, preference-elicitation approaches are the most complex of all and require knowledge of the interaction between a user and a dynamic environment. That is, it is necessary to observe not just the user's behaviors, but also the environmental context for those behaviors.

Relevant Time Scale(s)

The next critical question is what time scale(s) are important to consider? This axis varies from none—time is irrelevant (Breese et al., 1998; Foltz et al., 1998; Landauer et al., 1997)—to time can be measured synchronously at a single scale and all important behaviors are exhibited at that single scale (Abbeel & Ng, 2004; Boutilier et al., 2004; Chajewska & Koller, 2000; Davison & Hirsh, 1998; Fagan & Cunningham, 2003; Lane, 2000; Ng & Russell, 2000; Royalty et al., 2002), to multitime-scale approaches that model behaviors hierarchically (Albrecht et al., 1998; Nguyen et al., 2003; Oliver et al., 2002; Zukerman et al., 1999). The predominance of single-time-scale approaches in this list is a testament to two factors: Temporality is critical to many human behaviors, and multiscalar temporal modeling is difficult.

The latter factor reflects the inherent statistical difficulty in indirectly estimating multiple layers of hidden variables. Consider, for example, a system with two temporal scales modeled as two layers of hidden variables—say, a low-level behavior variable that tracks the immediate activities of a user (editing document, working on email, Web browsing, etc.) and a high-level behavior variable that tracks long-term goals and behaviors (such as which project the user is working on). To estimate the high-level behavior variable, the user modeling system first has to achieve a complete and accurate model of the low-level behavior. Inaccuracies in estimating the low-level state of the system can translate to extreme inaccuracies in estimating the high-level state. In turn, estimation of the high-level state can force reinterpretation of low-level behaviors and cause them to be reestimated. Altogether, estimating a multiscalar temporal system can require vastly more data than estimating a single-scalar system. This difficulty can be ameliorated somewhat if intermittent observations of the high-level state are allowed (e.g., the user's timesheet is available or the user modeling system is allowed to ask direct queries of the user).

We note that, to our knowledge, nobody has yet attempted to couple multiple-time-scale modeling with preference-elicitation techniques. Both problems are individually extremely challenging, and integrating them together is indeed a daunting prospect. Nonetheless, there are numerous applications that would benefit from being able to do both simultaneously. For example, such an approach would allow us to model how a user assesses the costs and benefits of immediate activities (open a document via a menu vs. via a hotkey combination) versus longer term activities (work on Project A vs. Project B).

Representation and Learning Algorithm

With the prior issues decided, it is possible to select a representation for the cognitive state and an algorithm for estimating that state from data. In many cases, the representation will simply be the set of relevant cognitive variables. Often it is tractable and even preferred to maintain posterior estimates of small sets of cognitive variables directly. For example, many temporal models explicitly maintain temporal probability models, as in Eqs. (11) or (14). The parameters of these models (Θ—typically transition and/or output probability distributions) can often be estimated from data via maximum likelihood (ML) or maximum a posteriori (MAP) estimation techniques (Duda et al., 2001; Hastie et al., 2001), possibly augmented with an expectation-maximization (EM) procedure when there are hidden variables in the system (Dempster et al., 1977; Moon, 1996).

For nearly all of these parameter estimation techniques, there are both batch-mode and online (recursively updated) versions depending on the needs of the designer. Although both batch-mode and online learning algorithms should converge to the same model in the limit of infinite data (assuming stationarity of Eqs. [12] or [13]), in practice batch-mode parameter estimation is generally more stable, yields better estimates given bounded amounts of data than does online estimation, and is marginally simpler to code. Nonetheless, if the task requires that the cognitive model adapt to the user in real time, while in use, online estimation methods may be preferred. Furthermore, it is usually overly strong to assume perfect parameter stationarity, and thus an online estimation method may be preferred because it is more easily adapted to track changing parameter distributions.

Not all models fall so nicely into standard parameter estimation techniques, however. In some cases, both representation and learning algorithm can be quite a bit simpler. Memory- or instance-based models, for example, represent the model simply as a large collection or library of instances of previously recorded behaviors (Breese et al., 1998; Fagan & Cunningham, 2003; Lane, 2000; Lane & Brodley, 1997). In these cases, the cognitive state is stored implicitly as an interpolation among some or all of this instance base. The learning step, then, is simply recording and storing the behaviors, possibly with some data pruning or reduction (Aha, Kibler, & Albert, 1991; Lane & Brodley, 1998). The difficult step in such approaches is almost always quickly and accurately retrieving the relevant set of instances for comparison to any newly observed behavior. Sometimes it is possible to take an intermediate position and, rather than literally storing an entire instance base, precompile the instance base into a representation that makes later retrieval simple. Latent semantic analysis (LSA) methods, for example, essentially precompile a large instance base into a small set of principal directions by performing a singular value decomposition on the data matrix (Foltz et al., 1998; Landauer et al., 1997).

At the other end of the spectrum are preference-elicitation techniques, for which we would *wish* to be able to perform standard parameter estimation, but where such techniques utterly break down in the face of the scale of the problem (Abbeel & Ng, 2004; Boutilier, Dean, & Hanks, 1999b; Boutilier et al., 2004; Chajewska & Koller, 2000; Ng & Russell, 2000; Royalty et al., 2002). In these cases, it is not possible to directly model the cognitive state of interest—a complete utility function—so it is necessary to change the representation. These approaches all spend significant effort to decompose full utility functions into some collection of smaller, easily parameterizable functions. Parameter estimation is then carried out in this space of compact functions via standard estimation methods (e.g., ML or MAP, plus EM, as discussed earlier). These decompositions will almost certainly sacrifice some descriptive power, but in practice it seems to be a useful tradeoff as humans do not usually appear to employ the full potential of general utility functions. That is, it is rarely the case that a human will have an extreme and difficult to represent utility function such as "having soup, fish, salad, and cake for dinner has high utility, but having any proper subset of that has zero utility and adding anything extra also has zero utility." The key to designing a good decomposition of utility function space is to take into account such regularities in human preference structures. Identifying these regularities, however, remains a question largely for cognitive psychology.

CONCLUSION

Although we have reviewed user modeling techniques largely from a statistical and machine learning point of view, there are more vital roles to be played by other disciplines. In particular, all of the infrastructure we have described here rests on the assumption of a specific modeling task and a focus on particular cognitive variables. The choice of these components depends on the role that the cognitive model is to play and the type of cognitive state that the designer wishes to monitor. Those questions remain the domain of system designers, implementors, cognitive scientists, and customers. Only when such issues are fully decided can the techniques overviewed in this chapter be brought to bear.

ACKNOWLEDGMENTS

This work was performed in collaboration with Sandia National Laboratories and supported, in part, by the U.S. Department of Energy under Contract DE-AC04-94AL85000.

REFERENCES

Abbeel, P., & Ng, A. Y. (2004). Apprenticeship learning via inverse reinforcement learning. In R. Greiner & D. Schuurmans (Eds.), *Proceedings of the Twenty-First International Conference on Machine Learning (ICML-2004*; pp. 1–8), Banff, Canada.

Aha, D., Kibler, D., & Albert, M. (1991). Instance-based learning algorithms. *Machine Learning, 6*(1), 37–66.

Albrecht, D. W., Zukerman, I., & Nicholson, A. E. (1998). Bayesian models for keyhole plan recognition in an adventure game. *User Modeling and User-Adapted Interaction, 8*(1–2), 5–47.

Angluin, D. (1987). Learning regular sets from queries and counterexamples. *Information and Computation*, 75–87.

Boutilier, C., Brafman, R. I., Domshlak, C., Hoos, H. H., & Poole, D. (2004). CP-nets: A tool for representing and reasoning with conditional ceteris paribus preference statements. *Journal of Artificial Intelligence Research, 21*, 135–191.

Boutilier, C., Brafman, R. I., Hoos, H. H., & Poole, D. (1999a). Reasoning with conditional ceteris paribus preference statements. In *Proceedings of the Fifteenth Annual Conference on Uncertainty in AI (UAI-99*; pp. 71–80), Stockholm, Sweden.

Boutilier, C., Dean, T., & Hanks, S. (1999b). Decision-theoretic planning: Structural assumptions and computational leverage. *Journal of Artificial Intelligence Research, 11*, 1–94.

Breese, J. S., Heckerman, D., & Kadie, C. M. (1998). Empirical analysis of predictive algorithms for collaborative filtering. In G. F. Cooper & S. Moral (Eds.), *Proceedings of the Fourteenth Conference on Uncertainty in Artificial Intelligence (UAI-98*; pp. 43–52), Madison, WI: Morgan Kaufmann.

Brémaud, P. (1999). *Markov Chains: Gibbs Fields, Monte Carlo Simulation, and Queues* (Vol. 31 of *Texts in Applied Mathematics*). New York: Springer-Verlag.

Card, S., Moran, T., & Newell, A. (1983). *The psychology of human–computer interaction*. Hillsdale, NJ: Lawrence Erlbaum Associates.

Chajewska, U., & Koller, D. (2000). Utilities as random variables: Density estimation and structure discovery. In *Proceedings of the Sixteenth Annual Conference on Uncertainty in AI (UAI 2000*; pp. 63–71), Stanford, CA.

Davison, B. D., & Hirsh, H. (1998). Predicting sequences of user actions. In *Proceedings of the AAAI-98/ICML-98 Joint Workshop on AI Approaches to Time-series Analysis* (pp. 5–12).

Dean, T., Angluin, D., Basye, K., Engelson, S., Kaelbling, L., Kokkevis, E., & Maron, O. (1995). Inferring finite automata with stochastic output functions and an application to map learning. *Machine Learning Journal, 18*(1), 81–108.

Dempster, A. P., Laird, N. M., & Rubin, D. B. (1977). Maximum likelihood from incomplete data via the EM algorithm. *Journal of the Royal Statistical Society Series B, 39*, 1–38.

Duda, R. O., Hart, P. E., & Stork, D. G. (2001). *Pattern classification* (2nd ed.). New York: Wiley.

Fagan, M., & Cunningham, P. (2003). *Case-based plan recognition in computer games* (Tech. Rep. TCD-CS-2003-01). Dublin: Trinity College, Computer Science Dept.

Foltz, P. W., Kintsch, W., & Landauer, T. K. (1998). The measurement of textual coherence with latent semantic analysis. *Discourse Processes, 25*, 285–307.

Hastie, T., Tibshirani, R., & Friedman, J. (2001). *The elements of statistical learning: Data mining, inference, and prediction*. New York: Springer.

Heckerman, D. (1999). *Learning in graphical models: A tutorial on learning with Bayesian networks*. Cambridge, MA: MIT Press.

Kemeny, J. G., & Snell, J. L. (1976). *Finite Markov chains. Undergraduate texts in mathematics*. New York: Springer-Verlag.

Landauer, T. K., Laham, D., Rehder, B., & Schreiner, M. E. (1997). How well can passage meaning be derived without using word order? A comparison of latent semantic analysis and humans. In M. G. Shafto & P. Langley (Eds.), *Proceedings of the 19th annual meeting of the Cognitive Science Society* (pp. 412–417). Mahwah, NJ: Lawrence Erlbaum Associates.

Lane, T. (1999). Hidden Markov models for human/computer interface modeling. In *Proceedings of the IJCAI-99 Workshop on Learning About Users, Sixteenth International Joint Conference on Artificial Intelligence* (pp. 35–44).

Lane, T. (2000). *Machine learning techniques for the computer security domain of anomaly detection*. Unpublished doctoral dissertation, Purdue University, W. Lafayette, IN.

Lane, T., & Brodley, C. E. (1997). Sequence matching and learning in anomaly detection for computer security. In *Proceedings of AAAI-97 Workshop on AI Approaches to Fraud Detection and Risk Management, Fourteenth National Conference on Artificial Intelligence* (pp. 43–49).

Lane, T., & Brodley, C. E. (1998). Approaches to online learning and concept drift for user identification in computer security. In R. Agrawal, P. Stolorz, & G. Piatetsky-Shapiro

(Eds.), *Proceedings of the Fourth International Conference on Knowledge Discovery and Data Mining* (pp. 259–263). New York: AAAI.

Lenat, D. B. (1995). CYC: A large-scale investment in knowledge infrastructure. *Communications of the ACM, 38*(11), 33–38.

Luger, G. F. (2002). *Artificial intelligence: Structures and strategies for complex problemsolving* (4th ed.). New York: Addison Wesley.

Moon, T. K. (1996). The expectation-maximization algorithm. *IEEE Signal Processing Magazine, 47*–59.

Murphy, K. (2002). *Dynamic Bayesian networks: Representation, inference and learning.* Unpublished doctoral dissertation, UC Berkeley.

Ng, A. Y., & Russell, S. (2000). Algorithms for inverse reinforcement learning. In P. Langley (Ed.), *Proceedings of the Seventeenth International Conference on Machine Learning (ICML-2000)*, Stanford, CA: Morgan Kaufmann.

Nguyen, N. T., Bui, H. H., Venkatesh, S., & West, G. (2003). Recognising and monitoring high-level behaviours in complex spatial environments. In *Proceedings of the IEEE International Conference on Computer Vision and Pattern Recognition (CVPR-03)*, IEEE Press.

Oliver, N., Horvitz, E., & Garg, A. (2002). Layered representations for human activity recognition. In *Fourth IEEE Int. Conf. on Multimodal Interfaces* (pp. 3–8).

Papoulis, A. (1991). *Probability, random variables, and stochastic processes* (3rd ed.). New York: McGraw-Hill.

Pearl, J. (1988). *Probabilistic reasoning in intelligent systems: Networks of plausible inference.* New York: Morgan Kaufmann.

Puterman, M. L. (1994). *Markov decision processes: Discrete stochastic dynamic programming.* New York: Wiley.

Rabiner, L. R. (1989). A tutorial on hidden Markov models and selected applications in speech recognition. *Proceedings of the IEEE, 77*(2).

Rosenbloom, P. S., Laird, J. E., & Newell, A. (Eds.). (1993). *The Soar Papers: Research on integrated intelligence.* Cambridge, MA: MIT Press.

Royalty, J., Holland, R., Goldsmith, J., & Dekhtyar, A. (2002). POET: The online preference elicitation tool. In *AAAI-02 Workshop, Preferences in AI and CP: Symbolic Approaches*, Edmonton, Canada: AAAI Press.

Russell, S. J., & Norvig, P. (2002). *Artificial intelligence: A modern approach* (2nd ed.). New York: Prentice-Hall.

Smyth, P., Heckerman, D., & Jordan, M. (1997). Probabilistic independence networks for hidden Markov models. *Neural Computation, 9*(2), 227–269.

Sutton, R. S., & Barto, A. G. (1998). *Reinforcement learning: An introduction.* Cambridge, MA: MIT Press.

Zukerman, I., Nicholson, A. E., & Albrecht, D. (1999). Evaluation methods for learning about users. In T. Dean (Ed.), *Proceedings of the Sixteenth International Joint Conference on Artificial Intelligence (IJCAI-99)*, Stockholm, Sweden: Morgan Kaufmann.

CHAPTER TWELVE

Metacognition—What a Cognitive System May/Should Know About Itself

Michael L. Bernard
Sandia National Laboratories

The question of whether computers can think is like the question of whether submarines can swim.
—Edsger Wybe Dijkstra (www.amusingquotes.com)

As far back as 1960, academic and governmental visionaries such as Joseph Licklider mused that, "in not too many years, human brains and computing machines will be coupled together very tightly, and that the resulting partnership will think as no human brain has ever thought and process data in a way not approached by the information-handling machine we know today" (p. 2). Although this vision has yet to be truly realized, efforts have been made toward this end. Nevertheless, until Licklider's vision is brought to fruition, the relationship between humans and computers will generally be an uneasy one. That is to say, the complexity of computer systems will continue to regularly burden the mental capacity and patience of humans.

There are many reasons for this current relationship, the main reason being that we have yet to fully adapt the computer to the user, rather than forcing the user to adapt to the practices and conventions set by the software design. In addition, as programs become more sophisticated, the complexity of this human–computer relationship will invariably change and intensify. Advances in computing power *will* tend to exacerbate this situation by permitting more complex systems to operate. Indeed an increase in complexity inevitably necessitates expanding the time needed to learn how to use these systems. As Ron Brachman, the Director of the Information Processing Technology Office at the Defense Advanced Research Projects Agency (DARPA), suggested, "we can't afford merely to increase the speed and capacity of our computer systems. We can't just do better software engineering. We need to change our perspective on computational systems and get off the current trajectory" (Brachman, 2002, p. 67).

To accomplish this undertaking, computer systems need to be fashioned into an appliance that can truly learn from the user—that is, a cognitive system that can learn from experience, understand the intent of the user over time, and develop an understanding of what it knows and does not know about its environment. This notion is not by any means new. In fact people such as Licklider (1960) suggested that computers should have the capability to understand their user to the point of developing idiosyncrasies through experiential learning corresponding to the idiosyncrasies of the user, resulting in a symbiosis between the two. In essence, a computer system should have an ability that allows it to form a cognitive symbiosis between itself and the user. The effect will be an intelligent behaving machine that mimics, in some ways, human thought processes. As Evans forecasted in his book, *The Micro Millennium*, 20 years ago:

> We are about to embark on a massive programme to develop highly intelligent machines, a process by which we will lead computers by the hand until they reach our own intellectual level, after which they will proceed to surpass us. . . . But what will we do with the Ultra-Intelligent Machines when they arrive? Clearly, the first thing would be to put them to work on some of the numerous problems facing society. These could be economic, medical or educational matters, and also, perhaps, strategic modeling to forecast trends and produce early warning of difficulties or crises. . . . It is unlikely that there will be any serious objection to this apart from those of an emotional or doctrinaire nature. (cited in Winograd & Flores, 1987, p. 4)

Yet how can this effort become realized? To achieve this, computer systems need to not only understand the data being processed, but also why it is being processed to fully assist humans in our endeavor to understand our own environment. More important, these systems would also need to integrate this information with previous experiences to form an internal representation of their environment. Moreover, as Brachman stated, the next generation computer system should be able to be taught and operated by nonexperts, should be cognizant of its own role in organizations and/or teams, and should be able to rationally interact with other team members in a natural way (Brachman & Lemnios, 2002).

METACOGNITION IN HUMANS

All of the previously mentioned requirements necessitate a computer system having some form of metacognitive ability. *Metacognition* has been defined as "one's knowledge concerning one's own cognitive processes and products or anything related to them" (Flavell, 1976, p. 232). What is implied here is a process of self-monitoring that not only occurs alongside experience as it takes place, but also retrospectively as one considers previous experiences as they have occurred (Schooler, 2002). This internal knowledge about one's own knowledge often takes place without awareness, such as when an individual evaluates his or her decisions after conducting a task.

A general distinction has traditionally been made between several different forms of metacognition (Jacobs & Paris, 1987; Schraw, 1998). The first form is the appraisal of one's own cognition. Here we seek to reflect on and self-evaluate the information that is known to us, how something is done and the process behind it, and the conditions that apply to certain strategies or situations. The appraisal of one's own cognition involves the knowledge of oneself as a learner, as well as recognizing the most effective and efficient manner to learn. This may involve both the use of certain strategies that promote learning and the understanding of when to implement these strategies.

In contrast to the first form, in which one periodically reflects on their cognitive process, the second form is an ongoing self-management of one's own thinking. This entails the dynamic evaluation of an individual's thought process and the mechanisms that control these processes. Metacognitive self-monitoring enhances the efficiency of the thought process by increasing an individual's awareness of their strategies, resources, and general understanding of the learning task (Schraw, 1998). For example, Schraw (1994) found that college students' performance significantly correlated with their ability to monitor their reading comprehension.

As one becomes more practiced with a particular task, he or she tends to develop global, abstract planning (Schraw, 1994). Indeed a study by Schoenfeld (1987) found a difference between novice and expert mathematicians, wherein novices quickly adopted a strategy for solving the problem, but concentrated on implementing this strategy with insufficient thought as to whether their strategy actually moved them toward accomplishing their goals. In contrast, experts sought to first reduce ambiguity by studying the problem before attempting to solve it. Once the problem was understood, they tried different approaches until they found one that was the most logical for solving the problem. The experts' attempt to first analyze the problem and then monitor their progress resulted in a much higher success rate than just seeking to tackle the problem without first considering it thoroughly and without attention to the success of their efforts.

Not surprisingly, both forms of metacognition can apply across a wide spectrum of subject domains. For example, Schoenfeld (1989) found that students' knowledge regarding how to actively manage their thinking is critical to their success in school. Moreover, at least for certain types of problem solving, Schoenfeld (1985) argued that four categories of knowledge and behavior exist: resources (general subject knowledge), heuristics (problem-solving techniques), control (metacognition), and belief systems (attitudes). Often the problems that students encounter are generally spawned from a breakdown with the last two categories—namely, their metacognitive control and their attitudes concerning the subject matter. Specifically, they may not use the knowledge they have, properly applying it to the problem at hand, because of an initial lack of appropriate evaluation and monitoring of their success (Gourgey, 1998).

METACOGNITION AND COMPUTERS

It is certainly conceivable for a need to have computer systems that produce some degree of "insight" as to their own abilities and knowledge. This is particularly true in instances in which the system has great autonomy and/or operates in a dynamic environment. For instance, a computer system could have metacognitive abilities that would allow it to know its current capability with regard to its environment, know what it does not yet know, and make changes to acquire the knowledge that it currently does not have. This knowledge would be gained either through experience or by means of direct instruction. In a sense, the system would know itself.

There are many examples where initial forms of this technology could currently be applied—such as with robotic devices that operate at remote distances. In essence, any environment in which unforeseeable events occur would benefit from this technology. Instead of preprogramming a computer for any contingency, which is terribly inefficient, computers with metacognitive abilities would recognize their strengths and weaknesses and plan a response with these strengths and weaknesses in mind.

This seems to be an extremely ambitious undertaking. Yet if one accounts for the progress that has been made in such a short time, it may be conceivable that a computer with extensive, humanlike metacognitive abilities could exist sometime before the middle of this century. In fact efforts by computer scientists, psychologists, and the like have worked toward this end with encouraging success.

If Moore's law—which predicts a linear growth in computing power and memory, in that the number of transistors on integrated circuits doubles every 18 months—continues to accurately predict computational growth, we should have the equivalent storage capacity of a brain (i.e., 4 million Gbytes) by approximately the year 2030 (Buttazzo, 2001). Of course great breakthroughs in information processing, as well as advances in computing and our general understanding of our own mind, are also required, which is no small feat.

The difficulties in implementing such a system may rest more in our lack of understanding of how humans think. Namely, we currently do not truly know all of the mechanisms that underlie our own metacognitive abilities. Having said this, simple elements of metacognition could be applied to computer systems in the near term. Even basic elements of metacognition would be a vast improvement in the way computers interact with humans. Producing the first instances of true metacognitive ability would also enable the system to mimic, to a small degree, the behaviors associated with our notion of human self-consciousness (see Minsky, 1985).

Of course enabling the computer system to have a certain measure of actual self-consciousness would in essence provide it with a critical ingredient that makes up the human mind—that is, what makes us who we are. However, many would argue that no computer system will ever be able to achieve a true sense of self-consciousness—assuming we can actually determine what makes up self-consciousness. As Professor Lister argued in 1949, ". . . not until a machine can write a sonnet or compose a concerto because of thoughts and emotions felt, and not be the chance fall of symbols, could we agree that machine equals brain—that is not only write it but know that it had written it" (cited in Turing, 1950/1988, p. 60). Most people do not write sonnets or compose concertos, however. What is really important are the simple abilities of humans. That is, the ability to basically know what we are doing at any given moment in time.

Yet even if a computer developed a metacognitive sense of self-consciousness, how would we know? The question has been posed by people such as Alan Turing, who is considered to be one of the founders of computer science. If a computer can be shown to exhibit *some* metacognitive ability with regard to *any* subject matter, it is considered to have reflective thoughts about what it is doing—at least for a particular subject matter (Turing, 1950/1988).

One of the most noted methods to test for metacognitive awareness is the Turing test. The test basically determines whether a computer can understand, deliberate, respond to questions, and have a dialogue with a human over a wide range of topics. If humans cannot determine whether they are communicating with either a person or computer after discussing a wide range of topics (e.g., politics, weather, values), the computer has passed the test. Currently, computers only had successes with the test when the topic was narrowly defined.

In a type of Turing test, IBM created a computer named Deep Blue in 1997 to challenge world chess champion Garry Kasparov to a chess match. Remarkably, and for the first time in history, a computer actually beat a chess champion. Of course this does not mean that the computer is more intelligent than Kasparov or even that it has intelligence and understands the game of chess and knows the significance of each move. What it does mean is that computers now have the capability to apply their computing power in the form of programming rules to calculate the best chess positions as the game unfolds—without a true understanding of what it is doing or why it is doing it. The ability to interact with humans and even beat us at a game of chess does show that computers can *perform* in an intelligent manner, but only that. This capacity to mimic human intelligence does, unfortunately, make it difficult to determine whether a computer has metacognitive reasoning.

Even the general notion of metacognition is a difficult concept to fully grasp. For example, attempts to correlate human metacognitive accuracy with the ability to learn new concepts have often met with nonsignificant results (Kelemen, Frost, & Weaver, 2000). In addition, metacognitive performance has generally been found to be unstable over time (Thompson & Mason, 1996). Most important, we do not know exactly how the mechanisms that underlie metacognitive self-consciousness for humans actually work.

Theories that are currently receiving attention postulate that awareness is generated by the brain's electromagnetic field, which is produced by the 100 billion or so neurons that reside there. A contributor to this theory, Johnjoe McFadden (2002), proposed that self-consciousness occurs when sensory information from the environment passes through the electromagnetic field in the brain to the individual's neurons and then back again to the electromagnetic field, creating a loop that forms our consciousness. Explicitly, information contained within the neurons are pooled and integrated to form an electromagnetic field. Consciousness is consequently a byproduct of electromagnetic field information transmitted to specific neurons (e.g., motor neurons), which then decode this information, producing a self-referring loop and, ultimately, determines our free will and potential actions. As the complexity of conscious thinking increases, so does the complexity of the electromagnetic field (McFadden, 2002).

There is measurable support for this hypothesis. For example, researchers such as Klimesch (1987, 1994, 1996) and others postulated there is strong evidence for the assumption that electromagnetic oscillations serve as the communication mechanism between neurons. Synchronous oscillations of large assemblies reflect a resting state of the brain. During mental activity, certain neuronal networks may begin oscillating with different frequencies. Each of the networks that are in some way connected in function may oscillate synchronously with each other while out of phase with the larger cell assemblies (see Fig. 12.1).

For example, if one attends to a bird, then neurons associated with recognition and representation of that bird would fire synchronously in a particular pattern. These patterns may be physically separated in the brain, but all contribute to the sensation of seeing the bird. At the electromagnetic field level, all aspects of information representing the bird, such as its form, characteristics, and the like, are physically linked such that it generates a unified field that represents conscious perception.

Klimesch contended that electromagnetic oscillations at certain frequency bands (i.e., alpha) facilitate encoding, accessing, and retrieving codes that are stored by means of a widely distributed and highly interconnected set of assemblies. It is thus possible that the electromagnetic oscillations and the neuronal networks together produce (or at least contribute to) our sense of metacognitive self-consciousness. If consciousness is a function of the brain's electromagnetic field, it *may* be possible to create computer systems that could duplicate this process in some form. However, as Bruce MacLennan, an expert in the field of computation, stated, such a computer may be possible, but not in the foreseeable future. "I cannot exaggerate how far we are from being able to construct a robot with the real-world cognitive capacities of a simple mammal, let alone a human. . . . We are even further from being able to make a principled claim that any artificial system is conscious. We have so much more to learn" (cited in Viegas, 2002, p. 1). Indeed McFadden (2002) argued that having a mechanical replacement of neural functioning that has field-level repre-

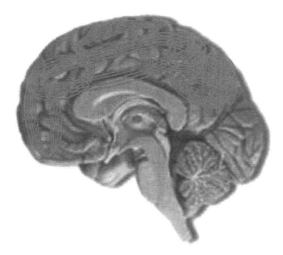

FIG. 12.1. A representation of multiple synchronous oscillations in phase with each other.

sentations of information would not behave in the same way as a biologically conscious person if the brain were not modeled in a physically similar fashion.

CURRENT ENDEAVOR TO SIMULATE METACOGNITION

An effort is currently underway at Sandia National Laboratories (Sandia) and other laboratories to do this by modeling aspects of human cognition in a plausible manner. Namely, work is being done to actually model the functioning of a human brain as accurately as possible to create a cognitively driven computer system. As discussed in chapter 1 of this book, Sandia's cognitive framework seeks to model naturalistic human decision making, as opposed to using more rule-based approaches (Forsythe, Bernard, Xavier, Abbott, Speed, & Brannon, 2002; Forsythe & Raybourn, 2001; Forsythe & Xavier, 2002). The Sandia cognitive models incorporate oscillating systems ideas concerning the neurophysiology underlying human cognition (Klimesch, 1996) to simulate elements of metacognition (Mazzoni & Nelson, 1998), multimodal memory of humans (Solomon & Barsalou, 2001), and the cognitive–affective interplay (LeDoux, 1998).

In the cognitive model, streaming inputs from the environment feed perceptual algorithms that perceive the system's environment. These algorithms operate in parallel and, depending on the corresponding cue in the associative network, provide either a continuous or discrete level of activation. For a given perceptual algorithm, if the level of activation is sufficient, a response is elicited from the corresponding node in an associative network. The associative network is modeled as an oscillating system, wherein each node is a separate oscillator. Perceptual activation causes corresponding nodes to begin oscillating, with activation spreading to other nodes for which there exists an associative relationship. Spreading activation between nodes in the associative network may be sufficient to cause a node, receiving activation, to begin oscillating or may prime the node such that the node exhibits a lowered threshold for activation by perceptual processes.

Recognition of situations occurs when there is activation of a pattern of nodes in the associative network that corresponds to a given situation. Computationally, recognition is based on an evidence accumulation[1]

---

[1]The evidence accumulation approach to situation recognition is based on a synthesis of findings from the EEG literature that included Coles et al. (1995), Kok (1990), Kounios et al. (1994), and Wilding (2000).

process, in which cues differentially contribute to or subtract from the evidence for different situations, and the evidence for each situation is periodically (i.e., every 250 msec) updated providing an ongoing level of evidence for each situation. At any given point in time, multiple situations may have sufficient evidence for their recognition (i.e., multitasking).

Although comparatively new, it is asserted by the developers that the underlying oscillating systems model emphasizing pattern recognition; integration of perceptual, cognitive, and affective processes, including multimodal memory representations; and other features provides the basis for a substantially more realistic and flexible representation of human metacognition. However, it is recognized that this model is still an initial effort to help understand and represent aspects of human cognition.

Implemented in augmented cognition and modeling and simulation systems, a customized model could be developed to reflect the metacognitive knowledge of a particular operator as the person interacts with a specific system. Operating in real time, this model can be used to interpret the ongoing state of the current system and the operator by comparing the difference between the expected behavior (the computer's understanding of what the operator should do) and the operator's actual behavior.

CURRENT EXAMPLES OF METACOGNITIVE SYSTEM APPLICATIONS

Mode Discrepancy Detection

A frequent problem with computer systems, particularly those employing automation, occurs when the human operator assumes the system is in one state when in fact the system is actually in a different state or mode. The potential for these occurrences increases under adverse circumstances (e.g., fatigue, stress, workload, etc.) or with intermediate levels of expertise. As a consequence, an operator(s) typically behaves appropriately given his or her understanding of the situation. However, his or her behavior may be inappropriate or erroneous given the actual situation.

One solution to the mode error problem, referred to as "Discrepant State Detection," begins with a customized model that reflects a specific operator's understanding of the system. The purpose of discrepancy detection is to accurately infer in real time the metacognitive processes of an operator using an individualized cognitive model of the operator. Discrepancy detection provides the foundation for a variety of concepts for augmentation that rely on the capability for a machine to accurately model the cognitive processes of an operator.

The machine first obtains an understanding of its own ongoing state to produce a machine model. Next, creating a separate model, the machine attempts to infer the operator's ongoing recognition of the state of the machine. This may involve input from a variety of sources (e.g., mouse movements/clicks, keyboard input, eye tracking, etc.). Finally, through comparison of the machine model and inferred operator model, discrepancies may be detected and corrective actions initiated. Discrepant state detection algorithms provide the computational mechanism for comparing a machine representation of situation awareness with that of an operator or multiple operators.

Through discrepancy detection, the machine not only detects that the operator has committed an error, but also recognizes the nature of the error within the context of the operator's overall knowledge and understanding of the system and associated tasks. Consequently, the machine may interact with the operator in a manner substantially more meaningful than the familiar error messages presented by current software applications and operating systems. Furthermore, to the extent that deficiencies exist in the operator's knowledge of the system and associated tasks, there is a meaningful basis for training intervention to correct deficiencies in the operator's knowledge.

The use of eye-tracking data to supplement operator actions would provide an even richer insight as to the intent of the operator, in that actions provide explicit data concerning an operator's interpretation of situations, and eye-tracking offers a more subtle indicator. To the extent that recognition of a situation requires that an operator process visual cues within the environment associated with the situation, data indicating visual cues that most likely have or have not been processed should enable better predictions.

Another approach to improving the machine awareness of an operator is to provide input from electrophysiological and brain imaging sources. These data offer the potential for systems to more accurately model the ongoing cognitive processes of an operator. Where physiological measures are employed to derive a real-time indication of workload, these indications may be enhanced by input supplied by a cognitive model. For example, the cognitive model may indicate the operator is actually faced with a different set of situations than first encountered. Such data could then be used as a modifier for physiological measures (i.e., if the cognitive model indicates that workload should be high, this serves to confirm physiological measures suggesting that workload is high; Forsythe et al., 2002).

DARPA's Augmented Cognition and Cognitive Information Processing Technology programs and the Army Advanced Decision Architecture programs are creating programs that are currently funding some of these initiatives. Through these initiatives, fundamentally different approaches to bridging the cognitive gap are likely to emerge. For example, the DARPA Augmented Cognition program seeks to develop capabilities whereby real-time physiological measures serve as the basis for machine adaptation in response to the cognitive and physiological states of an operator. Here the rate at which information is displayed to an operator may be adjusted in accordance with workload. If there are heavy demands being placed on one sensory modality (e.g., vision), urgent information may be presented using an alternate sensory modality (e.g., auditory and/or haptic; Brachman & Lemnios, 2002).

Human Behavior Modeling and Simulation

Another application area for metacognitive systems is the accurate modeling and simulation of human beings. In assessing human behavior modeling capabilities, it is fair to say that representing realistic human behaviors is "in its infancy." In modeling and simulation codes, "when human decisions are called for, a doctrinally based decision rule is inserted that reflects what the human ought to do in the ideal case" and human performance limitations are largely ignored (Pew & Mavor, 1998, p. 44). To exceed the capabilities found in current modeling and simulation technologies, an emphasis on psychological realism needs to be made—specifically, the cognition and behavior of humans.

It is also important to note that human modeling and simulation is not typically designed to specifically forecast what an individual or crowds will do in a given situation (e.g., "There is a 75% likelihood that X will happen"). Rather, the effort behind this is to demonstrate the range of possible outcomes given a certain set of input parameters, including crowd size, demographics, and so on, as well as physical location and other physical variables (e.g., temperature, rain, snow, etc.), and the original reason for the occurrence of a crowd—which is a more realistic and useful goal. It is anticipated that one potential use of crowd behavior models will be in training response forces for the military, police, and other agencies that interact with civilians in many different environments. However, using simulation for training purposes can be problematic, in that unrealistic simulation of human behavior and physics can lead to negative training, which gives soldiers an incorrect model of their actual environment. Thus, simulation is best served as a training tool when trainees are presented with a range of real-world outcomes rather than a single canned scenario. To accomplish this, simulated humans need to have lifelike characteristics and behaviors, and the simulated environment should be a realistic characterization of the actual environment they will face. Ultimately, the simulated humans should be able to act on their own, recognizing where they are and what type of situation they are currently in.

Implicit to recognition of a situation is recognition of one's goals (or attainable states) and the actions needed to realize these goals, including likely intermediate states. The human ability to quickly and accurately recognize a situation and respond accordingly, as opposed to a lengthy internal discourse in pros and cons, is one of the differentiating features of the current cognitive modeling efforts by Sandia and others. Just as recognition of situations leads to the development of a context and associated expectations, this method of interpreting the world also lends itself to immediate recognition of events or objects that do not fit in the current context.

In Sandia's cognitive framework, a cognitive subsystem serves as a point where the diverse emotions, stressors, memories, and other factors can be integrated into a decision for action (or inaction) to effect a transition to a next state (or return to the same state). Because the cognitive subsystem is a human characteristic, behavior can be made to realistically change as a function of the culture and their level of fatigue and stress over time, and in different situations.

Within this framework, it is recognized that metacognitive processes are inseparably interwoven with emotional processes (Bower, 1981; Bower & Cohen, 1982). This approach accounts for emotions, and other organic factors, through representation of the underlying neurophysiological mechanisms. Specifically, the computational framework is based on oscillating systems theories of cognitive function, such that a separate oscillator represents each subsystem component. Thus, different emotions are modeled as separate components, each correspondingly represented by an oscillator.

When constructing a model, concepts may each be attributed with associations to specific emotional components. Activation of a specific concept or situation produces activation of associated emotional components. Emotions then have a reciprocal effect on cognition, causing increased activation of the concept or situation that triggered the emotion and active inhibition of other concepts and situations. This interaction between emotion and cognition is consistent with neuropsychological findings of Le-Doux (1998) and allows certain neurophsyiological phenomenon to be demonstrated by the model (Forsythe & Raybourn, 2001; Forsythe & Xavier, 2002).

Representing the effect of culture in the shaping of a human's metacognition can be a difficult task. Where culture is known to play a role, it should be incorporated into the cognitive framework. For example, Hofstede (1991) determined there are at least four characteristics that help define the character of people within a specific country or geographical region, which can arguably lead to common patterns of behavior. These are power-distance,[2] individualism,[3] masculinity,[4] and uncertainity avoid-ance.[5] These characteristics, along with specific information regarding cultural norms and mores and expectations of society, would produce a metacognitive framework that realistically incorporates culture and its impact on how humans digest and assimilate information. All cultures comprise a diversity of people who often have opinions and beliefs in complete opposition to one another on national issues. Nevertheless, it is possible that a crowd composed of humans, with some cultural peculiarities and knowledge of key things particular to events and geographical area, is sufficient to generate the plausible range of crowd behaviors in specific situations.

CONCLUSION

The desire and need for computer systems to have at least some form of metacognitive ability is genuine. To accomplish this feat, a paradigm shift needs to take place in the way we construct computer systems, as well as what we know about the processes involved that make up the human mind. It may be that research being conducted to create these abilities in computer systems will actually provide important information as to how humans cognitively function. That being said, creating computers with true metacognitive abilities that have actual self-conscious behaviors may be a distant or even impossible dream. Perhaps it may even emerge on its own, without any directed help from humans. Indeed computer-generated, metacognitive self-consciousness could thus be a byproduct that is not even truly understood by its developers.

Even if actual metacognitive abilities could be created, this would not produce such important things as creativity, intuition, and the like. These qualities will probably stay as a uniquely human attribute. Indeed computers will never have the same type of creativity that we humans have—because computers will never have the same life experiences as us. That is not to say that computer systems of the future will not bring new qualities that are currently unknown to us. As with any entity that can perceive their environment, computer systems of the future may impart to humans a

---

[2]*Power distance* refers to the degree to which individuals with less power in a society expect and accept unequal distributions of power.

[3]*Individualism* refers to the degree to which a culture emphasizes the self and immediate family over the society at large.

[4]*Masculinity* refers to the degree to which traditional masculine roles of assertiveness and competition are rewarded by society.

[5]*Uncertainty avoidance* refers to the degree to which individuals have anxiety about certain events.

new mental quality that is wholly different from how we think. As such this quality would engender computers' greatest achievement—the ability to think for itself in a manner that is wholly unto itself.

Currently, we should be satisfied with existing accomplishments to generate the most minute and basic form of metacognitive ability. The two applications mentioned earlier can be described as first-step examples of efforts to implement metacognitive abilities in computer systems. These examples are by no means an exhaustive list of possible applications using current technology, but they do represent the immediate goals of the funding agencies driving this research. It is probably impossible to predict what type and form of cognitive abilities computer systems will have in the far future. Most likely, the only accurate prediction is that it will be wholly different from what we can now envision.

ACKNOWLEDGMENTS

This work was performed at Sandia National Laboratories. Sandia is a multiprogram laboratory operated by Sandia Corporation, a Lockheed-Martin Company, for the U.S. Department of Energy under Contract DE-AC04-94AL85000. Work discussed in this chapter was also the product of a grant from DARPA through the Augmented Cognition program to Sandia National Laboratories and through internal Sandia funding.

REFERENCES

Bower, G. H. (1981). Mood and memory. *American Psychologist, 36,* 129–148.

Bower, G. H., & Cohen, P. R. (1982). Emotional influences in memory and thinking: Data and theory. In M. S. Clark & S. T. Fiske (Eds.), *Affect and cognition: The 17th Annual Carnegie Symposium on Cognition.* Hillsdale, NJ: Lawrence Erlbaum Associates.

Brachman, R. J. (2002, November/December). Systems that know what they're doing. *IEEE Intelligent Systems,* pp. 67–71.

Brachman, R. J., & Lemnios, Z. (2002). DARPA's new cognitive system vision. *Computing Research News, 14*(5), 1–8.

Buttazzo, G. (2001, July). Artificial consciousness: Utopia or real possibility? *IEEE Perspectives,* pp. 24–30.

Coles, M. G. H., Snid, H. G. O. M., Scheffers, M. K., & Otten, L. J. (1995). Mental chronometry and the study of human information processing. *Electrophysiology of mind: Event-related brain potentials and cognition* (pp. 86–131). Oxford: Oxford Science Publications.

Flavell, J. (1976). Metacognitive aspects of problem solving. In L. Resnick (Ed.), *The nature of intelligence* (pp. 231–235). Hillsdale, NJ: Lawrence Erlbaum Associates.

Forsythe, C., Bernard, M., Xavier, P., Abbott, R., Speed, A., & Brannon, N. (2002). Engineering a transformation of human-machine interaction to an augmented cognitive relationship. *Proceedings of the Human Factors and Ergonomics Society 47th Annual Meeting* (pp. 302–306), Denver, CO.

Forsythe, C., & Raybourn, E. (2001). Toward a human emulator: A framework for the comprehensive computational representation of human cognition. *Proceedings of the Human Factors and Ergonomics Society* (pp. 537–541), Minneapolis, MN.

Forsythe, C., & Xavier, P. (2002). Human emulation: Progress toward realistic synthetic human agents. *Proceedings of the 11th Conference on Computer-Generated Forces and Behavior Representation*, Orlando, FL.

Gourgey, A. F. (1998). Metacognition in basic skills instruction. *Instructional Science, 26,* 81–96.

Hofstede, G. (1991). *Cultures and organizations: Software of the mind: Intercultural cooperation and its importance for survival.* New York: McGraw-Hill.

Jacobs, J. E., & Paris, S. G. (1987). Children's metacognition about reading: Issues in definition, measurement, and instruction. *Educational Psychologist, 22,* 255–278.

Kelemen, W. L., Frost, P. J., & Weaver, C. A. (2000). Individual differences in metacognition: Evidence against a general metacognitive ability. *Memory & Cognition, 28*(1), 92–107.

Klimesch, W. (1987). A connectivity model for semantic processing. *Psychological Research, 49,* 53–61.

Klimesch, W. (1994). *The structure of long-term memory: A connectivity model of semantic processing.* Hillsdale, NJ: Lawrence Erlbaum Associates.

Klimesch, W. (1996). Memory processes, brain oscillations and EEG synchronization. *International Journal of Psychophysiology, 24,* 61–100.

Kok, A. (1990). Internal and external control: A two-factor model of amplitude change of event-related potentials. *Acta Psychologica, 74,* 203–236.

Kounios, J., Montgomery, E. C., & Smith, R. W. (1994). Semantic memory and the granularity of semantic relations: Evidence from speed-accuracy decomposition. *Memory and Cognition, 22,* 729–741.

LeDoux, J. (1998). *The emotional brain: The mysterious underpinnings of emotional life.* New York: Touchstone Books.

Licklider, J. C. R. (1960). Man-computer symbiosis. *IRE Transactions on Human Factors in Electronics, 1,* 4–11.

Mazzoni, G., & Nelson, T. O. (1998). *Metacognition and cognitive neuropsychology: Monitoring and control processes.* Mahwah, NJ: Lawrence Erlbaum Associates.

McFadden, J. (2002). Synchronous firing and its influence on the brain's electromagnetic field: Evidence for an electromagnetic theory of consciousness. *Journal of Consciousness Studies, 9,* 23–50.

Minsky, M. (1985). Why people think computers can't. In D. Donnelly (Ed.), *The computer culture.* Cranbury, NJ: Associated University Press.

Pew, R. W., & Mavor, A. S. (1998). *Modeling human and organizational behavior.* Washington, DC: National Research Council, National Academy Press.

Schoenfeld, A. H. (1985). *Mathematical problem solving.* New York: Academic Press.

Schoenfeld, A. H. (1987). What's all the full about metacognition? In A. H. Schoenfeld (Ed.), *Cognitive science and mathematics education.* Hillsdale, NJ: Lawrence Erlbaum Associates.

Schoenfeld, A. H. (1989). Teaching mathematical thinking and problem solving. In L. B. Resnick & L. E. Kolpher (Eds.), *Toward the thinking curriculum: Current cognitive research.* Alexandria, VA: Association for Supervision and Curriculum Development Yearbook.

Schooler, J. W. (2002). Re-representing consciousness: Dissociations between experience and meta-consciousness. *Trends in Cognitive Sciences, 6,* 339–344.

Schraw, G. (1994). The effect of metacognitive knowledge on local and global monitoring. *Contemporary Educational Psychology, 19,* 143–154.

Schraw, G. (1998). Promoting general metacognitive awareness. *Instructional Science, 26,* 113–125.

Solomon, K. O., & Barsalou, L. W. (2001). Representing properties locally. *Cognitive Psychology, 43,* 129–169.

Thompson, W. B., & Mason, S. E. (1996). Instability of individual differences in the association between confidence judgments and memory performance. *Memory & Cognition, 24,* 226–234.

Turing, A. M. (1988). Computer machinery and intelligence. In D. R. Hofstadter & D. C. Dennett (Eds.), *The mind's I: Fantasies and reflections on self and soul* (pp. 53–67). Toronto: Bantam. (Original work published 1950)

Viegas, J. (2002). How does human consciousness work? *Discovery News.* Retrieved October 20, 2004, from http://dsc.discovery.com/news

Wilding, E. L. (2000). In what way does the parietal ERP old/new effect index recollection. *International Journal of Psychophysiology, 35,* 81–87.

Winograd, T., & Flores, J. (1987). *Understanding computer and cognition: A new foundation for design.* Reading, MA: Addison-Wesley.

Author Index

Subject Index

Printed and bound by CPI Group (UK) Ltd, Croydon, CR0 4YY

17/10/2024

01775656-0006